Books by Jane Roberts:

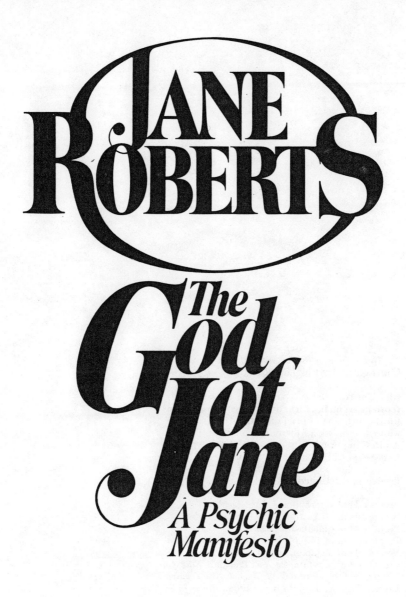

JANE ROBERTS

The God of Jane

A Psychic Manifesto

Prentice-Hall, Inc., Englewood Cliffs, New Jersey 07632

Prentice-Hall International, Inc., *London*
Prentice-Hall of Australia Pty. Limited, *Sydney*
Prentice-Hall Canada Inc., *Toronto*
Prentice-Hall of India Private Limited, *New Delhi*
Prentice-Hall of Japan, Inc., *Tokyo*
Prentice-Hall of Southeast Asia Pte. Ltd., *Singapore*
Whitehall Books Limited, *Wellington, New Zealand*
Editora Prentice-Hall do Brasil Ltda., *Rio de Janeiro*

Library of Congress Cataloging in Publication Data
Roberts, Jane (date).
    The God of Jane.
    Includes index.
    1. Psychical research—Case studies.   2. Roberts,
Jane (date).   I. Title.
BF1029.R6   133.9'3   81-321
ISBN 0-13-357517-9   AACR1
ISBN 0-13-357492-X (A Reward book : pbk.)

ISBN 0-13-357517-9

ISBN 0-13-357492-X {A REWARD BOOK : PBK.}

This book is dedicated to all of those individuals who insist upon interpreting the nature of reality for themselves.

e e cummings' ghost

by Jane Roberts

e e cummings' ghost,
slippery as polished smoke,
slipped through
time's keyhole.
his thoughts like silver rain,
seeped out of his brain,
and found themselves alive
and growing,
in a place where
all matter is mind.

now he rides
the backs
of the bronco molecules,
and like
a microscopic cowboy,
lassoes his dreams
with a silver cord.
he shouts, "yahoo,
god bless america,"
having at last found
his innocent beginning land.

he is
the rollicking pioneer
of a brand-new planet,
with endless mindprairies
roamed
by great thoughtcattle,
the very first settler
of lands that form themselves
into the shapes
of his desire.

his feelings roll out into new
miniature infinities,
receding
into worlds that open up,
as the silver smoke of thought
turns solid,
as you can see
if you even peek
through time's keyhole.

Contents

The God of Jane

Part One

CONFLICTING VIEWS
OF REALITY

Chapter 1

A History of Trancetime and an Alternate View of Reality

Since late 1963, I've clocked approximately 4,000 hours of trancetime, during which the Seth sessions have been held twice weekly. For eight of those years, while I conducted my "E.S.P." classes, though, there were three Seth sessions a week, averaging from two to three hours. This estimate of trancetime doesn't include other altered states of consciousness with which I've experimented, but represents only my regular schedule of speaking for Seth, my trance personality, through the years.

The tally constantly rises, of course, as Seth continues to dictate his books and other material, so that now I have what amounts to a reliable, steady alternate framework of perception and experience—a trancelife. This framework presents its own body of data, its own hypotheses, and its own evidence, even as my normal state of consciousness does. What I learn at the trance level is transmitted through Seth's dictation so that it becomes a part of my ordinary knowledge—though how much of it I may put into practical use at any given time is something else again; and a matter I'll return to shortly.

My trancetime is more concentrated than regular time. I'm not unconscious but conscious in a different way, at another level, with a greater capacity for attention. Trancetime presents its own rich blend of consciousness, a blend in which my own altered awareness is only one of the psychological ingredients.

This state of perception has nothing to do with classical pathological dissociation; and its products—Seth's five books— display a highly developed intellect at work and give evidence of a special kind of creativity. In those trance hours I "turn into someone else." At least I am not myself to myself; I become Seth, or a part of what Seth is. I don't feel "possessed" or "invaded" during sessions. I don't feel that some superspirit has "taken over" my body. Instead it's as if I'm practicing some precise psychological art, one that is ancient and poorly understood in our culture; or as if I'm learning a psychological science that helps me map the contours of consciousness itself. Not that I'm doing as well as I could at this endeavor, but after all this time I'm finally examining the trance view of reality and comparing it to the official views of science and religion. To say the least, those views don't agree.

My own trance experience shows me that normal consciousness is just one focus of many alternate (and natural) ways of perceiving reality. For example, usually we use our consciousness much as we use an automobile, going along at ground level, past "blocks" of hours, traveling along a rich but cluttered highway of sense perceptions where the scenery is more or less shared by everyone else on the same road. And I operate at that level much of the time. In a Seth trance, though, it's as if the automobile turns into an airplane (or sometimes, a rocket) lifting off, rising above the normal routes of perception, leaving the runway, and mind-sailing above the highways with their traffic jams, detours, and other obstructions.

This takes practice; that is, it does if you want a steady rise and a dependable vehicle. Then you can afford to look around and view the usual landscape from a "higher" perspective. You can put your airplane on automatic pilot, turn your attention to the atmosphere through which you're traveling, and try to identify and understand the mental phenomena that appear in the skyscape of the mind.

We aren't really talking about physical vehicles, of course, but about consciousness and its motion. No normal automobile turns into an airplane, for example; we have to get out of the

car first, and then into the airplane. And I get out of my usual mode
of consciousness and into another.

This is almost always an exhilarating experience, like
riding some perfect gigantic ninth wave of energy, knowing exactly
how and when to "jump in," and feeling absolutely safe and
supported even when embarked upon such a strange psychological
flight. But the energy and power of *this* wave carries me above and
below usual reality, sweeping me into contrasts that are microscopic
and macroscopic by turns.

In this analogy, Seth is that ninth wave of energy—an
energy that is aware, unique, individualistic, and yet endowed with
all of the general characteristics of energy itself; as if *his* consciousness rises like some superreal mental creature from the tidal waves
of a primal ocean of energy, so that he is himself and yet a part of a
greater reality. And by prearrangement, I wait by the shores of my
own private mind until I sense the approach of that psychological
surge. Then throwing off the clothes of my usual consciousness I
mentally jump in, striking that wave at a certain point and making
an intersection with it that results in the phenomenon of Seth as he
appears in our sessions.

Such a trance is private, but it is hardly lonely. I sense all
kinds of action. I mix with, collide with, and glide through psychological events almost impossible to describe. I'm not talking about
encounters with other entities or with the denizens of some
shadowy underworld, but of events that seem to involve an exploration of the hidden contours of consciousness. Riding that wave of
personified energy, I sense where currents from other realities enter
our own world, how our own consciousnesses circle around
probable events like fish deciding which morsels to nibble upon;
and mostly I sense the eddies and underground caves within our
minds where our ideas mix and merge; yours and mine.

Then, sometimes, that ninth wave of energy seems to
carry me higher than I think possible, cracking whitely past the
most distant peaks that my own consciousness has ever known; then
pausing, poised, waiting for something that almost happens but
hasn't so far, while I rest in a place that's like the calm eye of a
storm. Times and places seem to swirl around me with explosive
force, yet where I am it's peaceful.

I can usually feel that energy returning me home, gently,
with no psychological or psychic bumps. Almost always I'm re-
freshed and invigorated. My eyes have been wide open while I've
been in trance, and as Seth I've been speaking for the entire time.

I'm not sure when his expression recedes from my features and mine returns, but this happens very quickly. Then I look out of my own eyes as usual, seeing my husband, Rob, on the couch on the other side of the coffee table. Usually he's still writing down Seth's last words.

Actually Rob's written the equivalent of several large books himself through the years as he faithfully transcribes Seth's words, adds notes about the sessions or events connected with them, includes notes about the subjects Seth discusses, and generally provides the framework that connects the sessions with everyday reality. That's the reality I return to, of course.

Mostly though, Seth has left our world alone in his dictated books, not commenting on current events unless we specifically asked him to. In his latest book, *The Individual and the Nature of Mass Events,* however, he turned his attention to the arena of national and world affairs, explaining how our private beliefs and impulses are connected to mass experience. He looked at our institutions and beliefs and explained how conventional Darwinian, Freudian, and religious concepts have hampered our imaginations, creativity, and psychological development.

Actually, when Seth announced the title of that book in the spring of 1977, I was a trifle upset by it. I knew that his material would be pertinent and I *was* intrigued, but I didn't particularly want to be reminded of the world at large with all of its problems. They were with us constantly, I reasoned; no one could escape them. So why did they have to invade my trancetime?

I forgot that my questions about that same world back in 1963 were partially responsible for the beginning of the Seth sessions, for certainly they answered my need to find a greater framework from which to understand a world that seemed to glory in chaos.

And the sessions did provide such a framework. From the start, Seth's ideas about the nature of reality were the most convincing that Rob and I had ever encountered. For some time, though, I considered them as fascinating theories or evocative alternate hypotheses. As long as I did that, I didn't have to come face to face with the many sharp differences between Seth's views and those of the official world.

For one thing, I felt that it was my responsibility to keep a certain distance between myself and Seth's material to insure my own objectivity and mental independence. No one evaluated his material more critically than I did (and do). As time went on though, it became obvious that my own growing experience with altered states of consciousness and Seth's accumulated material were adding up to an entirely different picture of the world in which we all spend most of our time.

What is that picture like? As most of our readers know by now, Seth states that each of us forms our own reality, according to our beliefs about ourselves and others. Through all of his books Seth stresses that point and emphasizes the importance of the spontaneous self. In *The Individual and the Nature of Mass Events,* Seth carries these ideas further, clarifying and refining them.

In fact, he carries his concepts an important step further, stating that our impulses come from the deepest sources of our beings, and are meant to promote our own fulfillment and also to insure the most beneficial developments possible for mankind and for all other species as well. According to Seth, our impulses are our most natural aids to help us "find our way" in physical reality. In *Mass Events,* he describes our impulses as emerging from an innate, profound knowledge of the probable shape of events for the entire planet. Though we aren't consciously aware of those implications, Seth states that we *are* "impulsively aware" of the best possible future events, and our impulses are meant to lead us toward those areas of development best suited to our individual and collective good.

Actually, Seth began to explain these ideas in some private sessions when he introduced "Framework 1 and Framework 2," just after he began *Mass Events.* Framework 1 is the usual reality we're used to, and Framework 2 is the creative framework from which the ordinary world emerges. In a fascinating series of private sessions, Seth described how the two frameworks operate and how we can all draw help from Framework 2 in order to increase the quality of our lives in Framework 1. Then, later, he introduced this material to his readers in *Mass Events. How* do we actually change the events of our lives for the better? How can our impulses serve as reliable inner directives? Seth discusses these subjects thoroughly, and I'm including some excerpts from the unpublished material in the following chapter.

When Seth first began delivering this material I didn't realize that it would lead me into beginning what amounted to an accelerated course in higher education, forcing me to look into my own beliefs as never before, or that it would inspire me to write this book, which is my most personal one thus far. Actually this manuscript is the story of my efforts to put Seth's latest material to work in daily life; to free myself from many hampering cultural beliefs; and, most of all, to encounter and understand the nature of impulses in general, and mine in particular.

Seth's material on impulses did, in fact, lead me to an impulsive psychological journey of my own. But I learned long ago that such journeys, while mine, are also taken on behalf of others. This particular pilgrimage into the realm of personal beliefs and impulses must be taken by each of us in one way or another, I believe, if we are to rid ourselves of the many limiting concepts that are backed up by the official establishments of science and religion. There *are* some exciting alternate views of reality, though, as I hope to show in this book.

Chapter 2
Seth: On Framework 1 and Framework 2

The fall of 1977 was a subjectively exciting one, mostly because Seth's new material gave Rob and me the feeling that the vast world of events was opening up, so that we could at least glimpse the "psychic mechanics" that connected objective and subjective experience. At the same time Seth was dictating that material, I was typing *The Afterdeath Journal of an American Philosopher,* a surprising manuscript that had "come to me" during the summer, day in and day out, even while construction men invaded the house, tramping back and forth, building the small back room that was to be my new studio. Rob was busy preparing Seth's previous book, *The Nature of the Psyche,* for publication. And during our regular sessions, Seth began his introduction to Framework 1 and Framework 2:

FROM PRIVATE SETH SESSION FOR SEPTEMBER 19, 1977

"... Framework 2 represents the medium in which the natural and the source of the natural merge in a creative gestalt.

That gestalt forms your physical being. Nature, without nature's source, would not last a moment.

"In Framework 2, extra-natural help, energy, impetus, and knowledge are 'naturally' available. . . . But only when your own beliefs are clear enough so that the help is not blocked. By super-natural, again, I mean the source from which nature springs. . . .

"Your ideas come and go effortlessly, without impediments, with a sense of ease that is taken for granted. Your freedom to think is so transparent and natural that you are scarcely aware of it. That freedom comes from Framework 2, as does the great creativity it makes possible. . . .

"Framework 1 [in which you usually operate] deals with predictable behavior, predictable results, and dislikes surprises."

FROM PRIVATE SETH SESSION FOR SEPTEMBER 24, 1977

"In Framework 2, the mind affects the physical brain in a more complete and effective manner than usual, and can spark images, thoughts, or correlations that exist in a context outside of the time that is happening in Framework 1. Time occurs at a certain regulated rate, then, obviously, in Framework 1. A certain amount of time is needed there to do a certain amount of work, and according to scientific dictates, a specific amount of effort is required to perform each different kind of work.

"Framework 1, to some extent or another, however, is always influenced by Framework 2. There [in Framework 2], the same correlations do not apply between the effort expended and the work performed, or the time required for such procedures. Very little effort, there, comparatively speaking, has a very definite effect here in [your] Framework 1. That is, a small amount of effort in Framework 2 can result in extraordinary work done in Framework 1, and with a foreshortened time effect. . . .

"Suggestion purposefully applied while in a relaxed state, which is a connective to Framework 2, can be most effective."

FROM PRIVATE SETH SESSION FOR OCTOBER 22, 1977

"Now: as I told you, Framework 2 is the creative medium that is responsible for physical life. It is not true, however, that positive and negative feelings and beliefs 'take' there with equal vitality. It is true that your beliefs form your reality; however, you do have a certain leeway in that those desires that lead to fulfillment and positive creativity are more in keeping with the natural leanings of Framework 2 itself.

"Relatively speaking, then, these 'take' more quickly and accelerate in a more direct fashion. Limiting beliefs have to meet certain resistances, for they are not in keeping with the overall creative framework.

"It is easier for a body to be healthy than ill, and in the terms of this discussion, for example, old age does not basically bring with it any particular diseases or susceptibility. Practically speaking, now, negative beliefs often catch up with an individual, leading to various diseases. I want to emphasize, however, that Framework 2 is not a neutral medium. Negative beliefs have to be inserted there with great repetitiveness before you meet their physical results."

As Seth gave more Framework 1 and 2 material, Rob and I woke up each morning with a new excitement, trying to sense when we were "tuned into" Framework 2, and looking for evidence of its existence in our daily lives. Seth also stated that dreaming involved Framework 2 activity. As Rob's mentioned in his notes for Seth's books, I've had considerable trouble with stiffness through the years, an arthritic-like condition that makes it very difficult for me to get around normally. So after one Seth session, I asked for a dream that would give me more insight into the problem. Seth has helped all he can, but I make my own reality just like everyone else does, and I knew that "I had my reasons" for the situation. But with Framework 2 in mind, I gave the dream suggestion—and promptly fell to sleep.

The dream was vivid in my mind the next morning; and it packed a double wallop, as you'll see. The dream location was Turkey, and I was the very young son of a sultan who sent me on a journey around the world in a very small boat. The boat had no roof because roofs hadn't been invented yet, and I was afraid of getting wet or cold. So I stood in the palace garden and demanded that the sky stop from raining during my entire trip. Actually, I ordered the sky to remain clear.

And so it was: I set out on a small river that was to go to the ocean. Each day the sun shone until I was sunburned and rather miserable. Worst of all, though, the river began to dry up, until finally there was no water beneath my boat at all. Then a voice out of the sky thundered: "Work with nature, not against it."

End of dream. The message was clear enough to me. I was embarked on an inner journey, and I didn't want to be bothered, or put out, or distracted one little bit. So I held back strong parts of my nature so that my journey would be just the way I wanted it. I wrote down the dream, but when I started, the dream began to rewrite itself into a story about a young boy called Emir at the beginning of the world. And each day there was more, until I had a delightful and power-packed little book about beliefs and how they're connected to Frameworks 1 and 2. Besides that, I began to feel a good deal better.

So I divided those autumn days between typing *The Afterdeath Journal* and getting new chapters of what finally developed into *Emir's Education in the Proper Use of Magical Powers.* It's really a book for children of all ages, and in a way it marked the start of my new education too. I also saw that *The Afterdeath Journal* and most of my other books were the results of Framework 2 activity, for they came with little effort on my part in Framework 1. Writing is also the area of my most positive beliefs, of course, so there I was relatively free.

Rob and I still had endless questions about Seth's new material, though, and he answered some pertinent ones in a private session on faith that's pivotal for any understanding of Frameworks 1 and 2, so I'm including almost the entire session here (*Rob's notes are in italics*):

FROM PRIVATE SETH SESSION FOR OCTOBER 24, 1977

"Now: In the most basic manner, each person and creature possesses faith, whatever its degree or nature. Without it there would be no family groups—animal or human—or civilizations or governments. It may seem that the retribution of law holds society together and keeps criminal elements down, for example, so that you have operating processes that insure more or less stable living conditions. The laws, however, are necessarily based upon man's faith that those laws will be largely followed. Otherwise they would be useless.

"You 'go on faith' that there will be a tomorrow. You operate on faith constantly, so that it becomes an almost invisible element in each life. It is the fiber behind all organizations and relationships, and it is based upon the innate, natural knowledge possessed by each creature—the knowledge that it springs from a sustaining source, that its birth is cushioned by all the resources of nature, and that nature itself is sustained by the greater source that gave it birth.

"You cannot be alive without faith, yet faith can be distorted. There is faith in good, but there is also faith in 'evil.' In usual terms, faith takes it for granted that a certain desired end will be achieved, even though the means may be unknown. In usual terms again, there is no direct evidence, otherwise you would have no need for faith.

"When you fear that the worst will happen, you are often showing quite real faith, but in a backwards fashion. For with no direct evidence of disaster before your eyes, you heartily believe that it will occur. You have faith in it. (*This last was delivered with emphasis and irony.*) That is, indeed, misplaced faith. . . .

"It is then quite to everyone's advantage that Framework 2 is not neutral. Faith in a creative, fulfilling, desired end—sustained faith—literally draws from Framework 2 all of the necessary ingredients, all of the elements however staggering in number, all the details, and then inserts into Framework 1 the impulses, dreams, chance meetings, motivations, or whatever is necessary so that the desired end then falls into place as a completed pattern.

"You must begin somewhere, so you state your purpose clearly in Framework 1. Then you have the faith that the event will be brought to pass.

"Your own creative abilities are instantly mobilized in the proper direction. Your behavior in Framework 1 must automatically change. The ways and the means, however, cannot be questioned, for they will come from a greater source of knowledge than you consciously possess.

"I am trying to give you some kind of overall picture so that you can make your own helpful comparisons, and understand what is involved more thoroughly. . . .

"Someone, for example, may plan an airplane trip. Everything will be arranged, the last detail taken care of. The person may take great precautions to see that the plane is not missed. Persons may have been contacted to care for the house during the time of absence. Children may have been sent to camp, neighbors assigned to care for pets, and every logical situation cared for.

"Let us say that this particular plane may well crash; and, in fact, does. After all of this person's planning, hard work, and effort, at the last moment everything seems to go wrong. The children do not leave for camp in time. One of the animals runs away. A ticket is lost. Our individual comes down with indigestion or a cold. Lo and behold, for while everything seems to be going so poorly, our friend's life is being saved, for he misses his plane.

"Later he wonders what happened, that his life was saved and his plans altered at the last moment. Our friend wanted to live and had faith that he would. In spite of all his conscious lack of knowledge, he was brought to operate according to the information available in Framework 2, though he was not aware of it. He lost his ticket—a stupid error, it seemed. The lives and events of all those connected with his trip—the neighbors, the children, and so forth—all of those issues were arranged in Framework 2, so that while the events seemed most unpleasant, they were highly beneficial."

(Seth doesn't mean that other people were manipulated in Framework 2, but that, as he explains elsewhere, they also made moves that benefited themselves as well as their neighbor.)

"If our friend learned of the plane crash, he saw this only too well. If he never learned of the crash and did not have faith in the beneficial nature of events, then he might simply remember the entire affair as highly unpleasant, stupid, and even think that it was just another example of the fact that he could do nothing right.

"The entire pattern of your lives is taken for granted in Framework 2. There is no need for bargaining there. . . .

"Framework 2 contains all the dreams, plans, and thoughts of all human beings of any time. There, the spacious present is operative. There, it makes no difference if an undesirable condition has lasted a day or a lifetime. There, you are not impeded by the past.

"If your beliefs in Framework 1 make you assign great power to the past, then you impede your progress. I have said many times that spontaneity knows its own order, and I am speaking of true spontaneity. I say this because often anger, for instance, may seem spontaneous—and may be—but it is more often the explosive, finally forced expression of reactions long withheld or repressed.

"True spontaneity, however, comes directly from Framework 2, and behind it are endless patterns of orderliness and complexity that are beyond your conscious Framework 1 comprehension. . . .

"It is not simply that in Framework 2 there is no resistance to creative, fulfilling, natural, life-seeking desires, but that the medium of Framework 2 itself automatically adds its own magnification to them, so that once you get rolling, so to speak, the acceleration is spectacular, in whatever issue is involved. . . ."

Not only were these ideas fascinating to Rob and me, but they presented a model of the universe that was in direct contradiction to the official model of a meaningless cosmos, and a physical world in which each species fought against each other one in the struggle for survival. Seth had always stated that each act is meaningful, but with the Framework 1 and 2 material he seemed to be introducing a workable method to help us attract the events we wanted and avoid those we didn't want. So I was really ready to "run with the ball." At least I thought I was.

Chapter 3
Impulses, Impulses, Impulses

I finished typing *The Afterdeath Journal* late that fall and was working on *Emir* as the snowy winter of late 1977 turned into the even snowier winter of early 1978. Seth continued to give us more information on Frameworks 1 and 2, and he also devoted a block of sessions to personal matters. In 1978 I wrote *The Further Education of Oversoul Seven*. Finally, Seth returned to his dictation of *The Individual and Mass Events*. By then, his material on impulses was an integral part of his book; and I was growing uneasy. "I wish he'd used another word beside 'impulses'!" I must have made that particular remark so often that Rob got sick of hearing it.

But almost always he'd look at me with fake innocence and ask, "Why?"

I'd just sort of grumble under my breath, "I don't know. The word 'impulses' bothers me, that's all."

Then Rob would say something like, "Seth's been talking about the spontaneous self for years, and you went along with that." And that was it, I'd think. I could trust the spontaneous self because I connected it with my creative abilities. Besides, earlier I'd theorized about what I called "heroic impulses," separate from usual ones—superimpulses of a kind—meant to lead to our own greater fulfillment, if we could learn to distinguish them from ordinary ones.

I'd spent a good deal of time wondering why heroic impulses weren't easier to identify, and why mine hadn't led me closer to my "heroic self," as I called the part of the psyche that exists apart from physical reality. I'd also impatiently searched for these special impulses, ignoring any others that didn't live up to my standards. So naturally I began to wonder: What about the impulses I'd ignored as unworthy of my notice? Were these the ones, the *ordinary* ones, that Seth was talking about? What if I really followed his instructions to trust my impulses—even those distracting, annoying ones that tried to "tempt" me away from my typewriter, or "lured" me with "a million" different ways to waste valuable time? Suppose the very impulses that I'd been fighting so valiantly were the very ones meant to lead me where I wanted to go?

Hmm. I thought about it.

In the meantime, Rob and I planned to publish Seth's second volume of *The "Unknown" Reality*, his *The Nature of the Psyche*, and my *The Further Education of Oversoul Seven,* plus *Emir* in 1979 (and we did). During this time it seemed that we were reading galleys constantly. And even while we were doing that, I'd find myself brooding about impulses.

What about . . . the impulse to kill? I'd think, nearly with a shudder. Surely Seth wasn't saying that *that* impulse was good. Of course, *I* knew he wasn't, but what about all our readers? Didn't impulses imply unbridled hate or lust or lack of control? Then one morning before I began my day's work, a fairly unusual event happened: I felt Seth around, with some material that I was just supposed to take down in writing, without a usual session. We rarely work that way together, but the material was very immediate and clear, so I grabbed a pen and recorded it. It's a perfect capsule statement about Seth's position on the importance of impulses, so I'm including it here. When I read it back, I knew that he'd given it to me to emphasize its importance, not only to me, but in the larger context of his material. In our next regular session, that same evening, Seth referred to my material and asked Rob to add it to the session notes. The passages read as follows:

"Despite the beliefs and teachings of religion and psychology, impulses are biological and psychic directional signals meant to nudge the individual toward his or her greatest opportunities for expression and development privately, and also to insure the person's contribution to mass social reality.

"On a biological basis, impulses are like emotional instincts, individually tuned, so that ideally they are stimuli toward action that results as a consequence of complicated 'inner' computations. These computations are made by drawing upon the psyche's innate knowledge of probabilities on a private and mass basis.

"The authority of the self has been so eroded by religion, science and psychology itself that impulses are equated with antisocial behavior, considered synonymous with it, or with individual expression at the expense of social order.

"It should go without saying that impulses are the basis upon which life rides, and that they represent the overall motivating life force.

"Remind yourself that the best possible events *are* being brought about from Framework 2. Your impulses will automatically provide you with the proper balance of solitude and company, private and public activity, exercise and rest, for you."

I read that material often during the following months. In the meantime, the events of the world, particularly national ones, began to intrude on our private lives with a new frightening vigor. The tragic events of Jonestown flashed across the television screens of millions of Americans, and I thought, My *God,* how could men's belief in a God bring about such havoc? How could men's visions be so distorted? Why should so many people seek death? Why wasn't life, of itself, enough to satisfy us? What distorted *impulses* were somehow unleashed? How could men or women do so much harm in the name of good? What buried, unclean instincts still lurked in man from his evolutionary past?

So as Rob and I watched the events unfold on television and followed the newspaper accounts, it began to dawn on us that none of the learned explanations for those events made any sense. It also began to dawn on us that many of our own questions, particularly mine, were *programmed.* In *Mass Events,* Seth had been presenting a view of reality in which, for example, the Darwinian concept of the survival of the fittest had no part. Instead, it was the cooperative characteristics of species that led to survival. Yet when we forgot ourselves, watching the television news, it was only too easy to think automatically in terms of "man's evolutionary past" and to ask questions based on the assumption that man was a naturally deadly species.

Just the same, the tragedy reawakened my suspicions about impulses in general. And while I was still grappling with them, the spring of 1979 gave us the Three Mile Island drama of nearly tragic errors. So if religion could show an ugly face, what about science? Again through television's amazing technological achievement we saw or seemed to see another instance, even more chilling, of man's propensity for disaster. How could a creature like that trust its impulses?

And, more to the point, how could I trust mine?

To say that Seth addressed himself to such issues is an understatement. Not only did he discuss the Jonestown affair and the Three Mile Island fiasco in *Mass Events,* but his explanations made far more sense than anything else we came across on those subjects. And not only did he "redeem" impulses in our eyes, but when he was finished, we wondered how in the world we'd ever imagined that they worked against—instead of for—the private and public good.

Mass Events probably made the greatest impression on me, personally, of all Seth's books to date. It's an extension of his *Nature of Personal Reality* in a way, just as this book of mine is an extension of *Mass Events*: For it's the story of my attempts to come to terms with impulses in daily life, and to conquer those entrenched beliefs that made me doubt them. Seth was actually saying that we can't trust some hypothetical heroic self (or inner self or whole self) while distrusting the only self we're usually aware of being.

Around the time of the Three Mile Island affair, our three-year-old cat, Billy, died very suddenly of a kidney disease. He'd replaced Willie who had died at 16 years old. Seth broke off dictation on his Three Mile Island book material to discuss our private household sorrow. It was hard for us not to get caught up in the usual programmed thoughts like, "Well, the cat had been altered, so nature, having no use for him, found him dispensable." One day I even found myself upset for *daring* to mourn a cat's death when the world itself seemed headed for chaos. A friend gave us two new kittens, but we still missed Billy.

It was really strange: A part of me felt sheepish to even consider the immortality of a cat, in whatever fashion. The other, stronger part felt vehemently that if a cat's life and death had no meaning, then nothing else did either, including scientific statements that implied life had no purpose except for its own genetic survival. Somehow, meaninglessness ended up canceling itself out. Besides, Seth gave some excellent sessions on animal consciousness that we hope to publish some day, and he assured us that Billy's consciousness—like each of energy's personifications—continued to exist whatever its form.

Life, Seth said, has meaning or it doesn't. We can't really say that a person's life has meaning, but that a cat's or even an insect's life is meaningless. And, he stressed, we live in either an accidentally formed universe *or* a meaningfully created one. We can't scientifically prove either theory, but intuitively we do know the truth. And intuitively we know enough to trust our impulses.

So I decided to trust mine, and to see where they led me. I resolved to start my own modest journey with my impulses as my guides—a safe enough trip after all. I *mean,* I thought, what a fuss over nothing! I felt a touch of panic just the same: I was getting down to the nitty-gritty and I knew it.

I made this momentous decision one bright May morning in 1979, while at my desk in the rear studio. Then I rummaged through my mind for an impulse to follow: Nothing there. Rather embarrassed and a bit relieved, I began to work on my latest project, *Oversoul Seven and the Museum of Time.* I pulled the curtains but the sun kept shining in my eyes anyhow, when—happily now— I recognized an *impulse*: I definitely wanted to go into the living room to work where the windows were shaded. Rather abashed at this small harmless enough impulse, I "gave in" without a battle. What was to fight? Then at the last moment I had the urge to grab my daily journal and bring it into the other room with me. So I did, without thinking about it.

Actually it was that second, innocuous impulse that led directly to my writing this book; that, and a seeming mistake. When I sat down by the shaded living room windows, I picked up what I thought was my journal, only to discover that I'd grabbed the "wrong" notebook. The one I had was labeled "Heroics" and contained my old notes on the heroic self and heroic impulses. Hmm.

And in the next moment, the morning had completely changed. It was charged, filled with a stirring psychological motion that somehow combined the morning and me in a new relationship. The thick green rug on the floor seemed to blend with the green trembling leaf shadows just past the window ledges. The spring morning and I were part of each other. Some familiar psychic motion was starting up in me then; I was free to go ahead in some new direction. I knew I was ready to begin a new book in that moment.

I thought that the book would be on "Heroics," and the search for the heroic self. Instead it would lead me to encounter the limiting beliefs that stood in my way. But if I was "wrong" about the projected book's subject matter I was correct otherwise, because this present book began that morning. It would end up leading me back into my own past to confront the very beliefs that impeded my progress—beliefs that were not mine alone, but interwoven in the very framework of our society.

I didn't know any of this though that May morning; and I certainly didn't know that my impulses would lead me on a merry chase, or that they would provide the very framework on which the book would rest. I *was* a bit confused since I was on Chapter 18 of *Oversoul Seven and the Museum of Time,* and this impulse to start a new book meant that I'd lay *Seven* aside for a while. But I was used to following *creative* impulses! The thing is, I didn't realize how fully creative that impulse really was, or that it would involve my non-writing life so completely.

So for a few moments I sensed some internal processes of creativity and organization. I knew that I was in the act of moving into a new book's projected psychological space. Then, without warning, the feelings of certainty vanished. I sat there shocked. The impulse to start a new book might as well have been someone else's, I thought, because I certainly didn't feel it now. The morning and I were separate again. I frowned at the old "Heroics" notebook. I certainly didn't feel heroic, and right then I didn't have an idea in my head. What had happened to that impulse?

I brooded about impulses in general, and spent the rest of the morning and afternoon looking over my "Heroics" notes. My mood didn't improve when nighttime came either. I heard Rob in his studio typing up the last Seth session. The two kittens were playing on the rug and the damned birds, I thought, were singing in the twilight: everybody was busy but me. I was just brooding. And as I thought *that*, I realized that I'd been staring at the bouquet of irises a friend had given me the day before—and resisting the impulse to do an acrylic painting of them. Because—well, because I wanted an impulse to *write,* not one to paint.

Now we were getting somewhere; that was the kind of impulse I resented, I thought. Not that there was anything wrong with painting; I love to paint. But I'd often been afraid that my painting could take up too much time if I let it. So I shrugged mentally, set up my supplies, and began to paint. For a while I still worried: What *had* happened to the morning's terrific impulse to start a new book? Why wasn't I just content that Seth was doing so well on *his* book? Psychologically, I always think of Seth's books as his, even though I realize that my own creativity is also involved there; and, well, my books are mine. Seth's continue relatively independent of my own moods, while mine follow the upswings and downswings of my more usual creative activities. So I thought about that for a while as I painted. Then I wondered why I wasted my time with an art in which I certainly wasn't proficient. But finally my love of color and form took over, and I really enjoyed myself for several hours. By the end of the evening though, I thought nervously that I hadn't put in my full writing hours that day—well, I *had*, but I hadn't written anything—and I tried not to think what I was thinking: that my impulses would lead me into "goofing off." I'd trained myself for years to channel my energies, to ignore impulses that could distract me, and what on earth was I doing, tampering with that arrangement now?

Still, there had been something very satisfying about painting those irises. I fell to sleep wondering what it was. The next morning, determined anew to follow my impulses, I sat staring at the bouquet. It was really stunning, half in sunlight, half in shadow. And beside it sat my still uncompleted painting. This time I was aware of my own unformed thoughts suddenly rising from the background to the foreground of my mind. I grabbed a pen and scribbled down the following paragraph:

"Often we try to contact 'our source,' or the universe, or God, or whatever while acting as if that creative force is everywhere except where we are; as if it forms all of nature but ourselves. But we are each our own contacts with the universe. We *are* the universe as it transforms itself into private persons. Somehow we open up inside, and what we are intersects with what the universe is."

I stared at what I'd written, then I stared at the bouquet of flowers, caught up in a sudden rush of understanding, and I scribbled down the following notes:

"I see the connection between what I've just written and the irises, and in a way my painting of the flowers is teaching me something, though I'm not sure if I can verbalize it. When I paint, though, I'm noisy. I swear, shout, yell with delight or triumph or frustration. I acted that way last night, painting the acrylic of the irises. But underneath all that I felt that some inarticulate connection existed between the irises' mysterious creation and my attempt to duplicate them, though in a less complete form. I can't give life to my painted flowers of course; yet the thrust of creativity involved in the attempt momentarily united me with that greater creativity from which the world, you and I, and the flowers emerge.

"It seems that I'm only in contact with the irises since obviously they're what I see. Yet in a way the flowers are intermediaries, almost hiding the fact that they *are* the universe-turned-into-irises; particular irises, grown in a garden belonging to my friend's father, and now sitting beside my typewriter during this particular Thursday morning of May 1979.

"But again, what about the vaster time out of which the day itself emerges historically to our experience, containing the irises, myself, the friend who gave me the flowers, the paints and canvas board, and Rob typing in the back studio? I used the irises as models for my painting, but from what larger multidimensional model did those living flowers and all of the others in a million back yards emerge?"

This time I read what I'd written, grinning, because my impulse to paint (instead of write) had resulted in some writing after all. Besides that, I felt that the entire question of the origin of the world was intimately tied up with our feelings and beliefs about impulses in general. If we were really the deadliest species, half-crazed survivors in a meaningless universe, tainted with brutish impulses from our evolutionary past, then the poor reputation of impulses in the opinion of science and religion was justified.

But if the world and everything in it emerged from a meaningful pattern of multidimensional relationships—the pattern I sensed uniting me and the irises—then its reality was a cooperative venture as Seth states; and our impulses should help us sense that relatedness.

So I finished my painting, did some chores, worked on some poetry and went to bed tired but triumphant that night, sure that the very next morning I'd be writing more on "Heroics." Instead, I was to begin a rather dizzying journey into my own belief system, riding the bumpy thrust of my impulses, and emerging to my surprise on the crowded boulevard of mass beliefs.

Chapter 4
The Flawed Self

Rob wasn't having any difficulty with Seth's material on impulses at all, incidentally. I told myself that it was easy enough for him to be so nonchalant because he wasn't impulsive to begin with: He had a kind of built-in cool that I'd always admired. *I* was the spontaneous one. Wasn't I? Then I'd think glumly: If I was so damn spontaneous, how come my body parts were so stiff? And for the next few days I kept being drawn to my painting instead of to writing. Not exactly gritting my teeth, but nearly, I determined to *relax* and follow my impulses.

"Follow your *what*?" Rob would ask, as if he didn't understand. Then he'd laugh, but I wouldn't. Two excerpts from my journal show my frame of mind during the end of May. The first is the entry for Sunday, May 27, 1979:

"I get angry and discouraged. What happened to the book I'm supposed to be doing? I lay my novel aside, and what have I been doing? Painting! In fact, painting has really become more absorbing. For one thing, I don't think when I paint. I just paint, so lost in the creative processes that nothing else matters.

"In my writing and thinking though, an extension occurs in which I try to study and explore the creative processes themselves and seek their source or (again) that greater dimension from which they emerge. I know that such a search is also an extension of creativity itself, yet I do resent it sometimes, because it leads to so many tiresome questions that come up time and time again: one-hundred-and-fifty-million times, or so it seems. Sometimes, by contrast, a good little dogma to live by doesn't sound too bad. But that's the rub! There aren't any even halfway reasonable dogmas around nowadays, not one that doesn't offend or outrage either the intellect or the intuitions.

"So even though I know I create my own reality, sometimes I feel cheated and angry, having to take up so much of my life to find some sane reference to live it in. It would be difficult enough, I think at such times—like now—if I were completely free myself from all the nonsense I was brought up to believe was true. But obviously I'm not.

"It isn't particularly easy either to throw off all the idiocies connected with conventional religion, science in general, and God knows what else, but it takes an extra shot of adrenaline to dismiss Darwin. Goodbye, survival of the fittest! The religious fundamentalists are the only ones who question evolution, as far as I know, and *they* believe that the Bible is a book of facts."

And my entry for Monday, May 28, 1979:

"Uh. I've really been trying to relax and follow my impulses, trusting their overall subjective shape, as Seth suggests. There's no doubt that most people think of impulses as disruptive or contradictory—certainly one often seems to contradict another. The idea that impulses operate with an overall plan, that they actually shape our lives according to our own best interests and society's isn't popular to say the least. Western religion and science both put impulses down. The psychic field seems immersed in the idea that the impulsive self is the 'lower self,' devoted to 'mere' physical survival, and that man should be evolving toward so-called higher centers.

"Eastern religion, as it's practiced and understood in this country at least, stresses doing what you *don't* want to do, giving up the self that you know in the belief that an inner, more spiritual self will come out of hiding. In that line of belief, impulses and desires appear in opposition to the individual's search for fulfillment.

"Certainly I grew up believing that I must cut out all impulses except those involved with my writing and ignore all distractions, because left alone I'd be tempted to do other (less important, frivolous) things. I must have believed that my impulses would run in direct contradiction to my conscious dedication. I'm really spontaneous in my work. I didn't think that I dared relax for a moment though, or I'd backslide into laziness or apathy. For one thing, like many people I must have equated relaxation with sloth. And how many of our readers feel the same way? We can't just explore impulses theoretically. We have to deal with our own, practically, in daily life. . . ."

As May came to a close, the temperature was in the 90's for days at a time. Strangers began to knock at our door as some of our readers discovered our address one way or another, and came to call. Seth was still dictating *Mass Events* during our regular sessions. Rob was working on his own painting and typing Seth's material as well, and we were cleaning up the house after winter and putting summer furniture on the porches.

And to my bewilderment, on June 5 a completely new impulse came forcibly into consciousness: I found myself with an idea for still another book, one containing selections from my poetry through the years. Now what, I wondered, could *that* impulse have to do with the book on "Heroics" that I was supposed to be writing? If ever there was a contradictory impulse, this new one was it! But I was supposed to be following impulses, wasn't I? So I spent the next several days reading some old poetry of mine—notebooks piled all over the table; my paintings now forgotten, stacked in the corner of the room.

Impulsively, I began with the notebook closest to me. I suppose that I expected a somewhat pleasant nostalgic day, leafing through old notebooks, remembering favorite lines of poetry nearly forgotten. But the notebook I opened contained my poetry in the years just before the Seth sessions started—and if the May sunshine was warm even with the curtains drawn, the poetry was cold. Some of it was cold and brutal. I hadn't looked at that poetry in ages, and I was tempted not to read any further. But I was fascinated, too. Even the best verses were almost devastating in their pessimism. Worse, as I read them I remembered the sense of conviction with which they'd been written.

The morning was almost over before I realized why the poetry shocked me so. Poetry is a concentrated art form. There had been no distance between me and my beliefs when that poetry was written, so I was now presented with a concentrated picture of my own past beliefs. They were psychologically isolated by time now, so they stood out starkly. When I expressed those negative ideas, I accepted them as facts of life. I railed angrily against their implications but felt that the facts spoke for themselves.

My reactions to the poems didn't stop there, though. For a moment the June afternoon vanished for all intents and purposes from the year 1979. Mentally, at least, I was back in May of 1962, watching (nearly heartbroken) as another spring arrived, deceiving us (or so it seemed), with hopes that it never delivered. In the back of my mind I heard the poet, T. S. Eliot; his dry, cultured, melancholy voice on an old record reading from *The Waste Land*: "April is the cruelest month. . . ." And intermixed with that remembered voice there were snatches of college science lectures, dating back to the early 1950's: "The universe is running down . . ." and "Extinction is the natural conclusion to consciousness." A line of one of my own still older poems flashed into my mind: "Youth, beauty, and truth all give way to time."

With that, 1979 came back where it belonged, and I stared at the poetry notebook, startled by a new realization. The beliefs in those old poems, beliefs that I'd thought were highly personal, were instead my own interpretations of Darwinian and Freudian concepts. Why hadn't I ever seen that before? In *Mass Events,* Seth devoted a good deal of material to the fallacies of both schools of thought, and intellectually I'd followed him right down the line. He'd also alerted readers to be on the lookout for any Darwinian or Freudian theories that they had unwittingly accepted as facts. Look for them? I was suddenly *surrounded* by them. Earlier I just hadn't connected them emotionally with my "personal" beliefs.

I looked over the poetry again. There was no doubt of it: The poetry that I'd thought was so original when I wrote it was actually a showcase for beliefs that I'd picked up from college, from the newspapers and poetry journals, and from the culture in general. I'd considered those poems to be devastating comments on life itself. The ideas were expressed originally enough, and they were concentrated through the poetry form, where (I now saw, miserably) all of their flaws were brilliantly exaggerated.

I wondered how many other people still carried those beliefs, thinking them to be true statements about existence, the result of their own private experiences or deductions, never realizing that they were, instead, a kind of prepackaged cultural foodstuff, with little real mental nourishment.

Now the beliefs expressed in the poetry fascinated me. I sighed, and started reading again. The first poem I read was written in 1961, when I was thirty-one. I'm including this poetry for the benefit of people who don't have such a handy reference to pinpoint their own beliefs.

CARRIER

Old hates lie in wait for the infant
till he grows into a man.
Then they leap upon him
when he puts his father's coat on.
When the father's bones drop into the grave,
the lice flock up as the dark earth turns,
to feed on a son's guilt-love.

No man can look in his son's face,
for what was done to him, he does in turn,
and he carries the hate in his blood;
ghosts of times forgotten,
tragedies unseen, unspoken,
wait in the past's proud flesh,
and nothing will shake them off.

Heavy? I'll say! I thought I wrote that poem as I watched Rob's aging father with his three sons. Actually I wrote it as I interpreted that experience through my personal version of Freudian and Darwinian concepts: Our species itself is tainted by an evolutionary struggle for survival in which the young naturally overthrow the "leader of the pack" to gain control—a struggle played out again and again in each new family, as man—and all species—compete for life. Those tragic flaws were transmitted genetically from man's "brutal" past: He was simply a better killer than the other species. But the view also restates religion's ancient dictum that a father's sins are visited upon his children.

It was as if in all of nature, man alone knew the dreadful secret, that the universe and everything in it was meaningless, and that all of life was a preparation for extinction. So it seemed to me that love was the cruelest emotion of all, because it promised the most, in the face of certain disaster. Although my most optimistic poems were love poems to Rob, they always ended up with the feelings expressed in this stanza:

From LYRIC

Ah, my love, be my love.
Forget the last unknowing,
the misery of the finished flesh,
the time-wind ever blowing,
the summer bed's cruel skeleton,
the knocking at the glass,
and the tenant's final vacancy
from the borrowed flesh.

And death came in all shapes and sizes, I discovered. In the early 60's a favorite cat died, two goldfish, another cat, and Mischa, the dog I had when I married Rob. Back then, there were no alternate ways of viewing death as far as I was concerned: Nature (as science told us) had no particular use for individuals; only the species mattered. About the death of the last cat I wrote:

A SMALL INCIDENT

It wasn't just because the cat died.
I saw you or me brought to that,
and in the callousness of the man who came
to take the corpse, I saw the heartless weeks pass,
and felt the touch of hands
we will not see, while others watch.

In the cat's heavy-packed sleep
I saw the first light leap of her wiry haunches.
Flung into fur and muscle and sun, she even had her young
with no help from us. It was her final acquiescence
after all the living lust that hurt, the brevity
of yellow-eyed emergence, that stung.

I rush through the house scattering disinfectant
like holy water,
but germs are just another word for death.

While I read that poem about the death of our cat back in the 60's, our two kittens played on the green rug in the June 1979 living room, and I remembered my reaction to the death of their predecessor, Billy, a few months earlier. I *had* been saddened. So had Rob. But we had a far larger framework in which to consider Billy's death. Not only had we learned to question official views, but, to some extent anyhow, we'd refused to be emotionally smothered by them. We were cutting short some programmed emotional reactions.

The same event, the cat's death years ago, led me to anticipate my own death, rather dramatically and romantically, taking it for granted that death was final:

DEATH

I shall lie in the roomy earth, cool
and acquiescent as unborn.
No wish will quiver through my arm,
yet what I am will upturn stone.
My lips will have forgotten mouths.
No stars will shine within my brain.
The sun will whisper toward my thighs,
but I will have death's clothing on,
raiment no lover's hand will touch,
or lift the edges of one fold.

I saw our individual lives flickering like fireflies, briefly, before being extinguished forever. The following little poem was written in 1962 about my grandfather's death when I was in college, and again it anticipates my own death as well.

GRANDFATHER

Fireflies flickered, and he pointed,
a pyramid in their midst.
They flashed past his head, all burning,
and he flamed with them as he stood.

He laughed with their million descendants
for sixty swirling years.
Now they flash past my head, all burning,
and I flame with them, as he did.

The moods I had been in when I wrote the poems came

back to me as I read them, some very intensely. But in 1979 I could hardly relate to the following poem on time written in 1962, and now it's very difficult to imagine that I ever felt that way. Yet I recall sitting by the bay windows in the old apartment on Water Street one twilight, staring defiantly at the traffic in the road below, to write these lines:

THE BALANCE

It's the daily exchange
given and taken, that kills;
time's weight.
It's the mountain of the hours
that falls, stone by stone.
It's the daily bruise that wounds
till the soul weeps.
Know this and make your peace,
for the measured sun rays fall
as the moments drop,
and the sweet wind blows
from the mountaintop,
and the evening also rushes
past like a deep brook.
These too will vanish
when the pain stops.

I read the poem aloud when I came across it in the notebook, and that reminded me that I'd originally written it by saying the lines aloud, my voice catching; and that I'd felt rather disconsolate that evening in 1962, pinned down by time's weight. But as I read the poem nearly (Good God!) twenty years later, whatever else might weigh me down, time certainly didn't—I had trouble keeping up with it.

I vaguely recalled feeling stalled back then though, as if I'd come into adulthood with great energy, full steam ahead, only to come to a sudden, dismayed halt like some eager traveler expecting to arrive in a bustling city but finding only a bare, deserted spot of ground. And the next poem showed me why I'd felt that way. It expressed my feelings about adulthood, feelings that I've discovered many young adults have:

THE GAME

The children play hopscotch
on cracked moonlit sidewalks.
Spotlighted, they leap
from square to square.
Their parents sit watching,
from porch chairs rocking.
Inside, white beds in a starry row
wait crisply clean and bare.

The children play hopscotch
on cracked moonlit sidewalks.
On the sidelines their parents watch
as long as they dare.
"When will they discover . . . ?"
murmurs one mother.
The child leaps like a firecracker
into the air,
and back again, touched
as if by tissue's fire.
Crying and burning
the child crumbles there,
and rises exultant
in the cracked moonlight,
baptized and holy
and wickedly bright.

"Mommie," he calls,
but the porches are bare.
Insubstantial shadows inhabit
the rocking chairs.
"You've won the game,
as we knew you would—"
Scornful and sad
come the voices of blood.

"Take over. Take over.
It's your turn now."
Through the sober street
their ghostly voices blow.
The children stop and listen.
They shriek, "It isn't fair!"

But the game is forever,
the rocking chairs creak and glide,
and the children, in grown-up images
sit on cool porches in July.

  "That's still a damn good poem," I thought, safe enough
in the 1979 living room, divorced enough from those feelings to
think with a sense of triumph and relief, "Thank God, I don't feel
that way about adulthood anymore either." I wished momentarily
that I could visit that thirty-one-year-old self somehow and say,
"Hold on. Don't feel so badly. You're really going to get some
important insights. Life *is* as fantastic as you once thought it was,
but in a different fashion than you supposed." Yet maybe I'd
already done that, I thought, staring at the poem. Maybe some part
of me that was still in the future in 1962, somehow told the younger
self about the Seth sessions—for surely they existed, suspended in
my psyche, before they actually began.

  From my correspondence, I also knew that many young
people today feel betrayed or deceived by their own adulthoods, and
I wished that I could tell them that it wasn't life, but their beliefs
about it, that so distorted the will to live and develop. Not only our
beliefs about ourselves, but our beliefs about the species and the
world often hinder us, I thought; and again, the very next poem
illustrated this so perfectly that I might have chosen it on purpose.
It expresses the feeling that man will destroy himself and his world,
and you can see the same pessimism declared in newer form today:
We'll blow ourselves up or starve ourselves out; and individually we
each have a hand in this inevitable downfall.

I SAW A HAND

I saw a hand
plunge down the chaos switch.
Deathlight touched the maple streets.
The children, playing hopscotch,
were tinged, all unheeding.
Crisply their thoughts
dropped like burnt leaves.

The women sighed,
from porches leaning,
their moon faces hanging

like lanterns in air.
Their fingers like fire
trembled and whispered,
and deathlight kindled
their straw hair.

I shouted, "Whose hand? Whose hand?"
and bit it off,
dizzy with the taste of flesh.
But my hand flopped on without me.
The jigsaw world was lost.
My laugh was all I heard.
My hand was all I saw.

When I finished reading the poetry, again I felt a chill
that wasn't in the June afternoon air, but in an atmosphere of mind,
rising from some psychological season where it's always dark
and foreboding. For a few moments I felt intimations of disaster
swirl through my brain. Then catching myself, I muttered, "Hell,
no. We're going to short-circuit that sort of thing right now,"
because, I realized, the whole "we're-doomed-to-ruin-the-world"
bit was also a reaction to Darwinian, Freudian, and religious concepts. What else could you expect, for example, from a killer
species? From people who carried in their subconscious minds
remnants of a beastly heritage? (I use the phrase with apologies to
the beasts, incidentally.) And what could you expect from creatures
stained by original sin to boot?

The heroic self? Hardly. Certainly when those poems
were written, I believed that we were each mortally flawed, given
consciousness only long enough to understand our tragic fate. If we
were heroic, it was only in bearing our unfortunate situation with
some forbearance. We were chemicals and elements somehow gone
astray; demented creatures whose very presence might well present
a vital danger to the universe.

Sounds familiar, doesn't it?

As I closed my notebooks I felt uneasily that some of
those old beliefs still lingered, relatively unchallenged in my mind,
still affecting my thoughts and behavior to some extent. As I
thought that, though, suddenly I became aware of the day's entire
impulsive shape. It began with the morning impulse to read my old
poetry; with the idea of doing a book of poetry and personal
commentary—an impulse that seemed to distract me from my

conscious intent to do a book on the heroic self. Not only had I been led to encounter my own past pessimism, but to realize that it still held some sway in my life. And if I was still tainted by some of those beliefs, I knew that many of my readers were, too. And *then* I realized what I was up to: trying to disentangle myself more fully from official beliefs. For myself and my readers, I was beginning a new psychological journey with my impulses as my guides, though at this point I had no idea where it might lead me. My book had already begun. And the next day I began to choose the poetry for it that I've included in this chapter.

Something else became clear to me too. When I wrote *The Seth Material,* I said that nothing particularly unusual had happened to initiate the Seth sessions. But then, back in 1969, I still didn't realize how limited my beliefs had been in 1963 when the sessions started. Now after reading my old poetry, it became obvious to me that I had to find a new thematic world to live in. My restless creative energy could have found no suitable outlet other- wise, because it had gone as far as it could in that old framework. It had operated in a psychic and physical environment in which no meaning could be found anywhere. And the creative abilities, above all, seek new syntheses.

If I'd thought, back in the 60's, that I'd finally escaped the dogmas of religion, the sophisticated beliefs of psychology and science had been just as limiting, though I didn't realize it. They'd pressed threateningly, as my poetry shows, against the very edges of my existence. They denied dignity—a dignity that I somehow demanded—to life and all of its forms. If life had no meaning, though some part of me kept insisting that it did, then at least I had to discover a framework in which the *possibility* of life's meaning could be sanely considered.

In my daily experience back then, life had seemed dead- ended. Everything—birds, flowers, people—would sometime vanish into complete and final extinction. I couldn't live in that kind of world, and I loved life too much to consider suicide. I loved our apartment; Rob, painting in his studio; the way the sunlight swept across the walls. How mysterious and orderly it all was, to be meaningless.

In hindsight, the dilemma was clear. How could I trust my own growing comprehensions, since, again, I was a member of a flawed species to begin with, whose very impulses were tainted or deadly? More, how could I trust my impulses, when everyone knew that men and women were driven by primitive, self-seeking motives, no matter what they told themselves; and when the crafty sub-conscious was ready to sabotage their conscious ideals at every turn? Again, sounds familiar, doesn't it?

Moreover, psychology officially considered the very search for meaning as a neurotic symptom. In that framework, true sanity meant coming to terms with a meaningless universe. For that matter, psychology sees creativity itself as a kind of aberration caused by an imbalance of bodily hormones, or by unsatisfied neurotic needs. Before the Seth sessions, I interpreted this to mean that if I ever "plumbed the depths" of my subconscious and some-how solved whatever problems I might have, then my desire to write would vanish. Know thyself? Not under those conditions; not if I could help it! At least not when I was thinking according to established patterns.

Luckily our creativity is far more powerful and inventive than we give it credit for, so that those negative beliefs themselves turned into "grist for the mill," and the very writing of poetry itself initiated altered states of consciousness, inspiration, and some glimpses of the psyche's greater wisdom.

And during the time I wrote that poetry, I'd been too busy to brood intensely. I wrote religiously five hours a day. After-noons I worked in a local art gallery. For several of those years, Rob worked full-time in the art department of a greeting card firm, then switched to part-time. In between, there were normal chores and the other details of daily living.

In 1962, my science-fiction novel, *The Rebellers,* was pub-lished as an Ace double paperback. I must have been writing it about the same time that I wrote much of the poetry that I've just included in this book. I'd published a dozen or so science-fiction stories by then, too. Only in fiction did I dare suppose, back then, that established beliefs about the universe didn't really apply. They were the fictions—but if they were, what were the truths?

And while I've made progress, I realized that I'd still been looking over my own shoulder. And I determined not to do that anymore.

Chapter 5
Special Circumstances

In springtime not only do more visitors find their way to our door, but the mail increases and so do invitations to do workshops and other such projects. I wasn't particularly surprised the following day, then, to get a call from my publisher telling me that a movie studio in California was trying to reach me. Since our phone number is now unlisted, it was up to me to call the studio if I was at all interested in what they might have to say.

So I poured a fresh cup of coffee, smoked a cigarette, thought about it for a minute, and dialed. It *was* fun to sit there in the quiet, now shadowy living room—4 P.M. my time, noon their time—and hear an enthusiastic voice tell me that the studio was interested in doing a movie about my life. I admit I savored the moment. Rob came out from his studio and stood there, arms folded, grinning. I wiggled an eyebrow and shrugged elaborately, gestures that made a joke: Oh, I'm so bored with all of these invitations! But what *is* one to do?

I *have* had such offers before, and I'm really not sure why they haven't hit me right. Anyway, the person I spoke with asked if I'd write a few pages about my background, and any conflicts with society that arose as a result of my psychic activity. And my *impulse* suddenly was to do it—which really startled me, since I was pretty sure that I wasn't going to encourage a movie version of my life. Again, such ideas are fun to play around with, but as a writer I stay in the background and like it that way: my thoughts go mind-sailing out through books, even into other countries where I'll probably never go. And Seth's words go out into the world too, emerging from some *inner* country, barely explored.

But a movie of my life? And who would play the part? "And who would fake a Seth trance?" I said to Rob, when I'd hung up the phone. "Even the thought of that is too much!"

We joked about it for a few minutes, then Rob went back to work. And I started thinking: It was true that I didn't want to get involved in a movie, but I suddenly realized that I'd included very little personal background in my own books thus far, though my readers often shared incidents from their own lives with me in their letters. Rob and I had been determined from the first to stress the point that psychic events don't exist by themselves, apart from the rest of life. And—as reading my poetry had forcibly reminded me the day before—I certainly didn't just spring alive with the first Seth session. I had 34 years of other experiences behind me.

Yet sometimes, people who wrote or visited seemed to think that Seth emerged into some hypothetical life that just happened to be mine. A smaller percentage talked about my life being "charmed" in a way that theirs wasn't. And a much smaller percentage seemed to think that Rob and I are like psychic Barbie dolls, born sanitized, or plaster-of-paris people for whom everything has always come easily. We have our roles: Rob sits attentively on the couch with notebook in hand; Jane sits facing the couch, with prop cigarettes and wine or beer ready; then the real magic starts.

I gladly admit that only a minority of our readers see us in such lights, yet those attitudes had bothered me for some time. I knew that they were versions of another, more extensive view; that psychic abilities somehow exist apart from the lives involved, while of course the basic magic lies in that living context of consciousness that makes those abilities possible.

Another idea came to mind that really upset me. It was the belief that psychic abilities solve all problems, or are meant to do so. Psychic abilities, I thought more intensely, are almost always considered as a means to an end, instead of as a beginning. And in their enthusiasm for spiritual development, people again too often forget the magnificent medium of living itself, in which we're all equally immersed.

Almost without realizing it, I'd grabbed a pen and

started scribbling down my thoughts, thinking of all the things I'd
want emphasized if anyone ever *did* do a movie of my life and any
conflicts I'd experienced as a result of my psychic activity. A small
part of me whispered, "What are you wasting your time with that
for? You know you aren't going to send it to the movie studio." And
I answered rather grandly, "I'm following my impulses."

Still, I was aware of a certain feeling of reluctance too. I
wasn't particularly happy with the thought of telling the world that
I'd grown up on welfare, or that "ladies of the evening" often served
as our housekeepers when their usual places of business were
closed down in my original home town of Saratoga Springs, N.Y.
That background was once as much a part of my life as my
experiences today are, though, and it was from that living framework that the Seth sessions eventually emerged. So I decided that it
was time to fill in some of those past events for my readers, so that
the Seth sessions could be viewed in that context.

I guess I also wanted to say to others, "Look, if you're
having rough going right now, don't despair. Who knows what
redeeming events might happen tomorrow—events that are happening at other levels now, but haven't yet shown themselves?"

I was somewhat reluctant about another issue, too. In
his own notes for the Seth books, Rob mentioned my physical
symptoms occasionally, and it's my fault that he wasn't more
specific. I'm certainly not proud of my lack of agility. I've always
been gifted with energy. I still am, and I'm never bored. I find my
life and all life exciting. But for a while the idea people had of me, as
expressed in their letters, made me feel that any fault was doubly
reprehensible in me, or so it seemed, because "I had Seth." Besides
this, I knew that a few people at least, hearing that I was less than
perfect, shown to be human after all (dear God!), would say, wisely,
"Oh, yes, psychic activity takes its toll." It took me a while to
understand that both attitudes were unreasonable.

To deny that I have any ordinary human difficulties
denies part of my life, of course. Psychic abilities are *human* qualities,
appearing like all other such characteristics in the saint and sinner,
the wise man and the fool; but we've been taught to treat those
abilities with envy or dread, and to think of "psychics" as a breed
apart. So for those reasons, I decided that afternoon to speak
frankly about my physical symptoms in this book too, when they
applied to the subject at hand.

So, it goes without saying that I make no "supernatural"
claims. I don't materialize holy ash, or perform miracles at midday. I don't claim to be a healer, though I do believe that each of us
has the ability to heal ourselves, and that some people are uniquely

equipped to help us do so. I *do* proclaim the uniqueness of my own personality and its private connection with the universe, but I also maintain that each other individual is also unique, with his or her own connection to the universe. That's what this book is all about.

It took me three or four days to write the notes about my past, and during that time old memories seemed to pop up no matter what I was doing. Rob's notes in Seth's books *did* provide a steady reminder of life's daily framework in which the sessions took place, I thought again. But despite our efforts to relate psychic experience to daily living, a gap *had* developed in some people's minds—at least, between the unique subject matter of our books and my own life. Well, I was going to close that gap, I decided. So if my old poetry sent me mentally back into the 1960's, my impulsive reaction to the movie studio's telephone call turned my thoughts backward even further.

Each life has its own beginning in this world, of course; its own exterior history, its own special circumstances. To some extent, then, my own life has been marked by "special circumstances" also. These were unremarkable enough in life's greater context. Many people have had far more spectacular backgrounds, but in the context of my own early experiences, my life seemed to consist of "special circumstances"—and little in my life, from its start to now, has ever seemed to fit any norm.

My parents were divorced by the time I was three years old, but most of my childhood friends came from broken homes too, so that didn't particularly bother me. My mother was a bed-ridden arthritic invalid; I'd never seen her walk; and that I did consider a special circumstance. We were on welfare—hardly an unusual situation—but I was the only kid I knew who was being supported by taxpayers' money, and this was a special circumstance in my mother's mind and in mine; one we railed against constantly.

I wrote poetry as far back as I can remember, at home, in school, anywhere, everywhere, and at any time. To me this represented another special circumstance; one that seemed to give me some kind of uneasy status, as if I possessed a definite recognizable ability that no one knew quite what to do with—a remarkable but relatively worthless talent to someone in my particular position.

Again, those situations are hardly outstanding in life's larger context, but in my home town they seemed to set me apart. I also spent nearly two years in an institution called St. Vincent's Female Orphanage while my mother was in a hospital, and on my return home I didn't particularly feel like "one of the gang."

Other events that most people didn't know about set me

apart in my own mind too. One day my mother would say that she loved me, and the next day she'd scream that she was sorry I'd ever been born—that I'd ruined her life. She blamed me for the death of *her* mother who went out one evening to buy me shredded wheat for supper and was killed in an automobile accident. I was six. She also blamed me for the death of our favorite housekeeper, who died of a stroke in my arms when I was thirteen, right after the three of us had an argument. My mother would often stuff her mouth with cotton and hold her breath, pretending that she was dead, to scare me when I was small. In later years when I was in grade school and high school, she'd threaten suicide, sometimes saying that she'd also mail a letter to the police stating that I'd murdered her. And she did attempt suicide four or five times.

She was on all kinds of medically prescribed drugs, which helps explain some of her actions; and if she could be "a terror," she was also quite intelligent, imaginative, and above all, dramatic. She finally ran a telephone service from her bed, with my help. When I was in grade school she took creative writing courses by proxy, sending me to nighttime adult writing courses where I took notes for her and she did the assignments.

I mention all this now simply to make the point that my early life, like most of my readers', had its share of family misunderstandings and its own challenges.

It also had its own unique advantages. Our neighborhood bristled with vitality, and I used to sit on the porch steps and observe it all, and write my poetry when my chores were done. And listen. I felt even then that I had some direct connection with the universe. When I wrote poetry, the universe seemed to talk to me. Sometimes I talked back, and on rare occasions we spoke at once. There were even some cultural advantages that I quite took as my right at the time. These came along with rich doses of dogma from the priests, sent by our local Catholic church to be my "spiritual" fathers, and to compensate for my not having a male parent right at hand.

As I grew older the priests became younger, leading to some situations that in retrospect seem rather hilarious if unfortunate enough; then, they really shattered my idealism in certain areas. But, no matter. On the other side of that slippery ledger, the priests were highly educated men for the times. They introduced me to "good music," books, and philosophy. One old Irish priest read to us from a book of English poetry every Sunday afternoon for years. By the time I was in my middle teens though, the church and my poetry parted company when the priests objected to the

ideas I was beginning to express. Where my poetry goes, I follow—
so as I've written elsewhere, it was goodbye to the Catholic Church
and as far as I was concerned to conventional Christianity as well.

Some of my ideas certainly came from my mother's
father. She and he had a family argument and didn't see each other
for twenty years, though we all lived in the same town. Mother
wouldn't let my grandfather in the house. She let me visit him
though. He was part Indian and part French, a tiny, dark-haired
man with an Indian hooked nose; tight-lipped and stubborn. But
he talked to me about the spirits of the fire and the wind, and took
me for long walks in a nearby woods, while he told me Indian
legends.

I was popular enough in high school, though my boy-
friends had to wait on the front porch while I gave my mother the
bedpan before I went out. They could hear her yelling at me
through the open windows in summertime, "Hurry up, *bitch,*" if she
was really in a lousy mood, which was often. We had no furnace, so
in winter I had a coal stove and an oil burner to keep going, and
sometimes it seemed that whenever I went out, the fires did too.
Then I'd get a call to come home and restart them.

I got to college, again by special circumstances. Skidmore College is in Saratoga Springs. Then it was on the other side of
town. It had no real campus, but operated from a group of
beautifully kept old Victorian mansions. As a kid, I walked past
them often, telling myself that one day I'd be a student in that
college and know the insides of those mansions "like the back of my
hand." I insisted on taking a college preparatory course in high
school, instead of the business course that welfare authorities
suggested. Though my marks were only fair, I still applied to
Skidmore for a scholarship.

In the meantime, one of my high school teachers entered
some of my poetry for me in the National Scholastic Poetry Contest.
He didn't tell me about this until I received notice that I was among
the state winners; he'd asked to see some of my poetry, but I had no
idea that he'd entered it in the contest. I was still a good Catholic at
the time, and as we waited for the contest winners to be evaluated, I
prayed constantly to win.

I remember vividly walking through the snow to six
o'clock Mass, before school—cold, excited, chanting under my
breath: "I'll win the national contest. I'll win, I'll win, I'll win."

I would win! I had to win! I prayed to the universe, the
Sacred Heart, the Virgin Mary; to all of the saints I could think of;
and also to the bare treetops, the sparkling snow, the stars still
showing in those cold morning hours.

Well, I didn't win the national contest, but I did get honorary mention in it, and *that* led Skidmore to grant me the scholarship I'd applied for. The scholarship didn't begin to pay expenses, of course, so I worked at a series of jobs all through college—writing for the local newspaper, for the college itself, and anywhere I could during the summers.

The entire world seemed to open up for me. My writing brought me to the attention of a then well-known writer, Caroline Slade, who published in the national women's magazines and had a best-selling novel besides. Caroline introduced me at Yaddo, the famous writers' colony, which also happened to be in Saratoga (or rather, on its outskirts). I'd visited there often as a kid too—appearing at the back door with a stack of poetry, announcing that I was a poet. Once the cook who answered gave me a piece of cake, and once I was chased away.

Now, with some other college students, I was being invited to affairs there. At first I was dizzy with excitement, but as Caroline's protégée I was expected to serve tea, listen, look ladylike, and not interrupt the discussions. There was a cocktail party for the poet, Louis Untermeyer, at "Carrie's" house, and other heady meetings with some of the famous and near-famous members of the literary establishment. Once I argued about poetry with the actor Monty Woolley (of *The Man Who Came to Dinner* fame) in a local bar—and won. I went around dazed with self-importance for weeks.

In college I did well in subjects I liked, poorly in those I disliked, was president of the Day Students' Council, contributed to the school literary magazine, went wild reading a popular book on Einstein's theories, and very nearly flunked biology twice—I couldn't, wouldn't dissect the frog. I'd already been fairly well grounded in American and English poetry, and now I fell headlong into the world of philosophy and became much more aware of fiction and the novel.

I began a poets' and artists' club, fell in love and out of it several times, drank tons of coffee, didn't eat enough, and stayed away from the house whenever I could. And always I read poetry to anyone who would listen—but as if I didn't care if they listened or not. I was poor but talented. Disdainfully, I thought that the talented might one day get money, but the rich could never buy talent. So in that wealthy girls' college, I played it "poor but proud, thank you."

I never daydreamed about being a mother, or even about being married in conventional terms. Sometimes I saw myself living in Greenwich Village in New York City, as a proud and poor poet. Sometimes I saw myself as a college English teacher, spending my nights writing poetry until dawn. And I still like to write nights.

Looking back now, it's easy to see that I had no models for the socially accepted conventional female role, which was certainly a blessing. There were women galore and few men in my early background. Primarily there was my mother, of course, a bedridden woman on welfare who ruled the house (the housekeepers and me) through a series of tantrums and threats. The American Dream hadn't worked for her. She'd staked her future on her considerable beauty when she was a young woman, and lost, or so it seemed to both of us when I was growing up. She'd even married a man wealthy enough for the times, but she had a terrible temper, and she and my father never got along. She told me that he was perverted because he liked "unconventional" positions for love-making—"bestial intercourse." Dear God! She blamed her physical situation on the breakup of the marriage, and, I guess, on my birth.

Next door lived a woman in her eighties and her sixty-ish-year-old daughter. The story was that the daughter had given up her own life to care for her mother, and they argued night and day. So I thought, early in the game, "Not for me, thank you." My mother could out-threaten, out-scream, and out-lie that old woman any day, and I wasn't going to be around home when *I* was sixty. Or thirty. Or even twenty-one.

I was compassionate enough though; that is, I wasn't hard-hearted. I was up with my mother half the night for years, to give her the bedpan, fix her pillows, obey reasonable and unreasonable demands and fill the oil burner, which always ran out of fuel around 4 A.M. And I decided back then that if motherhood had turned a "young American beauty" into that unhappy woman, then motherhood wasn't for me either. That youthful, emotional decision (ill-formed and made for the wrong reasons) kept me from too much early sexual experimentation, and probably turned me into something of a tease. I'd "neck" but only go so far, because . . . well, because I was going to be a writer, "free and unhampered." At the very least, I wasn't going to get pregnant in my teens.

The women I knew *did* things. My mother's doctor was a woman. She even had two children (a fact I managed to ignore), and her family lived well on the welfare money paid for patients like my mother by the county. The story was that the doctor's husband was a "weak" man, and no one in the neighborhood even knew what he did for a living. So I resolved that if I ever did marry, it would have to be to a man who could hold his own.

But Caroline Slade was my mentor through high school and college, and her husband was a lawyer, though it was her show as far as I was concerned. They had a large summer house. In winter, though, the Slades lived in a town apartment, and I visited Carrie there often, agog over the book-lined walls, the manuscripts and other signs of the writer's world. She and her husband took Sundays for themselves, seeing no visitors. My mother, then in her forties, often snorted about that arrangement: "What a lot of bullshit. Lovey-dovey idiocy. That's all it is." But it sounded great to me.

Carrie wanted me to be a *lady* writer, though, which was something else again. I'd taken to gathering notes for dialogue in local diners and bus stations and sometimes (terrified, but feeling brave) alone in bars. So after a while, our relationship palled on both sides. It wasn't helped, either, by the fact that the college withdrew my scholarship and suspended me at the end of my third year because I'd attended an all-night party with three professors and three students. All we did was drink and discuss philosophy; at least, that's all *I* did.

My mother, who had attempted suicide several times in the past, tried again just before that party, and again several weeks after, by taking overdoses of sleeping pills. She'd become more and more irrational, and I suspected even then that the pills for pain she took contributed. Anyhow, I went to the welfare authorities while my mother was in the hospital, said that I was leaving, insisted that the authorities provide the care for her that I couldn't, and left for California—where my father lived.

I left with a fellow student who had just graduated. I'd been dating him regularly. He had a motorcycle, and the two of us took off on it. It was 1950. We crossed the continent on that cycle, and crossed it several times later by car. Eventually we married because we wanted to go back to Saratoga and didn't dare return without a marriage license.

My mother was back home by then. Her housekeeper had given notice, and she pleaded with me to take care of her until she found someone else; so I did, even though she wouldn't even let my husband in the house. He stayed with friends. After a few weeks of that, I found my mother a housekeeper myself, and moved out for the final time. For the next three years—the time my marriage lasted—Mother fought with one housekeeper after another, and I helped out when I could.

In that time I had a variety of jobs. I thought that I was working to put my husband through college. He was supposed to be working on his master's degree at the State University in Albany, but I discovered that he wasn't in school at all. When I left to work in a local factory, he left along with me each morning, and simply returned home to while away the hours.

All this time I wrote constantly, whenever I could. I met Rob in 1953 and we were married in 1954, after my divorce. I'd always known that writing was for me, and I knew that Rob was for me the minute I met him. After traveling around the country for a few years, we ended up in Elmira. Rob had his part-time job in the art department of the greeting card firm, and his devotion to his painting. I had my part-time job at the art gallery, and my devotion to my writing. By then I'd published my science-fiction stories, poetry, and my first novel.

So we're back up to the days when I wrote that poetry about the vulnerability of man and the briefness of time.

I was thinking about those past events constantly, of course, when I wrote the first notes for this chapter. If the woman hadn't called from the movie studio that day, and if I hadn't decided to follow my impulses, I probably wouldn't have shared so many personal details. (I began an autobiography, *From This Rich Bed,* some time ago, for example, but it sits gathering dust on a shelf.)

As I thought about the past though, it was obvious that my experiences had stimulated me to ask questions I might not have asked otherwise—questions that were to lead me to seek a greater framework. And as I wrote this chapter, I began to see more clearly how I'd come to encourage impulses that led to writing and curtail those that led in any other direction. Still, I didn't feel as impatient with myself as I had earlier. I even thought, with a grin, "You've come a long way, baby!"

Chapter 6

Goodbye Freudian Flaws, Darwinian Demons, and Crucified Gods

As I went rummaging through my past, I was mildly shocked when my own notes reminded me that Rob and I had been married almost ten years before the Seth sessions started. From my 1979 vantage point those early years seemed strangely telescoped and shortened, so that I thought of our marriage in one breath and the first Seth session in the next—as if there were hardly any time between. But I know we spent most of those years in our Water Street apartment, both working, painting and writing steadily, buying nothing on credit so that we'd have peace of mind, concentrating on our work. We went without a car for several years. We had freedom within the system, we figured, as long as we kept our wants in line. So even though we just had enough to get by, we felt quite triumphant most of the time: We were learning our crafts and supporting ourselves. When I sold a story or Rob sold a painting, we knew that it was all worthwhile.

47

So I had all that behind me when the Seth sessions started late in 1963, and since then I've acquired those 4,000-some-odd hours of trancetime, and more evidence of life's greater dimensions than I could reasonably expect.

But it's taken me a while to put it all together. For one thing, my psychic experience carried along with it a few of its own "shockers" as far as my relationship with the world was concerned, particularly in the beginning. I discovered early in the game, for example, that "psychic" books were considered "non-books" by the literary establishment I'd looked up to for years. There wouldn't be any of the reviews in respected journals that I'd daydreamed of as a child. Later I decided that I must be one of the most prolific non-writers ever. But my ideas about writing were changing also. The fact was that the old kind of fiction, the conventional novel form, no longer contented me, and the literary journals began to seem stuffy, limited, bound by concepts with which I could no longer agree. I was "hooked" by the glimpses I had of wider psychological experience. So after a while I forgot about the journals—or nearly.

And I discovered that psychics were either scoffed at, thought of as frauds, nearly idolized, or supposed to be all-wise and all-knowing—all attitudes that drove me up the wall. For example, on tour to publicize *The Seth Material,* Rob and I were almost yanked out of a studio just minutes before we were to go on the air. A secretary had been unable to establish the whereabouts of Raymond Van Over, the psychologist who wrote the book's Introduction. The studio suspected that he didn't really exist and that we were "frauds." Luckily, at the last moment, he was located. We were allowed to go on the air. *Then,* I was bewildered, embarrassed, and confused. *Now* I wouldn't have gone on if they'd plied me with gifts.

So I had to face the fact that I was blessed with abilities that were considered symptoms of emotional abnormality or mental derangement by psychology, often thought of as demonic by religion, and whose very existence was denied altogether by science. So in my darker moments I used to think that my psychic initiation and subsequent experiences were a mixed bag, to say the least.

But the fact is that I was very sensitive to criticism for the very good reason that often I still shared many of the beliefs that stimulated it. Coming to psychic awareness, strongly gifted in that area, I still carried along with me the beliefs that I'd acquired from my own background and the culture of the times. And I was always weighing my "new information" against the old.

Again, like almost everyone else in the Western world, I was brought up to believe that I was a part of a brilliant but flawed species, one bound for ultimate tragedy and extinction. More, being female, I numbered myself as second-best, which meant that I had to try even harder. And if we *are* flawed, how can we trust ourselves or our impulses or inner knowledge? So while I went my own way, I'd done so very anxiously, waiting for that flawed self to show its deceptive nature at last. One part of me watched the other part, ready to pounce upon any duplicity. And how could I trust *my* vision when it also seemed to me that those who were most sure of their beliefs were also the most fanatic?

It's taken me some time, again, but finally I realized that the most vocal salesmen of God and science alike defended their ideas so strenuously because they sensed the unwieldy foundations of their doctrines. Not that I cared—that was their right; but the realization cleared the mental air. I no longer had to feel that personal vision by itself was somehow suspect.

Of course I didn't! Yet as I wrote these notes about my past, as I sat there in those June afternoons of 1979 with those satisfying 4,000-some-odd trance hours under my mental belt, with all of my own psychic experiences and with Seth's books stacked neatly beside me, another chill rose up as if some freezer door of old beliefs suddenly opened, disclosing mental icetrays of fears I'd only stored away, not thrown away as I'd supposed.

For a while those beliefs thawed themselves out, and I felt flushed. It almost seemed dangerous again to believe that I was a good worthy person, a member of a decent species; or worse, to even imagine that some kind of divinity fashioned my being and gave it life. Because, I thought again, well, *Christ,* didn't Charles Manson believe that he was divine? And what about the Reverend Jim Jones? Look what self-expressed divinity did to him and his followers!

Then I realized that those particular fears came from *religious,* rather than scientific, beliefs that I thought no longer held any sway in my life. No wonder so many self-proclaimed messiahs dealt in bloodshed of one kind or another, I thought. We have a long history behind that one! There's the God of Vengeance, Jehovah the bloodthirsty, whose own son is a crucified victim. And, I mused disconsolately, our gods are even more flawed than we are. They exaggerate our deepest fears and most spectacular hopes. Good God, I thought—each of us in our private lives carries those beliefs in our own duplicity to some extent or another: Biologically we're a species surviving because of our deadly intent; and spiritually we're marred from the start. No wonder I didn't trust my impulses! And what about other people? They were as tainted as I was by such beliefs, and they didn't have the advantage of the Seth sessions.

I actually shivered. If Christ said, "Turn the other cheek," did the Crusaders pay any attention? Or the members of the Inquisition? It seldom occurs to us that to be divine might possibly mean that we could not kill; not even our enemies, or heretics, or the bad guys. But, some poor disturbed person believes that he or she is divine, and hears God's voice commanding the death of a neighbor, or ten neighbors, and for *that* (I thought ironically) we have Biblical precedent. Didn't Jehovah slay the enemies of the Israelites? Didn't God command Abraham to slay his own son, staying his hand only at the last moment? Now if I believed in the devil, I thought, *that's* when I would have said, "Get thou behind me, Satan." Was that the divinity that gave rise to my life? And yours?

I was back to that old question because, I thought irritably, it was impossible to think of our private impulses without considering their source and the nature of the self that gives rise to them. I knew, of course, that it was Seth's latest book (*Mass Events*) with its emphasis on impulses, that was bringing all of these questions to mind again. More, I suspected that this was just what Seth had in mind, not only for me but for readers of that book. We couldn't just shove those old beliefs under the rug (or back into that thematic freezer) because they still limited us too much in our daily lives. We couldn't—as Seth stated—look for "the inner self" while distrusting the self that we knew, and suspecting the very impulses that were meant to lead us toward greater fulfillment.

I was really upset. Although my beliefs about the world *were* overturned when the Seth sessions began, I thought, and although I had all those hours of altered perception, there was no doubt about it: To a considerable extent my methods of operating in the world still followed old habitual ways, so that my new beliefs must constantly vie with official, conventional ones.

I *was* aware of life's larger dimensions. I no longer automatically reacted to death as if it were the end of consciousness, and contrasting my late poetry with those earlier poems showed that I'd expanded my mental and emotional skyscape considerably. But in Seth's material I seem to have discovered an art of living, a new multidimensional art that requires not only the best of my writing and psychic abilities, but a practical expertise in all of life's other areas; and I don't have the techniques down pat, to say the least. The Seth sessions still continue so the "lesson plan" isn't finished yet. I hardly understand the millionfold nuances of thought, desire, and intent that together form the individual living picture of the world. So my own limitations in this living art sometimes strike at me bitterly—even though I know that like everyone else, I have to live and learn at the same time.

And only sometimes, I think that our readers can put the Seth material to work easier than Rob and I can, because . . . well, because they don't have to take those first strange subjective steps— and because we're so busy getting new material that we don't have time to study it as thoroughly as some of our readers do. But, when I think that way, I lose the sense of play and spontaneity that always sustains me in the sessions, and realize that I'm trying too hard and certainly not "hanging loose."

But anyway, it seems to me that I *am* trying to live up to an art that is entirely new and multidimensional, one that reaches into the most intimate aspects of life. Seth would probably say that he's referring to a natural homey craft of living that we've forgotten— in fact, he *has* said that in so many words, but from our level of reality those once-native techniques have to be relearned. We can each start by trying to distinguish between our own personal beliefs and observations and those that we've simply accepted from our culture, without examination.

And what can we actually say about life? After I finished stewing about the old beliefs brought so vividly to mind, I asked myself that question, trying to distinguish between what we experience about life and what we've been told. At the very least, I decided, life is characterized by sensation, individuation, growth, and purposeful motion; and in the case of humans this involves activity under the direction of the will. Life certainly seems to be a state of emotional, purposeful activity on the part of men and animals alike. As far as we're concerned, life usually seems almost inseparable from the body. The physical senses perceive activity only within their own range, however—so if there *is* life beyond their field of activity, they couldn't normally tell us about it. But the fact remains that on a normal conscious level we have nothing to compare life to except death, which appears to represent life's end.

As to the origin of life, any life, I thought, we remain ignorant. Our science theorizes about the beginning of the cosmos or the birth of life. Our religions postulate endless versions of a man-God, hardly more rational than we are, as the Creator. In the past I *have* sometimes thought that maybe life is meaningless after all. Then I'd think that maybe the Seth material is a kind of cosmic poppycock—the chemical composition of my mind somehow intelligent enough to understand the irony of its own meaninglessness, then spinning desperate yarns, as many psychologists would say;

futile fantasies leading nowhere. But then I'd think that a brain that could conceive of order somehow had to emerge from a greater order. Besides that, earlier I hadn't realized (I thought, feeling better) that science and religion had spun some pretty weird yarns themselves, and if poppycock was being measured on a scale of one to ten, in my book anyhow they'd each get a twelve and a gold star.

Watching news on television didn't exactly inspire confidence in man's destiny either, I thought, but behind the news is the arena in which world events happen—an arena as Seth constantly reminds us, in which all things grow according to their kind. Certainly purposelessness could not give us such well-ordered genetic activity, such elegant sequences of molecular activation. So there must be a purpose in life, I decided. But why is it hidden from us? Or at least, from the conscious mind?

As always, one question just led to another. If many scientists believed that life had no meaning outside of its own survival, most religions insisted that life's purpose was to serve God. But *which* God? I wondered irritably—the God who sent a flood to destroy an ancient world as punishment for sin? Who turned Lot's wife into a pillar of salt? Surely, I thought—for probably the thousandth time—our religious concepts are but dim visions that conceal far more than they convey, and close our eyes to a far greater divinity and a different kind of vision that might illuminate our position. And if the religious picture of God is parochial and prejudiced, embellished with the most primitive ideas of good and evil, science's version of man's source was equally nonsensical as far as I was concerned. In *that* picture, the universe consists of a meaningless conglomeration of elements, with life a curious and relatively unimportant by-product. And even the Eastern religions seem to see life only as an unpleasant condition of existence from which release is sought.

So what was the answer?

The answer, I thought vehemently, was to stack unofficial experience against official experience, to acquire our own body of evidence by paying direct attention to what actually *happens* in our lives, as opposed to interpreting those events as we've been taught. The answer was to begin trusting ourselves and our impulses now—and starting out with some sense of adventure, not looking over our shoulders at the official world. I was really talking about myself, of course.

So, somewhere during that week of June 1979, as I looked back into my own past and found in my present more old beliefs than I knew what to do with, I made some important discoveries about myself. Since my youth I've been a questioning person, for example, and I questioned myself most of all. I've certainly questioned my psychic experiences and the writings that resulted. And there's nothing wrong in that. Yet along with those intuitive knowings and growing collection of new concepts, I was always more than aware of the weight of conventional ideas. Even to myself, I was guilty until proven innocent; that is, the burden of proof seemed to rest upon me since so many other people were satisfied with the philosophical structure of our civilization. And as May turned into June, I realized that I was changing too—or I certainly intended to—from a Maylike, promising but still tenuous state of mind to the kind of sturdy definite flowering that June brings. It was time for me to really set myself as free as possible from the world's authoritative beliefs.

Seth wasn't just presenting an evocative theoretical framework through which we could view reality; he was initiating a new and superior philosophical system that explained reality more clearly than science or religion. It was as simple as that, I decided. So I simply had to shake off those old beliefs for myself and for my readers as well.

That means, I thought, that if we really want to form our own realities according to our *own* ideas, then we must rip out the beliefs that tell us we are evil, demented, powerless—the pawns of fate or chromosomes, the victims of genetics or society. It means forsaking not family and friends, but families of beliefs with whom we've become more than friendly, and in which we've already invested a good deal of time and effort. It means forsaking belief systems that define our existences for us.

And we're so used to them that their dogmas often pass unnoticed, in disguises that we never recognize. One example in particular came instantly into my mind—the television programs that deal with wild animals in their native environments. Nature programs, right? Half right: Through science's marvelous technology we do indeed see the splendid animals in their environments, but nature is interpreted through the "struggle for survival" concepts exclusively. Darwinian theories are taken for granted as being literal interpretations of the origin of the species; as literal fact, just as some Christian churches take the Bible's version of the world's birth as fact.

But science, I'd discovered, is as embarrassingly short of proving the theories of evolution as religion always has been in any attempt to prove that God created the world in six days and rested on the seventh. So I wasn't going to be bamboozled any longer by scientific dogmas either, or by the assumptions that went almost invisibly along with them.

So finally during those springtime afternoons I began to feel a delicious mental freedom. I didn't know if it would last or not, or where it might lead me, but I determined to follow it. I almost felt as if that thirty-two-year-old self, writing that poetry about life's meaninglessness, also sent me out on this subjective journey. In my mind she still sits in front of those bay windows, and I keep bringing her back tidbits of truth for her to nibble on. I give her the strength to continue; and she *did,* so that now I can write about her. But I still have a long way to go for both of us.

Chapter 7
The God of Jane

Even though I've had some marvelous and sometimes even awe-inspiring experiences in out-of-body states, I'm in no rush at all to leave this nest of the body to "try my wings" elsewhere. I'm more than willing to wait my place in line. That spring of 1979 brought death into our calculations though, as Rob and I made arrangements with a well-known university that agreed to accept for their library archives all our papers, paintings, and related materials upon the inevitable future events of our deaths.

Our intent was simply to insure that the Seth material would be preserved, available to the public, and presented in its true context—as a part of our lives. But how weird to imagine all of our paintings and books and private notes and Seth sessions—our *lives* in print and paper and canvas—stacked in some future library room, *surviving* manufactured products, while our flesh and blood was gone! For a while when I'd scribble a note in my journal I'd stop, dismayed momentarily, thinking that those funny squiggles of ink and how I arranged them would one day be deciphered by others. I wouldn't be around to mold them into an art form. And on a few occasions I imagined myself in some last future springtime, in my eighties, saying to hell with it all, having a wild bonfire

in the back yard—manuscripts, poetry, and notes all brilliantly
flaming; yellowed papers crinkling, sparks flying into that future air.
Then I'd think, "Rob would never do a thing like that." And I'd
think of all the painstaking work he's done and still would do on the
Seth material particularly—the careful notes and references—and
feel ashamed of myself. But the fantasy cleared my mind just the
same, and restored my sense of freedom.

And about the same time, the brand-new just-published
copies of my novel came, *The Further Education of Oversoul Seven,* and
shortly afterward the first copies of the German edition of *Seth
Speaks,* the first translation of one of Seth's books. Those shiny
editions brought my thoughts back to the present. So did the
springtime flowers in the yard. In-between times, I did acrylic
paintings of the forsythia and daffodils. Following my impulses, I
started the spring cleaning and shocked myself by also beginning—
and sticking to—a twenty-minute exercise period each day. And,
following a different set of impulses, I started on a new "round" of
poetry. I kept wondering where all those impulses were leading me,
and what events they were triggering in Seth's Framework 2 that
hadn't yet appeared in my daily life.

I accepted the impulse to begin exercising as a constructive, natural one, rising from inner Framework 2 activity into
the usual living area of Framework 1. And I reminded myself often
that as Seth states, the impulsive self knows our entire life situations
and takes these into consideration. Yet particularly in the beginning,
it seemed almost sacrilegious to take twenty minutes from my
writing to exercise. Why? Well, because! Because I'd trained myself
for so many years to concentrate all of my energies and spontaneity
into my work. Because? Uh, well because, left alone I'd be tempted
to do other things than write. Because? Oh, because, I couldn't trust
my impulses. Because? Because any fool knew that impulses were:
1. unsavory urges from man's bestial past; 2. unsavory, best-hidden
urges from the private, primitive subconscious; and, 3. at best contradictory and chaotic and unreasonable and dumb! I'd run
through the entire sequence of feelings and beliefs in my mind, *then*
tell myself firmly that I didn't believe any of that nonsense anymore. And finally, I'd do my exercises. Big brave Jane!

But it was easy to see that such beliefs made cowards of
us all, though in different areas. Some of my correspondents were
terrified of using their *creative* abilities because they were so suspicious of even creative impulsiveness and so afraid of their own
energies. With Seth dictating *Mass Events* in our regular sessions,
and with that new material fresh in my mind, it was easy to see how

those negative cultural beliefs were interpreted in all of our daily lives.

Just the same, as I worked with my own impulses on a physical level, sometimes "daring" to leave my desk during working hours if an impulse came to do so, I'd feel a touch of panic, thinking, "My God, I trained myself so well to cut out all distractions. What on earth am I doing? Trying to undo all that *good work?*" But that good work had gone too far: I'd cut down physical impulses to *move*. "And you can't do that," I'd say sternly to myself. Just the same, I had to admit that the restrictions still made sense to part of me or I'd be as physically flexible as the next person.

And while this was going on I was still working with some of the ideas discussed in the last chapter. Granted, we distrusted impulses because of their poor reputation in the eyes of science and religion, and because our own experience with them often reflected our beliefs; still it was impossible to even consider impulses as largely constructive and meaningful unless we also assigned purpose and meaning to the universe, and postulated a trustworthy self. And if I was throwing out the official explanations of science and religion in those areas, what was I offering instead?

I was offering the Seth material and my own vision, of course, but once again I wondered why I'd done so almost apologetically. I gave myself the same answer as I always did to such questions: I was afraid of leading myself or others down some hypothetical garden path. But this time, some powerful emotions came shooting into my mind, ripping the answer to shreds.

I thought vehemently: We can't find meaning in our private lives if we believe that the universe itself is without meaning. We can't live lives of honor if we believe that we're members of a dishonorable killer species (and in a meaningless universe, who makes that judgment, anyhow?). We can't trust ourselves or our impulses, either, if we believe that we're tainted by original sin or flawed critically by a spiritual or physical heritage.

So, we've already led ourselves down a garden path, I thought, by accepting as facts hypotheses that robbed us of any sense of integrity or honor in our own eyes. The Seth Material, at the very least, presents a picture of the universe in which we can be gallant, expressive, and effective; one in which our intellects and intuitions both have stature; and one that includes both order and spontaneity.

If that was a garden path, I decided (half tearfully, half triumphantly), then it sure was the best one I'd seen so far!

Moreover, I thought—really worked up now—Seth's

ideas *were* as factual in many respects as any other system of thought. Science couldn't prove that the universe began with a big bang or a small poof, or that birds came from reptiles. And if there were many statements that couldn't be proven in Seth's material, religion certainly couldn't prove that an objectified God made the world and topped it off by forming man in *His* own image. In *fact,* I decided, again, on a scale of 1 to 10, measuring the scientific, religious, and Sethian models of the universe according to their overall relative relationship to "the truth about things," I was now willing to admit that in my opinion Seth's ideas would win, hands down. Why hadn't I been willing to make that statement *whole-heartedly* before?

For one thing, it's obviously pretty difficult for any one person to stand against officially accepted knowledge, or to imagine that the individual *can* be right, and the culturally accepted ideas wrong. I'm not talking about absolute truths here or even of moral positions, but of various approaches to "truth," avenues of fruitful speculation and intuitive possibilities.

When we believe that science or religion "has the truth," we stop our speculations. While still referring to the *theory* of evolution, science accepts it as a fact about existence, and therefore any speculation that threatens that theory becomes almost heretical. So it often seems that there is no other choice in the matter of man's origin than a meaningless universe and an earth populated by creatures who fight for survival, or a universe created by Christianity's objectified God. And to me, at least, the Eastern religions present no acceptable answers either.

While I was engrossed in these speculations, now and then I'd stare at my paintings and think how innocent my painting seemed to be. On June 8 I scribbled in my journal: "How direct my painting seems. My skill, what I have of it, is clearly focused; my purpose simply to paint whatever's before me—usually flowers or some objects that seem 'right' at any given time; objects that stand for themselves and yet also imply a greater (and yet, intimate) source from which they emerge. I certainly don't feel I have to be 'as good as my paintings' or try to 'live up to them.' Why do I feel that way about my own writing or Seth's material?"

In the meantime the weather was turning even warmer. I moved all my things back to the cool small studio in the rear of the house, and though I didn't realize it at the time, my intense questions were even then leading me in some new directions. It wasn't until the middle of that June of 1979, when I looked back on my notes, that I saw the progression of those new ideas as rising from those earlier speculations.

As you can see, in this particular period the beliefs of organized religion were still stirring around in my mind. These notes are for Saturday, June 9, 1979:

"It's a very hot afternoon as I write. The local radio station is broadcasting national news right now, bringing me messages from the official world, and in these particular moments I enjoy that contact. I feel at one with the day, even though I'm rather miserable with the over-90-degree temperature. My studio door is opened to the screened-in patio, but the light is so bright in that direction that I have to face the opposite side of the room where the bare wall *used* to be. I had a window put in it, even though it's an inside wall. The new window just opens up inside the garage, but it's positioned so that I can look through it and through the garage's outside windows as well. Anyway, as I write I look through those double windows at the fence and trees. A picnic table sits under the inside window, loaded down with several plants, my paints and brushes, and some paintings in various stages of completion. So I'm surrounded by my mental and physical world, sitting in my own house. That house sits smack in the middle of the mass world, though. And my books go out from this room to affect other people.

"The world out there is established. It's the completed version of mass beliefs superimposed onto institutions, governments, science and religion. Not that the official world isn't changing, but that at any given time it defines what is and isn't realistic behavior, and outlines established roads for the individual to follow from birth to death, in health and illness.

"The Sethian concepts are still in the process of emerging, though, and the answers aren't all in. All of the questions haven't even been considered yet. The distortions of organized religion are all too obvious, for example; but so is the emotional power of, say, the Pope or any prominent religious leader. So religion certainly can energize and mobilize millions of people. And so far, what have I to offer in place of a sweet Jesus—a personalized God to whom people can relate? Can people get along without such personifications? And what is Seth's alternative?

"He offers All That Is—a spirit, if you will, that becomes the universe and is personified in all of Its parts; Its personality is expressed through the unique life of each being, whatever its stature in our terms of value. All That Is *is* more than the sum of Its parts; all of Its parts are separate, and yet united in the vaster gestalt.

"Transposed into religious terms, then, we are each continuous with what 'God' is, and any 'prayer' travels through dimensions of psychological validity that connect us with those portions of our own consciousnesses that are aware of that added identification. This isn't to say that we are each 'God' in absolute terms, but that we are expressions of 'God's' essence. We are part of All That Is, and All That Is is also the medium in which we exist. We are made of 'God Stuff.'

"We might picture All That Is in super*human* terms, personifying It as Him or Her—praying to a Christ, for example; a Christ quite legitimate as a reflection of our limited understanding, a Christ quite effective insofar as he would stand symbolically for us in our relationship with All That Is as best we could understand It. All That Is, however, is no parochial spirit—it is the force behind and within all species and beings, and could be projected quite as legitimately as a super*beast* or super*plant,* or whatever.

"According to Seth, All That Is is the entire creative pattern from which all realities of any kind emerge. Following these concepts, organized religions could operate quite effectively *if* each separate religion would see its version of God as a powerful, useful symbol for a greater psychic gestalt—as a way of perceiving a vast psychological being. But religion usually speaks in absolutes.

"And why should I care? Why should such thoughts even invade my private afternoon? Yet those questions and considerations aren't mine alone, of course. My correspondence shows me that all kinds of people are asking the same kind of questions, and it becomes more and more obvious to me that our personal and public problems stem directly from distortions in our ideas of who and what we are."

A psychiatrist who visited us that same week agreed with that last statement. His was the first of a series of visits with various professionals that we'd agreed upon earlier in the year. He told us that he was appalled at the closed-minded attitudes of many of his colleagues, who simply refused to take into consideration the value systems of their clients. He said that many people were having emotional and mental difficulties precisely because of conflicts related to their beliefs about right and wrong. "They're convinced they're bad people," he said, "even though none of them has committed a crime." Except, I thought dourly, the "crime" of being human.

Everything seemed to lead back to either the "blighted species" or to the Garden of Eden syndrome: How could we be "good" when our source was "bad"? And the more I thought about it, the more inconceivable it seemed to me that people could seriously accept the ideas of either religion or science in regard to the origin of man or the universe. (And doubly inconceivable that I had ever done so, or that I was still—unbelievably—tinged by some of those old beliefs.)

Some ideas that I'd had in the past came to mind. Surely, I thought again, as far as divinity was concerned, a many-spirited concept would be superior to the conventional one, so that we'd have the spirit of the tree, the spirit of the ocean, and so forth, as in many ancient religions. Since whatever gave birth to our world must still sustain it, then it must exist now as well as in the past, somehow distributed through creation. At least such an idea would conceptually distribute God among Its parts, delegate divine authority, and decentralize it. Each natural entity would at least have its right. And if God the Supreme Being wasn't available for dialogue, then when we addressed each creature we'd be addressing the divinity expressed through, say, the frog, the man, or whatever.

And, I thought, such a distribution of divinity throughout nature wouldn't necessarily mean a variety of isolated nature spirits either, but indicate the spirit of nature made individual, or individually manifested. In that view, divinity would be seen as flowing through the universe, pooling out to form our own individualities and the world.

No matter what work I was doing or what leisure activity I was engaged in, I was engrossed with these speculations. Again, though some old ideas of mine were involved here, they appeared in my mind with fresh vigor. Several times I berated myself or my own creative abilities for poking fun at Christianity and for thinking of Christ as a caricature-like figure: But he *has* become a caricature of whatever personage he once was, I thought irritably; and if the creative abilities and the intuitions can't see through such idiocies, then we are in trouble indeed. I could feel myself trying to get a better handle on these ideas. In retrospect, it's tempting to say that I half suspected where they were leading me. But I felt, instead, as if I were worrying some unnourishing metaphysical bone. The next notes though do show the progression of ideas and the direction in which my questions were leading. I wrote these notes one warm afternoon in my studio, while Rob mowed the grass out back and the two kittens slept on the porch:

"If there is a 'God,' why doesn't 'He' speak to us directly? The question implies a super-*person* God, of course, who can use the same kind of communication that we do—and even in those terms, perhaps we couldn't bear hearing a God's voice; or perhaps such a voice wouldn't carry in sound as we know it. Or perhaps, as I suspect, 'His' voice is the combination of all the voices of the earth so that we can't hear all of them at once. Or perhaps this 'God' speaks with living molecules instead of sound so that you and I and the entire world are his molecular voice—our atoms, cells and organs themselves the divine vowels and syllables whose 'soundings' form the living sentences of life.

"If so, then I am 'speaking Him' now, and so is my husband as he mows the grass, and so is the grass beneath the mower. Only if this is true, then in our wars we 'speak Him' poorly. We stutter biologically—an expression that certainly gives evidence of our need for greater visions of divinity and of humanity as well.

"I'm taking it for granted here that there *is* a Source or God, but that our visions of such a vast psychological reality are limited, even shoddy and destructive. The idea of a crucified God to me at least is aesthetically appalling, for example. Why not a God who loves earth and life for a change? If we're going to insist upon a superhuman God, then why a distant, tempestuous God 'the father'? Why not a God who has the finest human abilities carried to their fullest; God the superartist, superlover, superartisan or athlete or farmer? At least such designations would upgrade the conventional ideas of a godhead. And of course Christianity leaves out any goddesses, so that along with Darwinian and Freudian theories religion is not just parochial but 'sexist' as well. And no one ever talks about Christ, the lover of women. . . .

"The old version of a father God, a single deity, may have served to help form our own unique kind of consciousness so that we see ourselves as a species with a God of its own, set against the rest of creation, lifted up above the beasts. That concept may have helped unite us and let us find our own sense of identity at one time, but it's no longer serviceable, and it's turned a destructive face.

"And what dubious duality pervades our religions! We have Christ saying, Love thy enemies, turn the other cheek, and the meek will inherit the earth. But we also have his father who sent plagues to the Egyptians on behalf of the chosen people, and whose divine murders are wholesale. Even now each side in a war calls upon God to kill the enemy and almost any means is justified if the end is a *good* one—a subject that Seth discusses in full in his *Mass Events*.

"If we are to end our wars, we have to dispense with a threatening, vengeful, bloodthirsty God. If we're to have any kind of world brotherhood, we have to dispense with a God who reserves his favors for a chosen few. Life is given to all. The sun shines freely on each of us. Would a God be less kindly? More than this, we must also dispense with our species God, and extend our ideas of divinity outward to the rest of nature which couches us and our religious theorizing with such a steady gracious support.

"God-in-camouflage. I like that term, for certainly All That Is is camouflaged by our limited concepts, and on the other hand, All That Is appears within the camouflage of the world itself. In any case, we haven't been free to form any new conceptions of divinity. Any new visions of God seem to be blasphemy, because we feel so bound to the past, and to ideas that almost close our minds and hearts to any revelations that contradict ancient dogmas.

"Some people might argue with considerable vehemence that the gods have caused us enough trouble as it is; better dispense with the entire idea. I've given that considerable thought too, but I think that "god-making" is a part of our heritage—like it or not—and that if we studied the psychology of our gods as they appear in our histories and myths, we'd discover more about our own psychology than perhaps we're ready to know. And in reshaping our gods, we reshape ourselves."

As I finished those notes, it was nearly suppertime. Neighborhood people returned from work, driving from Elmira city proper up our hill to the relatively cooler air. Several cars went by while dogs barked, and I thought: What on earth was I doing, nursing that dumb metaphysical bone again? The "answers" were in that mysterious world right in front of me, appearing in the obvious trees and hilltop and dogs and people. Only, hidden in that public obviousness were secrets that I just couldn't see! So I said to hell with it and went in the kitchen to make Rob some cornbread.

That night though I just couldn't get to sleep. My body felt active. It kept moving around inside itself, and I kept muttering "Go to sleep" and ordering it to be quiet. Finally around 4 A.M., begrudgingly, I gave in and got up, only partially aware that I'd had the impulse to do so for some time.

The kittens awakened and followed me to the kitchen. I fixed instant oatmeal, two pieces of toast, and coffee. My body felt alert, yet I was still mentally complaining: I'd probably end up going to bed before Rob got up, and he'd have to eat breakfast alone; then I'd probably sleep till noon; and since it was Sunday, one of my answer-mail days, I probably wouldn't get a good start on the correspondence. All of those thoughts went through my mind as I took the rest of my coffee into the back studio.

The first bird calls came from the hill. I looked out the glass doors, instantly enchanted; and drawn as surely as if someone had called me, I went out to the patio. All of the trees were misted in morning fog. The big maple and oak trees in the back yard, the maples across the way, our new lilac bushes—everything looked like some masterful underpainting, yet an underpainting already endowed with life. In moments the gray-greens changed to June's richer shades, and all of the veiled details arose out of the morning. Our four gray stone steps suddenly emerged, as if newly formed, leading from the driveway up to the back yard.

We share the world with others, but portions of it carry personal significance. We see them as no one else does. So it was for me that morning. No one else was watching what I watched from my own personal viewpoint. I felt as if I were being privileged to view a beginning of the world—or my edge of it. Or, I thought suddenly, it was like seeing a new corner of your own psyche transformed into trees, grass, flowers, fog and sky—a hopeful, magical, ever-coming-into-existence part of the psyche that we'd forgotten or I'd forgotten. I felt as if I were viewing that part of myself that I'm always pursuing, the part that is as clear-eyed as a child, fleet, at one with its own knowing; the part that exists apart from daily concerns; the part that was my direct connection with the universe; the part that represented that section of the universe from which I emerged in each moment of my life.

And, in that moment, I named it the God of Jane.

I remember that at the time the concept seemed audacious, daring and somehow simple and inevitable all at once. It almost made me breathless. And in those terms, I thought, we *do* each have our personal "God," no matter who—or what—we are. There would be a God of Billy and a God of Mitzie for our cats. And why not? A "God" for each of us, a designation that would give us a sense of personal connection with the universe, yet be devoid of the nonsense that went along with the conventional idea of a personified God. The God of Jane, the God of Joe, the God of Lester, the God of Sarah . . .

An appeal to that "God" would be an appeal to that portion of universal creativity from which we personally emerge—the portion we're "plugged into," the hypothetical point from which our individual existences spring. It would stand for that otherwise inconceivable intersection between Being and our being, and hint of the universal pattern for each of us that must exist, out of which our private experience constantly happens.

I'd always thought that the universe knows us no matter who or what we are, and at times that knowledge had risen into vivid emotional awareness. But as I looked out at that June morning the feelings attained a new reality, almost as if I arose from *their* knowledge instead of the other way around. I didn't know if I was turning into the morning, or the morning was turning into me; but I did know that *The God of Jane* would be the title of my book.

I also remember feeling a touch of momentary alarm: Was I really audacious enough to title a *book*, *The God of Jane*? Now the concept seems so matter-of-fact and natural that it's hard to recall its first impact. I didn't write any notes until much later that morning. The experience was still vivid in my mind, and I was beginning to understand that it was the culmination of unconscious creativity roused by my own intense questions of the past month. My notes read:

"This 'God of Jane' idea, or 'God of Jim' or whoever, suits me in many ways. It suggests an intensely personal connection between each individual and the universe, for one thing. For another, it makes important distinctions between the private 'God' and the universal All That Is, while still maintaining the personal involvement. For instance, when I use the phrase 'the God of Jane,' I'm referring to or trying to contact that portion of the universe that is forming *me*—that is turning some indefinable divinity into this living temporal flesh. I want to avoid all other complications. I'm not trying to contact the God of Abraham, for instance, or the Biblical Christ, or the inexplicable power behind all of reality.

"My intent is more humble than that, more personal, more specific: I want to contact that tiny portion of All That Is that forms *my* image; that transforms itself or part of itself into my experience. That God of Jane must be continuous with the entire cloth of divinity, but I'm not asking that the entire attention of All That Is be turned in my direction. Besides, this would be quite unnecessary anyway, since according to Seth, any portion of All That Is contains the knowledge of all of its other parts.

"I really don't care what the God of Abraham said either. Since creation continues, the energy of that indefinable God is as present today as it ever was. And if 'He' doesn't speak clearly or 'His' messages seem contradictory, it's because we've transposed such ridiculous concepts over the entire affair. We no longer hear 'God's voice' in the buzzing bees, much less in the sound of our own breathing.

"Most churches wouldn't stand for such ideas, of course— a personal God for each one of us, so we'd each have 'a piece of the rock'? God forbid! Again though, what about those poor demented souls who interpret *their* God's words as licenses to kill their enemies? But now the answer to that question seems even clearer: Jehovah wrote *that* book and gave all the instructions. And again, what about that God killing all those first-born Egyptians and sending a pestilence of locusts and heaven-sent diseases, giving us probably the first biological warfare in history? And what about the God of the Inquisition, and what about Allah now in Iran, commanding the deaths of those who disagree with His idea of holy righteousness? Ideas of death and vengeance are so entwined with established religions that whenever some poor fool *does* think he's God, his first idea of proving it is to destroy the bad guys, to kill his enemies. And who taught him that?

"I think we *have* progressed. We don't think of war as the honorable affair we did in ages past, but it wasn't organized religion or science that led us away from our justification of war. Millions of men and women, after experiences in two world wars and other smaller ones, finally began to question its merits—even though religion still prayed for the downfall of our enemies, and science provided better and better means to that end. I really doubt that the God of Tom or the God of Whoever, denied that national following, would be capable of anything like such distortions of the meaning of life."

As I went about the next few days, the phrase "the God of Jane" kept returning to my mind, striking me with a certain sense of exquisite appropriateness. When my friend and former student Sue Watkins called, I told her about the concept. A few days later, Sue sent me the following poem she'd written as she interpreted the idea for herself:

THE GOD OF SUE
(With thanks to the God of Jane)
by Susan M. Watkins

She rides inside a dirty car,
one fender bent in a tinfoil sneer.
This is Her chariot of the sun.
Her world travels
(just like they guessed)
on the back of a grandfather turtle.
Pretty funny, my dear
God.

She walks down village streets and hides
Her God-ness fervently inside
Her pocketbook.
And sometimes She forgets
and accidentally lets
Her checkbook balance by itself,
or thinks about the fall and makes
the trees turn red and gold too soon.
Five demerits, my dear
God.

She thought the God of Man
kind was a jerk.
She loves desire,
She loves to love,
but as far as being loved, ah, well—
sometimes She simply isn't
sure She wants
the person who comes with it.
(She doesn't like
to cook).
Ah-ha! But this explains the
reason why
She threw aside
the book about
the God of Man—
the stupid S.O.B. eschewed
the use
of his own complimentary piece
of flesh!
Good thinking, my dear
God.

Once, after growing a fishy type
of thing into a
functioning adult, She said,
"I don't do anything
that's right."
Quite frankly, even
the God of Man
would laugh at that.
It took until She saw
that having faith was not
the snap
that all those martyrs claimed
they had while being stuck
with arrows or what-have-you.
In fact,
it took much less
than that—
Too bad for them, by God.

The God of Sue created the Earth.
I saw Her do it all Myself.

      The poem is Sue's excellent, exuberant, personal inter-
pretation of the ideas I had in mind. I was delighted that someone
else was so enthused, and that the concepts could be used in such a
highly individualized way. Sue's poem also surprised me in that it
visualized the God of Sue as She—reasonable enough, and almost a
feminine manifesto—but when I thought of the God of Jane, for
example, I just didn't think of sexual elements at all. And that's
great, because it means that each person *can* interpret the basic idea
itself in the most personally meaningful manner.
      Anyway, I wouldn't want to be confined to a one-sexed
God (neither would Sue, I know), and as I was typing her poem for
this book I came up with this humorous verse of my own:

The God of Jane said,
"I think I'll make
two sexes that can mate.
That sounds like fun.
And I'll be one or the other
now and then,
and sometimes, both,
or neither."

In any case, imagine your own God of Bob or Carol or whatever your name is, and as you do you'll learn quite a bit about yourself. And if you're personifying All That Is, at least you'll be aware of the process and know what you're doing. My God of Jane, for example, is primarily a poet or psychic, and I think I'd be involved in those same activities if I were a man instead of a woman. Other people might discover that their main identification is sexually attuned in a precise manner, but the characteristics you give your "God of ————" will represent your own focus in life. They will show how you center yourself in the world.

Anyhow, I'm simply offering the God of Jane idea as an *approach* to the entire question of our relationship with an indefinable Source from which our lives emerge, and I believe that the concept is psychologically sound. It reinforces our uniqueness in the universe and also emphasizes the source of that separateness in the unity of All That Is. Certainly this involves personification again: It's an attempt to provide each of us with the intimate involvement of a personal God that is a part of divinity—yet in our terms, not absolute. That is, if we're each getting "a piece of the rock," it's a small enough portion. And if we ever speak as oracles, then clearly we speak for "truth" as it appears through Janehood or Williamhood or whomeverhood: We don't take it for granted that we speak for or through an absolute God whose dictums must be followed without question.

The concept is exciting to me for other reasons too. Each person experiences reality as if he or she were at the center of it. Our experience of events is the immediate intersection point between ourselves and "the others." We must live from our own focus, and the God of Jane concept honors that focus while acknowledging its relativity.

Seth's view of subjective reality includes the existences of many selves connected with the self we know, however; and almost instantly I wondered how these many selves fitted in with the one-focus position that's necessary in each separate lifetime. In other words, how private is my focus in relationship to, say, reincarnational existences? The minute I asked the question, I knew I had the answer—in a poem that I'd written a few months earlier.

The poem is an imaginary dialogue between myself and a seamstress who is another portion of myself living in a past century. At least, that's *my* definition of her reality. *Her* definition is quite different, as you'll see from the poem in which she discusses her reality, mine, and the greater pattern of existence from which both of our lives emerge.

"The Seamstress" just "started coming to me" one morning, without preamble, and "kept coming" through the following days until it was finished. I felt that the seamstress knew me very well, whether she was a part of my creative imagination or a reincarnational self or both. And I now see that certain feelings about reincarnational experiences are expressed in the poem that would be quite difficult to approach in prose.

Actually, I wrote the poem in various places at various times—sitting at the kitchen table, at my desk, and some lines came to me while I was doing housework or watching television. The reality of the poem's events *did* seem to be oddly transposed over my normal activities, and certainly various states of consciousness are as much a part of the poem's framework as the stanzas are in usual terms.

Since the whole idea of reincarnation is scientifically unrespectable, it's probably no coincidence that our unofficial subjective experiences with it involve altered states of consciousness, trances, or dream events—when our own usual censoring habits are lessened. I should probably mention here too that reincarnation can be considered as part of an inner information-storing process that connects one generation to another in a kind of spontaneous, subjective "evolution." And if reincarnation is unprovable scientifically, at least at this point in time, again a careful reading of scientific literature on the theory of evolution will show that *it's* still not proven despite its respectability.

Anyway, how would reincarnation work psychologically? I think that "The Seamstress" gives some important clues as to how our personal identities could be maintained even through multiple existences. When I realized the connection between the God of Jane idea and the poem, I reread "The Seamstress" at once, and I'm including it in the following chapter.

Chapter 8
"Tale of the Seamstress"

1

"I was a seamstress once,"
she says,
sitting primly on a pillow
in my mind;
tiny silver needles, buttons, thread
in a blue woven basket,
scissors smiling in the busy air.

"I couldn't read or write,
but I could count my stitches
and get paid for every one.
I sewed the afternoons into britches,
capes and dresses,
for I knew that time
was part of any pattern,
stitched in between
the stitches that were mine.

"The ladies and gentlemen
came to my small room

and told their secrets,
those they tried to conceal
beneath their fancy dress.
The lies of fashion!
I was rich with gossip,
for I made my tongue as soft
as my needle was sharp,
and I stitched, stitched, stitched
away at their stories
in my mind.

"My days were turned
into other women's petticoats,
men's vests and waistcoats,
women's bonnets and shawls,
and I walked in my dreams
where those people went,
for I hid part of my heart
in the clothes that I sewed.

"Princess Marianne, I called her—
a woman of worth—
come to my room
by way of a coach.
I used to wonder
that she'd bother
to climb the stairs herself,
for everything but walking
was done for her.

"But I made her a hundred bonnets and skirts,
sewing by gaslight and candle and sun,
working all hours
until the damned things were done.
And she went to parties
and she went to balls,
and a part of me went with her,
stitched into her clothes.
So I danced when she danced
and I kissed when she did.
Though I sat all alone
in my own sewing room,
I smiled out

through button eyes
at the fashionable crowd.

"I told myself
that my thread was magical,
each spool
an extension of my soul,
smoothed out,
fine as a sunbeam,
so of course it would last forever,
mixed in with the coarser
visible thread of my trade."

2

"I hate to sew," I said.
"That's because *I* got enough of it,"
she replied, and slyly added,
"I always did want to read and write.
Now, words are power."
"Are they?" I asked, amused.
She smiled back at me
and cocked her head.

She said, "As I went abroad
in my magical thread,
so you travel outward
clothed in letters,
and smocked
in the alphabet.
You see, I know you
rather well."

I said, smooth as silk myself,
"Do you have proof
that we're related?"
and she stamped her foot.
"You dare check me out?
It wasn't me that beckoned
but you who sought *me* out.

"I'm not you. Can't say I'd want to be.
I'm me, but we're made from the same cloth,

if you don't mind
me talking shop some more.
It's as if each thought
or act or hope of mine
stitched itself into new form,
on a pattern
that was not yours or mine,
yet somehow both,
so that there are no replicas,
but—well, variations
of a pattern that's never really done.
We're tailored to ourselves only,
yet the magic stitches of our lives
wind in and out, back and forth,
so that somehow
we overlap."

"Where are you now?" I asked.
"In your head, as you can plainly see,"
she replied, sounding cross.
"I'm here for your edification,
endowed with words
better than any I knew then,
because you sent messages out
looking, in your terms, for a former self,
though as I've told you,
that, I'm not.

"But let me use analogies
I'm used to.
The soul has a wardrobe
of selves or images,
not identical,
but again, cut from the same cloth,
by a master tailor,
each suited to a special place and time,
yet all kept in the same
celestial closet,
hanging side by side
like costumes for period plays,
related but apart,
each marked by the overall style
and characteristics

of the soul.
And the patterns are originals
and exist forever,
even when their times are gone."

I muttered, "That closet
analogy sounds miserable,
and makes me think of corpses hanging
side by side, grinning, while one comes alive,
prances across the world's stage, and then
its image is hung
on a hanger of time,
where it dangles, discarded,
preserved, maybe,
but with its memories
calcified."

"My memories are no more calcified than yours,"
the seamstress said, scowling,
"and I'm as alive as you are.
My shop is still busy.
Patrons come and go.
Tonight I ate kraut for supper,
and the smell of it still
lingers in my clothes.
The scent fills the unfinished skirts
and petticoats,
and when my fine customers don *their* clothes,
they'll sniff my supper, poor as it is,
and wonder at the odor,
for it won't be that familiar,
used as they are to richer chowders
and beef of good report.
So how am I less real than you,
or my rooms less secure?"
She still sat there, saucy,
anywhere between nineteen and thirty,
scowling brilliantly as if
she prided her wit above her heart,
so I said:

"For one thing, it's you
who sits within my head,

and not the other way around.
My world is here, concrete,
while yours is a vestige
of the past, at best,
or perhaps
only a figment of my own imagining
of what the past was like.
I mean, I'm full of flesh and blood,
while you . . .
have to be just mental."

3

I turned my head. What was that smell?
Nothing was cooking on *my* stove.
The electric oven slept.
The button that lit up red
when the stove was on,
said "off."
Yet an odor, pungent, almost foul,
like rotten cabbages,
wafted strongly past my nostrils,
so sharply that I was sure
something almost foreign cooked,
invisibly, somewhere in my room.
Or was it rotten pork?
Knuckles filled with grubs?
What was I thinking?
The question made me dizzy,
and bleary and scared,
I looked around again.

Surely I was in a room of cloth!
I cried, mentally,
because my lips felt as if
they were sewn tightly shut,
and around me, bolts
of linens, wools, and cottons
were piled and stacked and stored,
and mountains of soft satin,
while dyes bubbled in a vat,
and the steam swirled above my head.

An old iron was in my hand.
I pressed, and pressed, and pressed.
How long had I been pressing
while the dye boiled
and the kraut simmered?
I settled in before
I knew what I was doing,
or rather, I changed I's,
forgetting what I knew,
chewing some tobacco gum,
bitter and brittle,
singing hymns,
cozy in the gaslight,
pressing, pressing, pressing down hard,
to do my work before
the iron turned cold.

But what was this?
I caught myself at the last moment,
or so it seemed.
"This isn't me," I shouted.
"This place isn't mine, and I swear
these aren't my eyes!
These aren't my hands."

I paused, knowing that
these bolts of cloth
surely must be dust by now.
Yet what woman's weight
pressed down
upon the iron in such
a familiar pose?
Whose fingers smoothed the cotton
in that quick automatic motion,
and why did I feel
those hands were mine?

"How quaint, the cluttered room!
I could stay in it forever,"
I thought, and frightened by the thought,
I caught myself again.
"I want out," I shouted.

"Out, indeed," she said.
"And 'quaint' offends me.
The clothes I make are fashionable
and quite in style,
and my room is furnished
no more quaintly than your own."
As she spoke,
I was myself again,
and breathless,
as if I'd done some
heavy work for hours,
or traveled too far
in too short a time.
So I said, as calmly as I could,
"Your room *was* quaint,
and if you want the truth,
impoverished."

"I had everything I needed,"
she cried, tartly.
"I was self-contained.
'Let the wealthy come to me,'
I said, as they did,
if they'd be dressed in proper form
for banquet, court, or ball,
for my authority
in that regard was paramount,
and the lift of my left eyebrow could make
the most stylish coquette feel
like a stupid clod.
Yet with my needles, there was magic everywhere,
and my dyes were more brilliant
than peacock tails,
so that even I wondered
at their odd intense hues.
And my fingers too were blessed with magic,
stitching universes more than clothes."

4

She said, "I was no more
a simple seamstress
than you are a lowly scribe,

writing other people's letters,
without adding any words of your own.
My hands were flawless,
not the slightest stain from dyeing
marred their surfaces.
I used stout sticks,
longer than my arms, to stir,
and the sunlight in the steam
turned the air
multicolored.

"But I clothed people
better than they were,
so they had to live up
to my invention,
knowing that they were finer
outside than inner,
for strut their stuff as they might,
they knew my art half made them
what they were.

"I dressed counts and countesses from birth,
bare bodies up,
and their skin wasn't made
of alabaster,
but was the same fabric
as yours or mine;
underneath was always flesh,
a fact I reminded them of
from time to time.
Now, my *hands* were royal,
with a built-in majesty
that no royal document could give
or take away.
My fingers moved
like ten slim swaying queens,
and all the rest of me
was grateful to them.
They stitched as naturally
as needles of rain fall,
dipping into
the satin, just so.
I was born just right,

with skills suited to my time,
and I fit into it as snug
as a bride in a wedding dress,
coming into life as innocent."

"But you're dead," I shouted,
"that's the difference."
And she flounced her skirts
and laughed, "Oh? Well, to me,
you're not yet born,
but still cradled in the womb of time—
poor thing—
but what noise you make
for one whose unborn thoughts
still wait a tongue!
You float, scattered,
in my dreams,
not even put together yet,
like a pattern
still unformed,
or an unwritten tale,
still awaiting wit and plot!

"In my scale of events,
your world may—
or may not—happen,
while even by your own reckoning,
mine is real enough
to appear in your history books.
But my world contains
no traces of your own;
and to me, your times are, at best,
probable.
So who is alive or dead?"

5

"We're each figures in a tapestry,"
she said,
"with threads of consciousness
cross-stitched,
and beneath each century's
prominent design,

others, only half visible,
weave in and out.
So I appear obscured
in your world,
and you, nearly invisible
in mine.
But the threads of consciousness
are never broken
and reach into each design.
We're counterparts
in a living tapestry
that changes all the time."

"For a seamstress," I said,
"you certainly seem
to know a lot."
I wasn't sure exactly what I meant
by the remark,
but she said, "And what are you?
You stitch thought
to thought,
and send your words out,
neatly tailored,
and you deal with mental clothes,
symbols and designs of mind
that appear seamless.
You rip apart old concepts,
and try to dress the world's soul
in new clothes,
one satiny word
at a time—
so you're as much a seamstress
as I am,
only you work with bolts of thought
instead of cloth.

"But wool provides good heat
against the cold,
and when I make a cloak of it,
I know it's warm.
But what about the mental clothes
you make?
Can you guarantee *their* worth

as well?
Now, *they're* immaterial.
So when you say to me,
'For a seamstress, you seem
to know a lot,'
then please grant me
the dignity you give
so freely to yourself."

"I do! I do!" I said
as quickly as I could,
but her image began to fade.
"It hardly matters though,"
she laughed,
"since at the best,
you're just a dream and a half
I've had in my head
while ironing,
but now I'm done,
and my supper's ready."

"No! No! I'm more, much more,"
I called, but she was gone.
Gone? But where?
I felt an odd vacancy as if
I'd lost a friend I'd
hardly met;
but closer, a friend-in-self,
not a twin,
but a curious version
of a self of a self of a self
I might have been.

Chapter 9

Lord of the Molecules, Divine Atoms, and Selfish Genes

When I finished reading "Tale of the Seamstress," I really did blink with astonishment, as the saying goes, because I realized that it actually presented an excellent psychological study of how reincarnation works—granted that reincarnation exists to work at all, of course. Earlier, I'd simply regarded the poem as purely an aesthetic production. That is, I hadn't thought of it as giving any information. But why hadn't I? The answer was obvious: We're taught to consider art as a symbolic statement, meaningful in its own context, but not necessarily bringing us any information as, say, a newspaper does.

The poem said that I had been a seamstress, for example, and I'd taken that as a symbolic statement of *aesthetic* fact. Now having read the poem again, I had to ask the question: Were the seamstress and I related in meaningful psychological terms? Even if all time is simultaneous as Seth states, was she somehow me, in a life I would call previous to this one? Or was I the seamstress in a life she would call a future one? Was the poem stating a factual psychological relationship?

And that question led instantly to another thought: Suppose, instead of the official evolutionary explanations for, say, man's instincts and individual differences, reincarnation acted as an inner directive and carrier of knowledge, affecting genetic patterns themselves. Hardly a new thought, but mentally placing the theory of reincarnation against the theory of evolution was immensely exciting. Surely reincarnation could account for an interior collective unconscious in place of instinct, and for individual characteristics and deviances as well. At any rate, the concept was certainly more gallant. If that were the case, then of course such information would color creative thought and express itself through the arts, and also through altered states of consciousness—when we were relatively free of entrenched official beliefs.

And when I allowed my own intellect some freedom from those old beliefs, I had to admit that reincarnation was certainly no more outlandish an explanation for human individual differences than evolution's natural selection, which was based on the thesis that *fish,* leaving the seas, dropped their fins, adapted lungs, paws, finally arms and legs, walked upright, and finally turned into—well, you and me. Now *that's* outlandish!

So is the idea that each of us is given one life by an omnipotent God who looks just like us, only better—a perfect God who creates imperfect creatures and then creates a hell to punish them for their blemishes. So against those ideas, the theory of reincarnation was suddenly making more sense. It was just that I hadn't intellectually compared those particular theories to each other in that way before.

And so instead of man's body carrying within it physical remnants of a mammalian heritage, why not, I thought, human beings carrying within their psyches at birth the memories of their own past consciousnesses? Again, why hadn't I thought of reincarnation before in relationship to man as a *species*? Once asked, the question almost answered itself. I'd granted reincarnation a psychic or intuitive basis but I'd taken it for granted that the theory of evolution carried an intellectual weight. Yet when you blinked your mental eyes, looked a bit to the left, shook your head—that intellectual weight was feather-light.

Then I thought: Suppose that sometimes aesthetic fact *could* be closer to truth than, say, scientific fact. For example, scientific thought doesn't grant the existence of clairvoyance or telepathy, and insists that all information comes to us from the outside, through physical perception; and, of course, it doesn't accept any kind of life after death, since sensation is seen as a bodily property.

I'd been used to thinking that science dealt with facts, while I dealt with—well, psychic knowledge that didn't necessarily involve facts as we're used to thinking of them. But, again, suppose that our psychic intuitions and private experiences with clairvoyance or telepathy (however small) were actually giving us not only a more aesthetic and psychic view of reality but a more *realistic,* factual one as well. And, of course they were! Why on earth had I ever felt that my way of "discovering the truth" about reality was *inferior* to science's? Because, I realized, I certainly had felt that way. Again, thinking about these subjects in this particular way was new to me, because I was so accustomed to taking it for granted, like almost everyone else, that the weight of evidence was all on science's side. But it was obvious that science couldn't accept in its framework some facts that were both aesthetic and intuitional, and that were also *facts* of personal experience as well.

Tracing my lines of thought backward, I saw that the God of Jane idea was the trigger for the comparisons between intuitional and scientific knowledge that I was now making: that, and my new understanding of what "Tale of the Seamstress" was really saying. One of the main points in the poem was that *my* line to the universe was direct in my time, whoever else I might be in other realities. The same would apply to the seamstress, of course. So the God of Jane would refer to that portion of the universe that constantly transforms itself into me, according to the heroic pattern that is, itself, a part of the entire universal fabric. And each other consciousness would be personified or individualized in the same fashion, experiencing physical reality from its own center.

We each do experience events as if we were at the center of reality, of course. That's a psychological fact, and one that I kept thinking about during those early weeks in June. How did that sense of personal centering fit in with, say, the origins of the world, or of our species? And again, if I didn't accept the views of religion or science as to the creation of the universe, what alternatives were there?

Sometimes I thought: To hell with it. Who *cared?* Our kittens were exuberantly enjoying their first springtime, playing together on the screened-in porches; inflation was sky-high; people were concerned about the present state of the world. So what difference did it make, how it all started? Yet stubbornly, I felt that it *did* make a difference. And thinking about it, I even forgot that I was supposed to be working on this book. Instead, following my impulses, I did what I felt like doing, which was writing poetry steadily. I still hadn't learned that when I thought I wasn't working on my book but only following other impulses, I was really doing my best work on my book after all. So while this was going on, I'd guiltily wonder why I felt like writing poetry instead of "doing what I should be doing." And right then, I'm rather embarrassed to say, I didn't see how the subject matter of the poetry fit into my conscious intentions.

I wasn't *just* sitting around wondering about the origins of the world and writing poetry, of course. Seth was still dictating his book; I was spending more time answering correspondence than I used to spend with my classes; and while books stay written, houses don't stay cleaned, so there was the usual housework. Besides that, the summer visitors were increasing. I don't mean that there was (or is) a steady parade to our door, but several times a week and sometimes several times a day, a visitor or two arrives in good weather.

If I ever thought of "general" readers, our correspondents and particularly our visitors quickly acquainted me with the fact that each reader is a delightfully unique, almost astonishingly creative person; and no visitor is like any other one. So in that summer of 1979, as I wrestled with generalized concepts, these visitors reminded me of each individual's specific nature; the sharpness of personal experience; and the impact that any and every person has, no matter how vast the universe may seem to be.

I'd be writing or doing house chores, hear a knock at the screen door, and look up to see a stranger looking at me from his or her own viewpoint—seeing Rob and me, our house and cats and grounds from a perspective that wasn't ours. That experience always gives me a quirky feeling, as if some part of me disconnects from myself and goes tiptoeing through the house, looking at it through other eyes. But in any case there's always a moment where I catch a sensation, at least, of a visitor's world view. And I realized that summer (as I do now) that each person who came walking or driving up our hill saw a different hill, a different neighborhood, even a different Rob and Jane, because individuality cast its own private glaze over the environment. The guests saw me from *their* centers.

I thought about that, too, one morning as I sat in my swivel chair at my table, staring out the patio windows. And I wrote:

NO MATTER WHERE I LOOK

No matter where I look, I seem to be
at the center of a world that forms
perfectly around me.
No lopsided vision ever shows
the world spread only to my left,
with my image on the last right edge;
nor has the world
ever appeared just ahead,
while nothingness began
just behind my back.

I sit in a swivel chair
with smooth ball bearings.
Without warning, I turn myself
around in a complete circle,
but nothing disturbs
my world vision,
and objects appear on all sides
with sweet precision;
as if a projector in my head
sends out invisible rays that turn
into images, so I
always seem inside
dimensions of depth
and weight.

     And, I reasoned, in the same fashion, we must be in the center of attention as far as the universe is concerned. Each of us must have the focus of the universe turned in our direction at the intersecting point between Being and our particular being, as that universal energy is transformed into our private experience. And again this would apply, I thought, to each consciousness—to cats, insects, plants, objects that we consider inanimate, and to atoms, whatever their organization.

     Surely it was this last line of thought that must have led me to write the next poem on the following day. Not until the poem was done, several days later, did I see what I'd been up to or understand that when I least expected it, I was being given an alternate explanation for the beginning of the universe. For one thing, Rob's birthday was coming up, and I started the poem as a love poem to him, intending to give it to him later with some ink sketches. It was

almost as if my love for him intensified my questions enough to
bring about a response from the universe itself, or from Framework
2; or simply (if you prefer) from other levels of the psyche. I could
feel myself click in and out of altered states of consciousness as I
scribbled down the lines.

LORD OF THE MOLECULES
A Poem on Origins
to Rob

1

In formal molecular gardens,
did you and I ascend
(strands of consciousness
interwoven
with ancient mental blood)?
How long did we pause
at the entrance of the world,
while our histories
spun our images
into time's cocoon?

Do our atoms recall their pilgrimage
through smooth passageways
of molecules?
Did they move once, inch by inch,
climbing cool reptilian dreams,
to find sunlight on prehistoric cliffs?
For now their worlds of knowledge
form our flesh,
and our personhood is a gift
of innumerable
microscopic donors.

2

Yet if God is within all matter,
then each atom of my body is divine;
a tiny deity in a cellular kingdom,
invisible as heaven,
electrons spinning in miniature galaxies

within my flesh,
each inch eternity-thick,
as well ordered as the planets.

3

Or have we, ourselves, dwelled
in miniature heavens,
content within a scale of perfection
small yet infinite;
one with what we were,
contained in tiny universes—
atoms, each of us once—
all secure in sweet spontaneous
order and reason?
Was that the Garden of Eden—
an inner landscape of perfect functioning,
each of us orbiting around some divine nucleus,
timeless, before any worlds were formed?
Perhaps we were silent invisible gods,
swirling inside our perfect worlds,
subjective atoms whose dreams
finally demanded images.

If so, what awesome innocence
propelled our eternal motion,
as filled with the weight
of immense probabilities,
all of us together weighed
a million times less than one feather
of a flying bird,
yet were each filled
with the burden of all
possible worlds,
which swirled hidden within us in the darkness,
which pushed against our perfection
and sang with potential voices,
demanding the independence of being,
pleading for the right of the flawed?
For how long
did the exclusivity of perfection hold,
before the desirous thrust
of all probable worlds burst through,

allowing the release
of the gods' dreams?

5

Or did they
(or did we, if we were they)
mix perfection with imperfection,
the whole with the incomplete,
in a divine blend
in which mortality was born?

Did those entities dwell
in an existence
unsegmented,
without mass,
yet so powerful
that their dreams culminated
in a creativity
second only to their own,
in which even flaws
were cast in a perfect light,
in which the knowledge of the whole
was hidden in each
imperfect part,
and each fragment contained
a center of eternity?

When I wrote that poem I was often in a state of mild
exhilaration. I felt at one with myself; tuned into a clear channel
that connected me or my consciousness to the universe. The poem
led me to feel that my body was *graced,* from its most microscopic
aspects to its now perspiring fleshy surfaces. And it occurred to me
that there was certainly no room in the Darwinian world for grace,
or in the Freudian one either, for that matter. I wasn't thinking
about some "odor of sanctity" or hypothetical saintly bliss, but of
natural biological grace such as the animals seem to have—a grace
that is physical and spiritual at once—and of the feeling that the
universe was with us instead of just neutral—or worse, against us.
      As I wrote the poem I forgot all about religion's "corrupt
flesh," science's "selfish genes," and psychology's theories about

the "insidious subconscious." For a moment I felt mentally weight-less, released from some psychic bulk, free to consider any hypo-thesis I wanted, without being held down to old theories.

I reminded myself for the hundredth time that our beliefs about the origin of man and the universe aren't just philo-sophic or scientific or religious concepts disconnected from our daily lives, but that they cause us to experience our daily lives according to their precepts. As Seth continued dictating *The Indi-vidual and the Nature of Mass Events,* for example, it became more apparent that our beliefs about our origins were becoming self-fulfilling: We were acting *as if* we were aggressively competitive, *as if* there were a territorial imperative, *as if* we were nature's deadliest species spawned without purpose. And we "read" nature so that its activities also seemed to reflect that same picture of reality.

And I thought, rebelliously, my divine atoms were no more outlandish than science's selfish genes—genes that sup-posedly create all living structures, including the human body, simply as vehicles to insure their own survival. Again, *that's* out-landish. Science insists that it doesn't deal with values one way or the other, yet it thinks nothing of personifying genes as selfish. Somehow that's supposed to be O.K., I thought. So I had every right to call my atoms divine.

Yet talk was cheap, I mused, because for all of my determination to short-circuit automatic reactions to established beliefs, sometimes a TV show or newspaper or magazine article could still send me back to an unthinking acceptance of such views. Now and then I thought, dryly: "Thanks a lot, Seth," because it was his latest book that had made me so aware of the impact of those old beliefs in my life. Moreover, I suspected that this psychological journey of mine would be followed by many of the readers of *Mass Events,* and most probably it was just the kind of self-examination that Seth hoped to arouse in others in the first place.

And my own poetry and trance states *were* teaching me something. I was asking questions at the intellectual level of con-sciousness, and getting answers at other levels. Whether or not atoms were divine, my poem, "Origins," wasn't just the carrier of *aesthetic* fact: I was convinced that it was a more factual statement about the origins of the universe than officially accepted theories.

It seemed almost impossible now that I'd ever felt guilty when I "gave into" the impulse to write poetry or paint during my "working" hours, and that for all of my deep love for poetry I'd felt that I had to justify it. I was beginning to understand, too, that *all* of my impulses were creative, whether or not they were connected directly with my work. But I still had some troubles with physical impulses.

One day in early June, for example, I suddenly felt the impulse to begin a second half-hour period of exercises. For a moment I was scandalized. I was busy enough as it was, I thought. I just didn't have a minute's more time. But I backtracked to the impulse again, and felt that stimulus toward action that I'd felt just before my objections started. I added the second period of exercises to my schedule, but for some time I felt, guiltily, that I should be at my desk instead.

And I didn't know that I hadn't even come to the nitty-gritty yet.

Chapter 10

Psychic Newscasts and Dramas. From The Library: Psychic Structures and a Personal Universe

Actually it wasn't until I'd read my poem, "Origins," several times that I finally realized where Seth's book and my own impulses were leading me. In *Psychic Politics* I'd written about the "Codicils," information that came to me from "the Library." The Library is a psychological place that I sometimes see mentally; a creative construct unconsciously organized. My perception of it varies. On some occasions I see the entire main Library room, with rows of books rising to a ceiling of sky; a desk, a few chairs, a south window looking out to green landscaped grounds, and closed doors leading to other rooms. Sometimes my own double is there, picking out a book, reading at the desk, or simply watching me across that strange invisible psychological boundary that separates us. And now and then, all I see is one page from an open book.

The Codicils just appeared in my mind as if transplanted there from the Library, and they were supposed to offer new codes or assumptions upon which to base individual life and civilization. They were to replace our official beliefs and hopefully lead us toward our fullest development as individuals and as a species.

The Codicils themselves were actually statements based on Seth's own material, presented in a different way. Seth mentioned them later himself, stressing their importance. They advocated basing personal life and civilization on the assumptions that all physical matter possessed consciousness; that the universe and life had meaning; that all of earth's species cooperated in forming physical life; and that inner senses allowed us to perceive precise and vital data that added up to a psychic system of communication.

I'd wondered why I hadn't been able to put those ideas to better practical use, and now I saw the obvious—these ideas weren't going to replace official beliefs by themselves, automatically: We had to get rid of the old concepts first. Otherwise we simply held two contradictory sets of belief. Seth's book, with each new chapter, and my own impulses were showing me what obstacles still lay in my mental path. I simply had to examine all official beliefs as they affected me personally; *I* had to replace them with new assumptions. And, I thought, each of us interested in human potential had to dispense with all beliefs that denied man dimensions of psychological heroism or power.

"Positive thinking" isn't enough. We can't just tell ourselves that we're good, worthy people, for example, while still fervently believing that we're nature's deadliest species or God's disobedient children, tainted by original sin. And we certainly can't trust our impulses, no matter what we tell ourselves, if we still believe that impulses are chaotic or primitive urges from our evolutionary unsavory past; or sent by "the devil"; or expressions of a devious subconscious.

And, I thought, we had to be *truly* scientific, which meant that we had to take into consideration all of our knowledge, not just that narrow area that was accepted by *official* science. We had to examine and evaluate those perceptions that appeared in our own experience—no matter what any system of knowledge thought of them.

And *that* thought brought me back to my Library again so that I saw it from another perspective—not only as a source of,

say, psychic knowledge, but as a source of information—of facts as
well. And why, I wondered, hadn't *that* occurred to me in just that
way before?

It wasn't that I hadn't been involved with my Library
since it first appeared: My books *The World View of Paul Cézanne* and
The Afterdeath Journal of an American Philosopher both originated there.
I'd considered those books to be excellent psychic constructs, con-
tainers of the psyche's greater knowledge—but not *necessarily* factual
in usual terms, because I thought of fact as something that was the
exclusive property of science. But science was censoring itself,
actually narrowing its scope when it refused to accept facts that
didn't fit within its own present system.

These thoughts may seem prosaic enough, but they were
beginning to reorganize my own way of viewing my experiences. I
had quite a bit of library material, for example, that didn't seem to
fit into any one category or another, that had just come to me in
odd hours; and when I finished reading "Origins," some of that
material came instantly to mind. Sometimes it takes me a while to
catch up to my own psychic information, and I could feel a mental
click, click, click as a whole series of ideas fell together relating to
some library material that I'd nearly forgotten.

I found the particular passages without too much trouble, only as I read them they came into brilliant focus, as if I were
reading them for the first time. And I thought, "These aren't just
fascinating hypotheses. These are statements of fact. One day,
maybe, we can prove that some of them at least are true; but they're
facts now, nevertheless."

At once I felt a flash of alarm: Surely I wasn't saying that
all psychic information (or so-called psychic information) was factual? But what about all those people whose "psychic sources" told
them that they'd been kings and queens, prophets or noblemen in
previous lives; or those who were supposedly in contact with spacemen from other planets—spacemen who were always going to
appear for the people, but never did? What frightening, slippery
chasms of ignorance and fanaticism could open if we even imagined that all psychic information was factual?

And in that moment, when the whole idea really frightened me, I got the answer. We know how to interpret usual perceptions. We know the difference between a TV drama and a news
broadcast, between a war movie and an on-the-spot documentary
shot in the middle of a real war, between a story meant to point out
a moral or theme, and a factual account of a life. But we haven't

learned to make distinctions as far as psychic perceptions are concerned—and they are far more wide-ranging than usual perceptions. We haven't learned to distinguish between psychic "news stories" and psychic dramas, between intuitive documentaries and morality plays, between symbolism and fact.

This vast area of psychic information would—*must*—include all such classifications and more; and what we were really presented with was an incredible, nearly unexplored system of inner communications that carried *all kinds* of data.

I sat there, suddenly grinning, feeling the kind of excitement I always feel when my thoughts go over old ground and unexpectedly turn a new corner, coming out in a completely new mental place. Vaguely I remembered reading about the panic that had broken out years ago, in 1938, when Orson Welles broadcast Wells' story, *War of the Worlds*: Thousands of people, hearing the radio account of the Martians landing, thought that New Jersey actually was being invaded; they'd tuned in to the program too late to hear the station's lead-in to the mock news event. And in somewhat the same way, it could be only too easy to interpret a psychic drama as a news broadcast, and in so doing miss the actual message of the drama itself—a point that I'll return to later in this book.

In the meantime though, I just stared at the Library material and realized that it hadn't really reached me when it came to me three years ago. I'd misinterpreted it—considering it fascinating as a symbolic (not literal) statement about the universe and man's place in it. How could I have been so opaque? And reading that material, I understood how it fit with the God of Jane idea, the concepts in "Origins," and how it also echoed Seth's material—but from a different direction.

Actually, I'd been getting the same "news broadcasts" from several levels of consciousness, each one giving a different but clear picture of an overall reality; but I hadn't quite put them all together. Yet, only by utilizing, understanding, and organizing data from all possible states of consciousness could we hope to assess our present position within the universe: I *was* sure of that much. So I read the Library material again with these ideas in mind. The first passages had come without preamble one day after I'd read a letter from a correspondent about the existence of black holes. Suddenly I'd sensed the Library, and was vaguely aware of my double there. She opened a book, and the words she read were transposed into my mind. I'd written as quickly as I could to keep up with the material:

FROM THE LIBRARY:
PSYCHIC STRUCTURES

"Psychic structures coexist stimultaneously; the 'points' of attention or focus changing constantly and forming concentrations of self-related consciousness or identities.

"Physically, the earth-tuned structure of consciousness alters its focus points, thus revolving in time, which is the 'drag' resulting from the nature of such a structure and its position in relationship to other, larger, sometimes overlapping structures. Hence, the earth identity (focus personality) escapes in death by altering its attention, which automatically changes its structure, and then by re-forming itself in time as per reincarnational existences.

"The self as we know it is one such psychic structure, but from it probable actions also constantly occur. Like relativity, this psychological or psychic motion is relative to the perceiver; i.e., to the particular attention-point that each of us accepts as our platform of action.

"The earth-tuned self with its reincarnational spinoffs is just one such psychic structure, however, or one part of a larger multidimensional one—according to your definitions and where you want to draw the line. These structures are superimposed one over the other, even one within the other, though at any given 'time,' separate identities are maintained. Actually, however, relationships and boundaries change constantly as new hookups are formed and new connections made. These are also reflected in the earth-tuned probable and reincarnational activities.

"These psychic structures *are structures*—multidimensionally fitted one within the other like Chinese boxes, only eternally mobile. They can turn themselves inside out. One can travel through another. Yet each connection or identity made is eternal (while ever-changing outside of time, yet manufacturing times through which it moves), while it is, itself, timeless. Actually each such structure *does* move through itself constantly. Each portion is a self with its own unique tone, or note, or attention-point."

The above material came with a delicious smoothness, each word mentally crystal clear. The following material is obviously my personal interpretation of those passages, but somehow to me there was no transition at all between them. Without pause, then, the material continued, but with this obvious change of viewpoint.

"As I become Seth, I attract a part of my greater psyche that intersects with my life, pulling in my version of the Seth structure within which my present being partially resides. So Seth is automatically personified by my focus point, and *his* attention (the part of it that I've attracted) is tuned into the direction of our world. What happens when I change focus in this way? Do I move out of or transform my psychic structure, or change my psychic direction? or motion? or both?

"Is our usual consciousness a psychic *posture* that shapes our experience (literally forms it), so that when I change that focus I'm actually taking on another psychic motion? changing psychic speeds? And maybe those new speeds literally put me in a different psychic *space*.

"Are my various states of altered consciousness my interpretations of psychological existence 'at different speeds,' or in different portions of the psychic superstructure of which I'm a part? If so, my own privileged viewpoint gives the entire superstructure a 'window' on physical life; an earthly livingscape, that to some extent has to add to the experience of the entire psychic superstructure.

"Again, usually we experience a relatively flat psychic self as we progress along the surface plane of space in what we call present time: But that present time is only somewhat enriched and 'thickened' by past memory and future anticipation. Actually there are vast *psychological* distances in the psychic structure, distances that we would interpret as past and future.

"Action even in these vast psychological distances, changes constantly; i.e.: Fresh action happens in the psyche's 'past,' and action is also changed *in the past* by motion happening (simultaneously) in the unimaginable future—which then changes the past or remakes it.

"On the one hand, our own consciousness might be the result of peaks of awareness on the part of our atoms and molecules—a gift from them to us, as each minute 'entity' leaps to life, consuming itself to one extent or another, so that we might reach for a cup of tea, smile, or walk across the floor. And, on the other hand, our own awareness might also be the result of the greater psychic structure that formed the cooperative venture to begin with. These psychic superstructures would also act as models as in my own book *Psychic Politics*."

As you can probably tell, writing this material I went from what I call my "Library consciousness," which seems to deliver information from another viewpoint than my own, to an inspired personal state and back again. This was like going up and down psychic or mental scales—very enjoyable, providing a steady sense of accomplishment even if I wasn't at all sure how the process worked. The rest of the material, coming as "automatically" and smoothly as the rest, was obviously the product of my own consciousness, but working at an accelerated rate:

> "Is our kind of being, then, inherent in our own cellular patterns; and are these superstructures (or heroic personages) inherent in *our* psychological patterns? Are we, as Seth says, immersed in death and life at once? Apparently, yes. Our particular focus simply rides over or ignores many microscopic deaths that happen physically within us constantly. And if portions of our psychological structures 'die' to us, or drop off into other probabilities, surely we go about our ways in blissful ignorance of such events.
>
> "But at some point we die, or at least from our viewpoint it seems that we end in a very vital way—the *only* way that seems to make any difference to us. Now, of course, we see death and life as contrasting states, although many people will argue that death can't be considered a state at all.
>
> "Yet, suppose that other portions of this psychic structure have a kind of existence that is composed of life *and* death; that possesses an attention span that straddles both, and bridges our limited psychological event-horizon—as, now, *ours* bridges the minute deaths of our cells which, after all, *do* compose a part of our reality.
>
> "In other words, imagine a psychic structure whose attention spans a 'series' of births and deaths in time—a superstructure that is a multidimensional outside-of-time version of each of our separate time-selves.
>
> "The time-self or focus personality would have its true being in those other (heroic) dimensions and the self that was aware *there* would correlate with my idea of the 'heroic personages.'. . ."

I remembered feeling that I was really onto something toward the end of those last passages. Yet a short time later, when I read them over, they simply seemed to be creative analogies; intriguing, but somehow just too disconnected from practical living. The entire question of man's personal experience of a basically impersonal universe must really have bothered me, though. I couldn't reconcile them *or* change my definitions.

As I read over that material now, with the God of Jane fresh in my mind, and the "divine atoms" mentioned in the poem "Origins," I made some further connections. My "heroic dimensions" discussed in *Psychic Politics* correlated with the dimensions in which the Library's psychic superstructures existed; and both correlated with Seth's Framework 2. So without realizing it, I'd been getting the same information from different levels of consciousness. Again, I just hadn't been ready to put it all together.

The second parcel of material that I found had come only a month after the first. As I read it, it was easy to see why it followed the earlier material, but it wasn't easy to understand why I'd merely filed the material away. For one thing, the instant the sentences began coming to me mentally, I'd known that the information was important. Once again, the words came as quickly as I could write them down; yet when I was done I'd felt an intellectual excitement, but no emotional contact with the material. As I read it over now, emotional acknowledgement was instant, and I knew that I'd finally caught up with myself.

Something else was clear, too: This material was more like a mental program from some psychic "University of the Air" than a newscast. Reading it, I thought that it was as if I'd been given a small segment from an advanced course of study; and only now was I able to really take advantage of it. The material came all at one sitting:

THE PERSONAL UNIVERSE

"The individual person *is* the center of the universe from our standpoint, responsible for his or her private physical and psychological experience.

"Through the individual, the energy of the universe is focused into physical expression, so that each person is immortal and mortal at once. In conventional terms, each person is part human, part divine; except that this transdimensional blend is seamless in heroic fact. That is, in life as we know it, human and divine elements are blended so perfectly together in nature that, looking for divinity, we ignore the divine blend present even in the genes, atoms, molecules, and cells. We are born and grow spontaneously: Our bodies and existences are 'given' by our divine attributes, which in our experience then seem human.

"The universe has as many 'centers' as it has 'points' within it. That is, the universe is, at every hypothetical point, a center.

"Each center, in our terms, is like a seed, growing into dimensionality, bursting into probabilities. In heroic fact, each center is not only its own focus, but the focus through which 'divinity' flows into probabilities. Each center is connected with each other probable center; and each *is the* center of the universe from its own viewpoint. Through this arrangement there is literally no beginning or end, and divinity pervades all realities equally—automatically translating itself into such dimensional activities, and knowing itself from all centers as All That Is.

"Psychological events exist on mental levels as psychic environment, in the same way that earth's physical features provide a physical environment in which action can happen. That is, we're given a definite supportive, invisible, psychological environment upon which or with which we build events in the same way that we build structures from physical elements. At our level, these two environments are intertwined. In heroic terms, both are actually local, sharing certain characteristics with all existence and all realities, and possessing other attributes that are peculiarly ours—in that we focus upon these predominately, while they may be only latent in other realities.

"While we are earth-tuned, then, we may return as individuals into other life spans. Though these lifetimes would actually exist simultaneously, we would experience them separately because our physical and psychological environments include the sensation of passing time. Other systems of reality without such a time system, would have no 'reincarnational' system.

"Each 'point' or center of the universe has an infinite number of equally valid identities, each inviolate; each using its own unique focus to carve out experience and being.

"In ways almost impossible to describe, these identities can meet, merge and intersect, while still retaining their inviolate nature.

"Memory seems necessary to us in any retention of identity because of our practical time experience. Without such a scheme, however, direct perception of events simultaneously would make memory unnecessary and needless. In heroic fact, all events exist at once, so to some extent our experience of memory is the result of faulty perception. We're only aware of a given event at one point in time and when we lose that direct perception of it, we begin to say that we remember it. Even then, we remember events one at a time. If we try to recall as many events as we can at once, we can glimpse the complexity of heroic perception.

"All of the events of our lives happen at once. While we

are unconscious of this, the divine elements in the body at micro-scopic levels do operate with that recognition. This operation is complicated by the existence of probabilities, however; as the cells, for example, expertly position our bodies in highly specific stances of psychological and physical activity while taking all other prob-able motions into consideration.

"The normal events of the world happen globe-wise 'at once' generally speaking, on any given day, though we're directly aware of events in our local sector only. Television and other physical methods of communication also bring such events into our private spheres. But the events of our private lives exist all at once in the same way, though we're only aware of what happens in our local *time* sphere—except for those other communications that come through memory, anticipation, and interior methods of communi-cation. These inner methods represent the inner senses [described by Seth].

"The gods of our religions are automatic psychological and psychic organizations, psychic structures at other levels, just as our cultural and political organizations exist in the social field. That is, the gods represent psychic organizations on 'higher levels'; they *represent* psychological structures more complicated than ours, more 'advanced' in the way that a body is more 'advanced' than a one-celled animal.

"We may be a part of these 'gods' in the same fashion that a cell is a part of our bodies; only in this case, the structures are psychological. [Note the change of viewpoint here from the pre-vious material.]

"Physically in a lifetime, we grow from a fetus into an adult million-celled organism. During this process, we call our selves, ourselves, though we go through many changes in size, weight, capabilities, and general expression as we grow into an adulthood that seemed almost godlike to the children we once were. At other levels, then, we may grow into a different multidi-mensional maturity that, from our present viewpoint, would seem quite as godlike. As there is a pattern for our physical growth, so there must be a psychological pattern for this more extended psychic maturity.

"*To this extent,* we would each have a private 'god,' as in life we have adult parents who serve as models for development, are intimately connected with our physical existence, and act as pro-viders. These gods or heroic aspects would act as unconscious patterns for psychological development in the same way that inner patterns for physical growth reside in our cellular structures. The patterns for physical development are *part of* the genes, and the inner heroic patterns are *part of* our psychological reality; one implies the other. This spiritual inwardness, then, is also a physical inwardness, and is present in the cells and tissues of the body."

Note here, the return to the earlier tone and viewpoint; the lessening of speculation; the confidence, and to my ear at least, the sense of inevitability.

"Each hypothetical point of the universe is identified; that is, each point in our conceivable space-time universe is aware-ized energy, with properties of consciousness and an identity or 'am-ness' which becomes a center of focus for experience—a threshold retaining certain characteristics of an inviolate nature through which, then, other elements are sifted.

"The overall energy of the universe is constantly coming into identification, then; into known, experienced condition. The 'within-ness' of the universe constantly turns into exteriorization; the undifferentiated becomes specific. On the other hand, this inwardness is not annihilated as it turns into exteriorization, and its undifferentiated aspect is never used up. This energy is self-generating, and therefore is also never completely expressed, since each expression and identification brings about additional inner activity and new generation.

"The universe is manifest and unmanifested at once.

"Again, in ways perhaps impossible to understand at our level, the manifest and unmanifest are not separate states—one flows through the other, and the two are blended. In the same way, each center springing into identification is also, by virtue of its unmanifest nature, a part of all other centers. Each identified portion of the universe knows through its own unmanifested level what is happening to any other center. The existence of one such center takes the existence of all other such centers for granted. Since all conditions spring out of the unmanifest, and since the unmanifest turns into the manifest, all centers or identifications are 'properly placed,' following inner patterns that take the entire (ever-changing) picture into consideration. As the identities fulfill their own patterns, they therefore also act in a way that is beneficial to the whole.

"The lives that we know are not less eternal because they are temporal. Our lives express eternity in temporal terms. Temporality is one expression of eternity. Our lives are temporal and eternal at once, then. Here, eternity takes a temporal stance. 'God' exists in eternal terms, and in temporal ones, through 'His' manifestations. 'He' does and does not exist, for in 'Him' the manifest and unmanifest would be equally expressed. In that regard, there would be a Source out of which 'God' springs, as 'He' emerges into identification, and however vast 'His' dimensions. We would tune into that portion of a godhead that correlated with our own understanding.

"In our terms, one part of the psyche is manifest in life as we know it, and one part is unmanifest. The known, manifest portion of our existence rides on the unknown, unmanifest portion— but the reverse is also true, since the unmanifest actively seeks manifestation. It is also true that the two states are complimentary and that each state is 'folded' in the other, immersed in the other, actually without separation, though even to speak of these states *as* separate causes us to artificially divide their unity.

"Again, our manifest and unmanifest states exist simultaneously: Our lives and deaths are now. We can't understand eternal being without thinking of duration from our viewpoint, yet eternity exists outside of time, even while it expresses itself through temporality. Eternity is also expressed through probabilities, some operating within our understood time framework, and some apart from it. At those levels, all events are equally valid. We stamp some with the imprint of our identification and these become actual in physical existence. The others are equally valid and operate in varying degrees at other levels 'beneath' the accepted framework of our experience.

"In the most valid of psychological, psychic, and physical terms, we live in a personal universe."

That Library material is some of the best I've received from any source. It was obvious that I'd been dealing with the same ideas, whether through Seth, the Library, or my poetry. But now I was getting it clearly at my usual conscious level; that is, I was beginning to get it through my head that more than symbolic material was involved. More and more I was impressed by the realization I was being presented with a picture of the universe that, again, just made more sense than official views; and this model of the universe could effectively change private life and world reality for the better, if it could be put to use.

Putting it to use meant discarding old theories of any kind that denied man's intuitive, psychic nature. But more, I thought, putting those ideas to work meant that I had to use them as a yardstick in daily experience. I had to change over my emotional alliance to the newer framework, and above all, I had to trust my own impulses. We were back to that again. I sighed, reconciled by now to the idea that I couldn't just deal with impulses as if they were theoretical. I had to start with my own.

So as the hot June weather of 1979 arrived, I determined to watch for different kinds of impulses with as much eagerness as I looked for different species of birds at our bird feeder; to study their eccentricities and emotional plumage, and most of all, to follow their emotional or mental flights to see where they might lead.

They led to the nitty-gritty. But before getting into that strange interplay of impulses and beliefs, I want to include this humorous poem, which describes the personal universe from another viewpoint. *How* personal is the universe? you may be asking. The poem gives an answer of its own.

ONE DAY AN ANT

One day an ant reared up, and addressed me, thusly:
"Oh, Thou, hold back Thy mighty foot,
which even now is poised above me.
Hold, I beg Thee.
I've run just ahead of Your approaching shadow,
zigzagged a breath away from Your giant stride,
but it seems You seek me out.
Why else, free to wander immense dimensions,
would You choose to intersect
my lonely path?
Would You, in Your mercy, move Your descending boot,
most gently,
just one inch to the right or left,
for if it continues as it's begun,
then this cry of mine
will surely be my last."

I paused in astonishment.
The ant said, "Would You please
withdraw Your foot completely, Lord?
Forgive my unease. My panicky wits
have forgotten how to move me, and I fear
that in a mood

of divine absent-mindedness, You might unleash
the power of Your mighty weight,
and drop Your foot,
without completely meaning to.
The results, unfortunately for me,
would be the same
as if You killed me by intent.

"I'm flattered, of course,
to so come to a God's attention,
but the sidewalk across the way is grander,
and I suggest You might find it
more suited to Your progress,
on Your next trip by,
but I am still too terrified
to take myself out of Your sight.
So speak. What is to become of me?
I cannot move.
Thy will be done."

I smiled and stepped aside.
The ant rose, shaking. He bowed and fled,
chattering hosannas nervously
over his shoulder,
and a heavy branch,
strong enough to kill me,
suddenly fell
harmlessly beside me.
One inch closer,
and I would be dead.

For those of you who might be too literal-minded, I'm
not implying that the poem's narrator would have been *punished* for
not helping the ant, but that each creature looks at reality and
interprets it from its own center of experience; and that at the same
time, the acts of all species are interrelated.

That interrelatedness between events *here* would have its
origins in Seth's Framework 2 or in my heroic dimension or in the
Library's "unmanifest" state—the names we give to that inner
reality are relatively unimportant. But it *is* vital that we realize that
all of our own actions don't show in daily reality, only their effects;

and that our impulses fit together at other levels of reality and then form the actions of the world.

Impulses open the doors to probabilities. That fact became clear to me as I began examining my own impulses, following some and discarding others, realizing that with each decision, I was moving through different Junes of 1979. . . .

Part Two

THE NITTY-GRITTY
AND RESOLUTION

Chapter 11

"Contrary" Impulses, Precognition, and "Coincidence." What's Going On in Framework 2 and the Woman from Big Flats

Just yesterday I had another example of a seemingly contrary impulse that actually proved to be remarkably constructive. I'd just finished typing the last chapter (on the Library material) and was all ready to begin this present chapter when my ambition deserted me. Suddenly I didn't feel like working at all. Instead I felt lazy and dissatisfied. At the same time I was annoyingly aware of a vague impulse to browse through an old book that had been sitting on my bookcase for several years.

So I sat there, mentally muttering. My conscious intent was surely to get on with my next chapter, I thought. So why should an impulse to do something else come to my attention? Because—I sighed—I'd been training myself to notice such intrusions. And just as I thought *that,* still another contradictory impulse popped into my mind. The kittens, now a year old, were gamboling at my feet and I was tempted to play with them for a while and forget the whole thing. Anyway, I combined the impulses, got the book, opened it up at random on my desk, and ran a piece of string along the floor for the cats at the same time.

It was impossible not to laugh at their antics, so gradually I forgot that I *should* be working, played with the cats, and read a few lines here and there from the book. Quite contented. Then my eyes fell on a seemingly innocuous sentence in which the author wondered what happened to personal identity after death, if reincarnation actually meant that we had more selves than one. What happened to each ego?

The question was hardly new, but I felt a flash of annoyance because I'd never really answered it to my own satisfaction in the past, and even Seth's explanations hadn't cleared up the issue for me. There was also a mild, brief sense of panic as I read the sentence: I was so convinced that the ego survived death even in the face of other equally valid reincarnational selves—but suppose I was wrong and our identities sort of equalized out or spread out evenly over all of those selves, our experiences blending in so smoothly as to be indistinguishable?

And in the next moment I had it! I saw how it worked—or rather, I understood it emotionally in a way I just hadn't before. I have no idea of the actual mental processes that must have been involved, but I *did* have an acceptable answer to a question that *had* plagued me for years.

We each experience existence from our own center, as per the Library material, and as implied in "Tale of the Seamstress." I'd more or less understood that, but now I saw how it worked. If I ever become aware of my reincarnational selves, I'll consider them *my* selves and think of me as the main self who lived all those other lives too. But the seamstress, for example, would consider *her* life the focal point and look at my life as one of hers. The ego of each self would continue to operate and develop on its own. Neat. And simple. Why had the entire matter seemed so difficult only a few moments before?

Then it came to me that if it hadn't been for the impulse to look through that book, I might still be trying to figure it all out. And the impulse to play with the cats had relaxed me enough to be receptive. Not only that, but as my eyes caught sight of my manuscript, I saw that the entire episode would make a much better opening for this chapter than the one I had. Once again, when I thought my impulses were leading me astray, they were leading me where I wanted to go all along.

The question about reincarnation must have stuck in my mind ever since I typed the Library material the day before. But since I was anxious to get my typing done, the problem must have "gone underground." Some part of me must have known what passages in that old book would act as the proper stimulus. *That* information could have been in my "unconscious" mind, since I'd read the book once or twice years ago.

Even in that June of 1979, though, it was becoming obvious that some impulses also seemed to rise from a knowledge of events that I couldn't have, even unconsciously, according to official psychology, and I began to sense how one personal impulse could involve several people in a highly unconventional psychological activity.

One such event happened late that month. I'd started out that morning determined to keep track of my impulses, as per Seth's instructions. I didn't have an idea in my head for *this* book, but I tried not to worry about that. Actually I was thinking about Seth's material on Frameworks 1 and 2, and contrasting his views with those of science. And before I knew it, I began some poetry. It took my full attention, and I lost all sense of time. I did my exercises at noon though, and looked forward to working on my poetry all afternoon. I felt great about the day; lines for the poetry went through my head as Rob and I ate lunch, while rainy June air rushed in the open back door.

Rob started talking about some chores he had to do downtown that afternoon. All at once I had the impulse to go downtown with him. I didn't say a thing, though. Instead, I started silently arguing with myself. I was angry at the impulse, to begin with. My thoughts went something like this: "Damn it! I wanted to do my poetry this afternoon. What did I have to think about going out for? I've got the breakfast and lunch dishes to do before I can go back to work as it is. I've already done my exercises once and I still have afternoon ones to do."

My good mood was gone. I felt all my old defenses rise up to do battle with any impulses that threatened my writing hours. The old feelings rushed up: The day would come and go, *vanish* for all practical purposes, and I'd have nothing to show for it unless I captured it somehow through my writing; unless I formed another pseudo-living platform above living itself to examine life from. The lunch we were eating would be forgotten, and the day's details, and all that would remain was whatever essence I could capture through my art. So why the hell should I squander my time going out with Rob while he did chores? I did my part too, chore-wise. So why did I get that impulse?

Why indeed? For a moment I squeezed all the day's available time out of eternity's tube: There it was, all used up! Feelings of being harassed returned. I guess I grumbled out loud, and Rob asked me what was wrong.

"Nothing," I muttered. I was tempted to tell him that I'd go with him, but I just couldn't commit myself at that point.

All of this may sound like much ado about nothing, but when we tackle our most troublesome impulses, we're up against all the beliefs we've connected with them too. I knew that, of course, so I went through the now familiar procedure of telling myself that: 1. Impulses were meant to be constructive. 2. They could be trusted. 3. They didn't operate contrary to my conscious intents.

So even though the impulse *seemed* in direct contradiction to my desire to work on my book and write my poetry, I *would* go along and see what happened. Before I could change my mind I said quickly, "I guess I'll go downtown with you, hon."

"Great," Rob said—grinning. His look told me that he realized I was having a bit of difficulty, so I swore sheepishly under my breath and grinned back at him. I was relieved. I felt virtuous: I was going to follow my impulses all day come hell or high water. The poetry would just have to wait!

The poetry would have to *what*? The thought sent me back to the doldrums. I was staring at the red and white checkered oil-cloth on the table top, frowning at the lamp and bottles of spices, and the magazines; and the table seemed as cluttered as time did, or vice versa. Then, a knock came at the door.

By now I was nearly furious. Dear blessed Jesus, I thought, what next? In walked a friend and former student. He'd made a special gadget for me to use in my exercises, and he'd taken time out from *his* day to bring it over. So I could hardly be angry at him for coming, I thought. Only why did he have to come now?

So while the three of us sat drinking coffee, I silently moaned that I'd lost still more time. Besides that, the already rainy-looking sky outside darkened even more, and in a few moments a heavy rain began to fall. I brooded: I couldn't let our friend go home in a storm, so he'd have to stay until it was over; and *then* I'd have to do the dishes before we went out—if *I* went out—so that I could get right back to my desk when we came back. In a matter of minutes I decided that my original impulse didn't stand a chance. So when our guest finally left, I did the dishes, grumbling to myself because I also remembered that I was behind in my correspondence.

"I'm ready. Are you coming?" It was Rob, all chipper, ready to leave.

"I guess I'll stay home," I said.

"Are you sure?"

No, I wasn't sure, I thought. I wasn't *sure* of anything. But Rob's voice was quizzical, concerned, and humorous all at once. It made me hesitate just long enough to let that beleaguered impulse rise once more to mind. In a series of quick mental images, I saw the two of us driving downtown, with the street scenes flashing by. With the mental images, all of my earlier determination returned.

"I changed my mind. I'm coming," I said.

The ride through the wet June afternoon was lovely. The luxurious trees were all dripping, and the thunderclouds almost touched the hilltops. Only a fine sprinkle of rain fell. I felt exhausted, triumphant, and somewhat of an ass. How dumb to feel it was wrong to "break training" in the middle of the day and go for a ride! Rob made several trips into various stores in the downtown mall and I sat in the car, reading. Now and then I'd pick up a notebook I kept in the car, and do a brief sketch of a passer-by.

I was reading when, mentally, I heard someone call my name. My head snapped up. A young man was walking by, and instantly I connected him with my mental impression. He was a fan, I thought, and in a minute he'd come over to the car. But he didn't. As I watched, he passed by. With a good touch of irritation, I decided that obviously I'd been wrong; yet the feeling that someone was about to come over to the car had been strong, and specific.

Frowning, I lit a cigarette. I should have known better anyhow, I thought: While strangers come to the house, we kept a very low local profile, and no one ever came up to us on the street. Then why did I still have the same feeling? Wishful thinking? Not that I knew of, I muttered. I just wanted Rob to return, so I could go home and get some more writing done. And while I sat there, trying to figure the whole thing out—you guessed it—somebody called my name.

I looked through the half-opened car window. A well-dressed, good-looking, plumpish young woman with brown hair came running from the front of the supermarket toward the car. At first I didn't realize that she was actually heading for me, though, and her face was so flushed with pleasure and delight that I wondered wistfully who she was running to meet. By the time I realized she was coming over to the car, she was nearly at the window. Grinning, surprised, I opened the car door.

She spoke in an excited rush. "I just met your husband in the grocery store. I've read all of your books. They've helped me and my family in more ways than I can say. And look! I just bought this at the bookstore next to the market." Triumphantly she showed me a copy of Seth's *"Unknown" Reality,* Volume 2, that she had in a green plastic bag. "And I recognized your husband from the pictures in *The Seth Material,*" she exclaimed, just as Rob came up behind her, pushing a basketload of groceries.

"Are you from Elmira?" I asked.

"No, that's it," she said. "We live in Big Flats, which is nearby, of course. But I don't come in to this market very often. I've always wanted to meet you, but I didn't want to try to visit and disturb your privacy. I just knew we'd meet somehow! I just knew it!"

Her warm voice was full of conviction, and in a few quick phrases she shared the main flavor of her life: She had four children, her husband had a biplane, and her husband and oldest children had also read all of our books.

"I told them that I'd meet you some day too," she said. "And now I have. Coincidence? Not as far as I'm concerned."

The rain had let up, but it was still sprinkling, so I said, "Come on, get in the car. You'll get all wet."

But she shook her head. "I have to go. But I'll tell you one thing, you really made my day!" She'd made my day too, and I told her so. And I didn't think that our meeting was any coincidence either.

Rob put the groceries in the trunk and got in the car. We watched the woman walk away toward the end of the parking lot when I remembered my earlier impression that the young passer-by was a fan and was going to approach me. I told Rob, and *he* told *me* that he'd been speaking with the woman at the checkout counter in the store, which was directly behind the young man's position on the sidewalk. So, I'd mistakenly ascribed the impression to the man, while actually it must have come from the woman who stood directly behind him, approximately ten feet away.

"It *could* just be coincidence," I said. "But my earlier impression about a fan coming to the car makes that really seem unlikely, even if I was mistaken about who the fan was. On the other hand, how did I know even a few minutes ahead of time that a fan *would* approach us? It's the first time someone's ever done that while I've been in the car."

Rob threw me a look of mock severity. "According to science or psychology, you just *happened* to get your impression that a fan was coming over to the car about the same time that the woman was speaking to me in the store. She just *happened* to be there and she just *happened* to have a new copy of your latest book under her arm—"

"And I just *happened* to go out with you today," I said, finishing the sentence for him. "It's one of those evocative little incidents that you can't prove one way or another."

"Proof or not, that's the way life works," Rob said soberly. "Think of the millions of events like that occurring in just one day. But people have been brainwashed to ignore the evidence of their own experience."

I nodded. He was right, of course. I thought of all the letters we get from people who have all kinds of "unofficial" experiences; experiences that shouldn't happen at all according to established fields of thought. So the significance of the day's events began to sink in as we drove home. The episode was important, I thought, precisely because it was indicative of the kinds of events that happen to many people—people who don't necessarily go into trances or specialize in studies of the mind.

I was tickled at the entire affair; positive that the woman from Big Flats had somehow impressed the universe (or our part of it) with her intent to meet us, and that the encounter took place as soon as the circumstances were right. But what conditions had to exist in inner reality or Seth's Framework 2 before we could meet in the ordinary world? I couldn't wait to get home to figure it out and write my notes.

We sped up the wet road, with the overhanging dripping foliage giving everything a secretive air, and I thought with delight that the universe or nature gave up its secretiveness once you started paying attention to the small details of living that we've been taught to ignore. And each coincidence that was more than a coincidence, each precognition no matter how small, was evidence that the world had a meaning never found by Darwinian or Freudian thought; and for that matter, never discovered by most religions. And each such instance should be dearly held in the mind, I thought, smiling at the trees through the windshield, because each bit of new data added to the larger picture of reality—a picture that hopefully would be as vivid and persuasive in the future as the official view was today. I wasn't thinking of scientific proof. I was thinking of self-evident proof, or proof through experience.

Anyway, we went home. I did my exercises. We ate dinner. Then I sat down to write my notes. As I went over the day's events in my mind, I saw that there was even more involved than I'd realized. It wasn't until I started writing that I remembered my morning impulse to go out with Rob, and all the resistance it engendered before I finally followed it. And if I hadn't, the woman never would have met me at the store. Not that day, anyhow. As I wrote my notes, the green evening twilight seemed to wink, as if the leaves had tiny eyes that opened and closed, and again I felt that nature's seeming secretiveness was actually an invitation to us to really look at its events, innocent of our preconceptions.

I wrote: "I keep thinking about the woman who approached me in front of the store today. How many impulses did *she* have that somehow or another resulted in our encounter? How many did she follow or discard? Did *she* think about staying home early this afternoon when it rained so hard? Did she stand in her doorway, in momentary indecision, as I did in mine? What inner connections reached between us so that at certain levels each of us must have known what the other one was doing?

"And what about our friend's visit? If he hadn't come precisely when he did, and detained us, we would have reached the store too soon to meet the woman. Or somehow knowing that, would she have changed her plans? In fact, I changed my mind several times about going out, so the whole meeting must have been up in the air until I finally made my decision.

"Did I actually know that there was a particular reason for me to go downtown today? Did that woman's intent to meet me account for the persistence of my own impulse to go out? In the face of all those questions, the matter of my apparent precognition is almost secondary. And how differently the world must really work, from the way we're taught it does!

"I'm convinced that such instances of unofficial activity can pile up and provide us with our own kinds of evidence, *if* we let them; if we trust our impulses, study them, and keep track of where they lead us. The entire episode *could* have been just coincidence as science would say, but science couldn't prove that thesis any more than I can *prove* mine. But my contention that we have an inner system of communication and perception does have on its side the evidence of experience.

"Anyhow, Seth says that impulses emerge from the deepest sources of the psyche; that they're meant to help us follow the paths of our greatest development and to interwork with the impulses of others so that the entire species is benefitted. And this affair certainly seems to suggest such relatedness."

I finished my notes, stared at them, and realized something: I'd be using the material in my book, so I *had* been working on it all day, even when I'd been worried that my impulses were carrying me in another direction. Hmm. I turned off my electric typewriter, and immediately heard the sound of Rob's machine coming from his studio: He was still typing up Seth's latest session on *Mass Events,* so I decided that I might as well work for a little longer too. By then it was 9:30, too late to start something new, so I glanced at the poetry I'd done that morning. I'd nearly forgotten how badly I'd wanted to get back to it.

I grinned. I chuckled. Reading it, I couldn't believe how pertinent the poetry was to the day's events. The poetry was asking the question, "How do we know what we know, when we aren't consciously aware of knowing it?" Or, really, "Where does our unconscious knowledge come from?" And both poems were stating the importance of self-evident knowledge, or experience. In a way, it almost seemed as if the poetry had set up a series of questions that were followed by the day's unofficial events, so that my art and my life were joined in the same intent inquiry.

Here are the poems:

IF TOES HAD EYES

If toes had eyes,
then I could see
how my feet know where to go,
but toes are blind.
And how is it that my tongue
speaks words it cannot hear?
Because for all its eloquence,
the tongue itself is deaf,
and flaps in soundlessness.

If tongues had brains of their own,
then I could understand
how they can talk of calculus
without an education,
or just speak sentences
without ever learning grammar.
And who taught my fingers how to spell?
For as I write, they form the letters
as if they'd read a spelling book
or studied vocabulary.

Scientists and men of worth
tell us that the brain
carries messages,
telling each body part
just what its purpose is,
so when a brand new brain starts up,
it knows it's made for thinking.
But how does it know what thoughts are,
if it's never thought a thought before?
And why does the new tongue begin to cry,
when it can't hear the sound it makes,
but lies, deaf, in the brand new mouth?
What moves the tongue?

If all we are is flesh,
and flesh is made of molecules,
then how wise atoms are
to teach themselves how to walk,
and train mute ears to hear
words that they can never speak.

FIRST THOUGHT

I've forgotten how shocked
I must have been,
when first my brain
discovered thought,
and brassy new molecules
went searching
after sentences.
All of my ignorant infant cells
must have lifted

their heads, and roused,
as the first messages
stirred the waiting
chromosomes.

My first thought must have broken
through pristine mental silences,
jingling ten million new neurons
that had been dozing,
with the first signals
that reached
even the smallest atoms,
hidden in the fresh corneas
of my newly opened eyes.

Not the first word,
but the first thought
is magical;
the mute but vigorous
first thought electrifying
unlettered molecules,
as anew, biology
turns godlike,
imbuing congregated particles
of animated dust
with the mental
properties of personhood.

Not just food,
but the first sweet taste
of thought entices us,
fattens the piths of our beings,
and sends us searching
through neural paths
to seek meanings.

When my brain first broke
its silence,
golden syllables suddenly whispering
grandly through my skull,
how did the brain cells
bridge that gap,
giving chemicals
the gift of thought?

How, indeed! The existence of any thought is mysterious when you *think* of it, and I'm not just speaking hypothetically, but about the specific thoughts I have right now and the private thoughts that each of my readers have as they read these lines. How do we read and decipher words? What connections are there between our individual nervous centers and the vast network of communication that unites civilization? No science or religion has any adequate answers for those questions. And if we're made of only atoms and molecules, where *did* they learn such tricks? By *chance*? Not likely, in my book.

Anyway, when I finished reading my poetry that night, I made a mental note to ask Seth to discuss the entire matter of the meeting with the woman at the supermarket, and to include a description of the interactions that went on between Frameworks 1 and 2. I still couldn't forget the day's events precisely because they were so innocuous in a way, so easy to assign to coincidence, so familiar to everybody's experience . . . and so definitely brought about by inner psychic connections and communications that exist all the while beneath the officially experienced world.

It was late. The supper dishes still waited in the sink and I wondered if the woman in Big Flats had done *her* dishes yet. And I thought: The God of Jane must have had a busy day.

Chapter 12

A Scientific Put-down and a Psychic Declaration of Independence

The supermarket encounter with the woman from Big Flats happened Friday, June 29, 1979, but that day's events stretched out to include the entire summer, in ways that will soon become quite clear. In fact, the repercussions began the very next day with another incident that Rob and I wouldn't soon forget.

We were eating lunch in the kitchen. I was still thinking about the Big Flats affair, the implications of seeming coincidences and their importance as possible evidential material. "If enough people kept track of such events and followed them through, then we might end up with a decent body of evidence based on observation," I said. "Now, *that* would be true scientific behavior."

"Well, get on with it," Rob said, joking. Then, more soberly he added, "I'm afraid that science isn't going to accept any evidence about anything that might upset the apple cart."

"Maybe you're right," I answered, but in a few flights of fancy I visualized "the people" keeping track of all those instances of telepathy or clairvoyance or seeming coincidences; collecting and categorizing their nightly dreams as carefully and systematically as if they were examining and labeling exotic butterflies or samples of some precious ores, until finally we had it—piles and piles of evidence that defied statistics and showed that "coincidences" were, instead, clues of a comprehensive order that united the largest and smallest of events in a field of relatedness; an order that implied that each act had meaning on both microscopic and macroscopic scales.

For if the universe had meaning, I thought, then each act within it did also; and conversely, if each act fitted in with each other act in a meaningful gestalt, then the entire combination of acts, culminating in the universe, was also meaningful. So once we started seeking with those ideas in mind, the universe would give up its secrets to our observation! Why not? We would be "psychic naturalists," taking our field trips in the mental and psychological environments, watching for species of perceptions instead of for birds or plants.

And (as my fantasy continued) there would be thousands of meticulously kept journals as the people recorded their private dreams, collected the strange varieties of dream life, and checked dream events against personal and even national and worldwide public events. For if established science was based on the hypothesis that the universe is a meaningless production formed by chance— almost a cosmic farce, but more deadly—so I imagained an alter- nate science based instead on the hypothesis that the universe had meaning. *This* science would examine all the data that official science ignored or dismissed, and I was willing to bet that the new evidence would far outweigh the old.

That was the gist of my thoughts that noon when the mail came and jogged my fantasies to a rude awakening. As Rob and I opened and read our correspondence, the entire character of the weekend changed.

Actually, there were many letters from people telling us that they'd been using Seth's material or mine to achieve more satisfying lives, or to develop their intuitive abilities—letters that should have cheered us considerably. But one letter was far dif- ferent. Now I can't remember who read it first, Rob or me. Actually the envelope contained three letters. The first was from a fan, an architect. Out of curiosity he'd written to a fairly well-known scientist, asking him if he knew about our work. He had enclosed a copy of the scientist's reply, with the comment that he was sure that we were too open-minded to be upset. (I'll explain the third letter later.)

Upset? It's a wonder people didn't hear me shouting my indignation blocks away. The letter really took me by surprise; but as an example of a scientific put-down, I had to admit that it was a classic. The scientist wasn't writing about some hypothetical woman, though. He was writing about *me,* so my appreciation was a bit jagged. In fact, he was defining my reality by his rules, and I was furious.

I'll call the scientist Dr. Camper. In the first paragraph of his letter he told the architect that as he understood it, "Ms. Roberts has published several books of mediumistic messages allegedly from Seth," and that Seth "simply conveys a philosophic message without making concrete, falsifiable predictions." In the next paragraph he said, "As far as I know, Ms. Roberts honestly believes that she is 'taken over' by another entity called Seth." Then he went on to say that again—as far as he knew—no one had ever accused me of conscious fraud.

I stared at the letter. O.K., I thought. What really upsets you, Jane, outside of the "messages allegedly from Seth"? You've got to admit that scientists love the word *allegedly.* The man doesn't mean any personal offense. After all, even newspaper reporters use the word when they don't know if a person actually committed a given crime or not. Like, "Mrs. Jorden *allegedly* picked up the axe."

"Crime?" I sputtered. "Of course." It was the suggestion of some kind of fraud that angered me, not a conscious fraud which might take some wit, but the insidious hint of a subconscious fraud so psychologically suspect that it could never be proven true or false.

And, I thought, what about Seth making no "falsifiable predictions"? That tricky wording almost escaped me in my first reading. I said to Rob, rather loudly, "You notice that he didn't say that Seth made no *verifiable* predictions. He takes it for granted that any prediction would be proven false. *Falsifiable.* And," I said, somewhat louder, "I don't believe that I'm 'taken over by another entity called Seth,' in the way he means at all. If he'd read any of my books, he'd know how much I've examined the psychological issues involved."

"He's read very little of your work or Seth's," Rob said, finally getting a word in edgewise. "He says as much somewhere. Toward the end of the letter, I think."

I read on, now filled with righteous indignation, and found the passage almost at once. It stated: "From what I have read allegedly from Seth (and I have not read that much), there is little remarkable about it that I could not imagine simply coming from

Ms. Roberts' unconscious." Then in the next passages, Dr. Camper went on to mention my work as being in the same league as some other books that Rob and I both considered to be on the level of psychic junk food, or well-meaning psychic pulp.

I saw the word *allegedly* again, as if it were a red flag, with me the attacking Taurean bull. But I tried to be reasonable, too. Camper didn't have to like my work or Seth's, of course. He had a right to his opinion. And, as I well knew the term, "unconscious" was another old scientific stand-by, used to explain the origin of events that science really wanted to dismiss. Oh, well, to each his own, I thought.

To each his own, indeed! When I read the rest of the paragraph, I was angry, bewildered, and confused all at once. Dr. Camper wrote: "You [the architect] are not correct in saying she has not built up a cultic following," and went on to say: "Ms. Roberts used to live in Elmira, N.Y. (she may still) when I was in nearby Ithaca. I gather that she had quite a local following back then (circa. 1960)." Then he told the architect that a particular exposé-type novel published at that time was "basically about her group in Elmira, by the way. . . . More important, she has earned very *large* sums of money from her books by Seth. The Seth books sell extremely well. . . ."

For a minute I really didn't believe what I'd just read. I hadn't even begun sessions with Seth until late 1964, and I didn't hold any classes or meetings of any kind until 1967. So it was impossible for anyone to have written a book back then about me and my "cultish following." And "large sums of money," he'd said, underlining the word, "large." Now what, I asked myself, did that mean?

I found out in the next paragraph, and scandalized, I read the passages to Rob: "Ms. Roberts has never been interested in having her message or trance states tested by skeptics. I cannot blame her. She has a very good thing going and probably a harmless one. . . ."

To each his own—hell, I thought: He had a right to his opinion when it was stated as such, but not to twist the facts, and not to present his own misconceptions as facts. And many of his "facts" were wrong.

Actually, though, the misstatements of facts didn't bother me as much as the innuendoes. Throughout the entire letter ran the obvious implication that I was a nutty, not-too-scrupulous lady out for a good thing, writing spiritualist nonsense with far more than any author's quite natural desire to sell in the marketplace, embarked upon an endeavor certainly marked, at the least, by subconscious fraud; and in any case, beneath the serious notice of lofty and objective men of science. And I was . . . alarmed.

The third letter made me feel a bit better, but that's all. The architect had also enclosed a copy of a letter from the author of the book that was supposed to have been written about my "circle." The architect had written asking if this was the case and the author replied in the negative, saying that my work hadn't come to her attention until years later.

But I reacted so strongly to Dr. Camper's letter because the affair of the day before was so fresh in my mind, and because of my fantasies of only a few moments earlier about the psychic naturalists. It would be a cold day in hell, I thought wearily, before science would ever really change. What had I been thinking of, to imagine that official science would grant any credence to personal experience? And how could science admit that subjective examination had any validity when it even refused to consider the question of consciousness in any of its calculations?

Other issues were responsible for my reactions too. Rob and I were aware of Dr. Camper's reputation as an open-minded scientist who was interested in investigating the paranormal. With some dismay, though, I thought that if Dr. Camper was the scientist most receptive to "the cause," then my psychic naturalists might as well be science-fiction characters; it would be some time before such investigations were ever taken seriously by science.

I wasn't angry at Dr. Camper personally, but at the entire situation. And I was sad, thinking of all the people who write us about their own instances of psychic events—events that our largest field of established knowledge simply ignored. But people's experiences weren't going to change, regardless of science's attitudes, I thought; and Dr. Camper's letter couldn't alter one minute of my trancetime. So I said to Rob, "I suppose we might just as well let the whole thing go, and forget it."

"No," Rob said slowly. "We have a right to set the facts straight, at least."

When I get angry, I usually rumble and yell and snort. When Rob gets upset, he gets quiet, and he was *very* quiet. It's never pleasant to have your integrity questioned, of course, no matter who you are. But when it's questioned by someone who doesn't even know you, someone who doesn't even have the facts straight, yet whose name carries the authority of science—well, that's not exactly guaranteed to make your day. Or your weekend. And Rob's integrity was being questioned as well as mine. It was being questioned automatically, without malice, but questioned all the same.

Usually Rob and I really enjoy our weekends. We take

more leisurely meals than during the week, and even though we
both work on our writing projects for a few hours, and I answer the
mail, still we always feel a kind of holiday air. Not that weekend,
though. Rob spent it drafting a letter to Dr. Camper.

To set the facts straight, Rob explained that in *The Seth
Material,* published in 1970, we'd described our early but unsuccess-
ful attempts to interest science in our work. One psychologist had
questioned my sanity in very insulting terms. One just didn't want
to be bothered. The only psychologist who showed any real interest
was a Dr. Instream (not his real name), and in his letter Rob
described the year-long, twice-weekly tests we did with Dr. Instream
through the mail. Rob also outlined the matching series of tests that
we conducted ourselves, and explained that when Dr. Instream
refused to give us the results of the mail tests (saying we had to work
without feedback on behalf of scientific objectivity), we ended the
venture: A year without results was a bit much, we'd thought. And,
as Rob told Dr. Camper, we then concluded that if we were going to
learn anything new about the nature of human personality, we'd
have to do it alone. That was O.K. with us, as Rob made clear in his
letter, only now it didn't seem fair to accuse us of *avoiding* scientific
investigation.

Rob also cleared up the issue of the book that was
supposedly about my "circle," but wasn't, and he concluded by
making some pretty pertinent comments about the limitations of
contemporary science. I added a rather lively one-page letter of my
own, but Rob's ran ten pages. It took him most of the weekend to
compose, because he also had to check our old records. So he lost
time painting and working on Seth's book, which didn't exactly
improve his spirits.

I spent most of the weekend writing my own notes, and
trying to sort out my feelings and reactions. Any animosity I may
have had toward Dr. Camper personally had already vanished. I
was even willing to admit that I thought that *he* thought he was
being quite open-minded when he wrote the letter to the architect.
So the question was: If that was scientific open-mindedness, then
what had happened to its old claim of being an objective explorer,
seeking the meaning of man and the universe? Because, I thought,
now science was seeking mechanisms, not meanings. It was seeking
meaningless mechanisms to explain life's meaningful spontaneity.
Now that just didn't make sense as far as I was concerned.

And I did make a distinction between official science
and people who happened to be in the sciences. Many practicing
psychologists were using Seth's ideas and mine in their work with

clients. Several physicists had expressed interest in our material almost from the beginning. Just the same, I thought morosely, I had classes for over eight years, speaking for Seth in good light, surrounded by "witnesses"; and where were those hard-nosed scientists then? If they'd wanted to see the "unconscious" in living stereo, there it was, all aglow, more or less in public view. And it occurred to me that maybe I'd needed that letter from Dr. Camper to help me crystallize my own beliefs. Perhaps I'd looked hopefully over my shoulder at official science for too long.

I sat by the living room windows, looking out at the mountains and vaguely listening to Rob's electric typewriter: click, click, click. I saw Rob in my mind's eye in "the writing room" where he types all Seth's sessions, prepares the manuscripts for publication, and keeps records of current events, giving the sessions an added framework. Surely his dedication deserved better from official science, whether or not it agreed with our conclusions. The objective study and observation of altered states of consciousness: Why *wasn't* that a worthwhile study? As I brooded another phrase from Dr. Camper's letter came to mind, to the effect that I hadn't encouraged investigation by *skeptics*. And for some reason, the word "skeptics" really really got to me. I felt the rise of a slow, sure, indignant stubbornness and, at the same time, a new sense of independence. The stack of unanswered mail sat in a basket in front of me on the table: The vacuum stood against the wall where I'd put it to remind me to clean the rug. The dishes were still piled in the sink, and the cats were prowling around looking for attention. But I grabbed a piece of paper and started typing as fast as I could, so that for a while the only sounds in our house were the double click-click-clicks of our two typewriters.

"Science worships skepticism," I wrote, "unless skepticism is applied to science, its hypotheses, procedures, or methods. What we need are more skeptics who are not afraid to judge the claims of science with the same fine discrimination used to examine other alternate disciplines and fields of endeavor. Like *The New York Times,* science publishes 'all the news that's fit to print,' meaning all of the news that fits into the officially accepted view of reality. That news is already invisibly censored, and yet we're supposed to live our lives in accordance with that official definition of experience.

"Human experiences that don't fit the picture just aren't included. Psychological events aren't even considered facts by established science. We live in a society whose scientific disciplines state that we have no real volition; our feeling that we have free will is seen only as an illusionary reflection from the state of our brain's condition. According to the theory of evolution, life itself came into being through the auspices of chance, without intent or meaning. Established psychology still states that our perceptions are mechanistic. Yet in that cultural framework, Rob and I have spent over fifteen years studying altered states of consciousness, and exploring other ways of perceiving reality.

"I should have realized that to conventional science all such pursuits must seem futile, caused by delusions, unsteady brain states, misfiring neurons, chemical imbalances or obsessive, neurotic need. As long as it holds its present beliefs, science must consider the human being as a sophisticated but mechanical psychocybernetic system that happens to run itself.

"When I first began to speak for Seth, Rob and I looked to science as the unrivaled arbiter of reality, within whose framework any phenomena could find its place. All these years, I've regarded my experiences with an objective eye. I tried to be my own subject and my own investigator at the same time. It's just occurring to me that I almost tried to be both heretic and inquisitor at once. Anyhow to a large extent, I still looked at myself through my understanding of science's framework. And it becomes apparent that science's dogma is as limiting as religion's.

"If I wouldn't let the priests tell me how to live my life or how to regard my own experiences, why should I give that privilege to science? Yet while I've gone my own way I've constantly looked nostalgically for some kind of scientific approval."

As I typed, I could feel my emotions rising. The stubbornness was coming on strong, and it pushed a new sense of conviction along with it. I knew that my feelings would moderate later, and I even thought how funny and futile—one woman railing against official science, as if science cared. But I replied to myself, *stubbornly* again, that while my feelings were mine, they also reflected the indignation of many other people—men, women, and children—whose private experiences happened not to fit science's "norms."

So I wrote,
"Intellectually and emotionally we must all cut ourselves off from official dictums; look at reality anew and try to form some

fresh, sane view of ourselves and the natural and social worlds. I write these lines with a finally felt sense of freedom, and yet with some nostalgia for the brave view of science I once held. Surely a field of endeavor that sent men to the moon could have enlarged its theories of psychological reality to include those inner mysteries of the human mind.

"And as I see it, each human mind has the right to question the beliefs of its time and the bases upon which those beliefs rest. Even animals explore their physical environment. Shall we do less with the mental environment that is so a part of our natural heritage?

"There's no room for negotiation as far as official science is concerned. If religion has its original sin, science has given us the survival of 'the fittest' and man, the predatory animal. Impulses become mere chemical reactions, a kind of chaotic biological commotion, against which we must exert all of our will and reason. In that framework, the idea of heroic impulses seems laughable or worse, highly misleading and dangerous.

"What weird romanticism in the face of such beliefs, to imagine that man is even a well-intended animal! How daring for any of us to fly in the face of centuries of official knowledge and scholasticism, to deny the tenets of religion and science both and insist, even querulously, that man is good and that his impulses can be trusted! And why is it that the most scientific and the most religious persons will both insist upon man's inequity? Only their reasons for it differ.

"But if we are even willing to agree that man *might* be good, then we must begin to recognize and trust our own impulses. And, ah, there's the rub, as the saying goes, since we've been taught that our impulses will betray us. They are the tempters. The voices of the devil. Or the lingering rages roused in our infancies. Or the disordered, random, chaotic desires rising from our evolutionary past.

"So let us be the first scientific Protestants, challenging the orthodoxy and authority of organized science as well as religion, denying science the right to define reality for us by insisting that its terms are the only terms; its version of truth the only version; its answers the only acceptable ones for intelligent adults. Let science be relegated to the making of better mousetraps and other handy household gadgets that can, at least, contribute to our domestic ease; since in science's pursuit of the nature of reality, it specializes in the production of better bombs and a nuclear technology that threatens to send us 'to our maker' all too soon.

"I refuse to let such a science define my reality. I hope that my book can serve as a rousing call to action: Let us be truly objective, examining the claims of science with a very careful *skeptical* eye, particularly in those areas where its dictums encroach upon our private realities. And they do, constantly.

"Such an approach won't be easy, though. If organized religion considers non-members sinners to be converted, science believes that its membership is the only fitting place for the elite, the thoughtful, the reasonable and the reasoned. Anyone with views considered unscientific is thrown into the mental trash heap of the mentally or emotionally blemished.

"Regardless, here I state my own psychic declaration of independence, refusing any longer any dependence upon versions of reality that strike me as limiting and senseless, whatever their power in the world or their own strength in my own background. I refuse to feel guilty by responding almost automatically to the built-in pressure hammered by science, religion or psychology. And I hope that individuals within those fields will rouse themselves, bringing official views closer to their own private experiences with reality; refusing to scale down their lives to fit outmoded theories.

"But whatever they do, I hope that my decision frees me from any lingering loyalties to officialdom, and that I'll be daring enough to use whatever abilities I have to continually explore those further reaches of subjective reality with which I have contact.

"I don't flatter myself, of course, by thinking that science cares if I excommunicate myself from its framework. It never considered me part of it to begin with. But it occurs to me that science had better take care that too many people don't leave the fold, for its projects are financed by funds from the people—from you and me. If enough of us flee the fold, the umbrella of government funds could no longer provide its public shelter. And in such a case I think that all of us would suffer. I also think that science's attitudes are causing many people to turn to fundamental religions in a backlash effect. Also unfortunate.

"Actually, I'm making a plea that we return to true science; the science that the established foundations have forgotten, a science expanded to include a really objective exploration of man's subjective reality—and a science that dares to be its own subject."

So, rather dramatically, alone at my table, I dedicated myself to true science. It was twilight. I'd written myself out for the day. My sweet electric typewriter was still; and now that its click, click, click no longer filled my ears, I heard the birds chirrupping and feeding at the window box. And I wondered: Was it true science and its technology that developed my electric typewriter, so that I could argue with "untrue" science so eloquently? Hmm. Nothing was ever simple.

And, I reminded myself, the same technology had given us the Three Mile Island accident, numerous medical and scientific errors like the swine flu vaccine fiasco, and a planet polluted as science tried to "control" a natural environment with which it had lost rapport. And I knew that I was reacting to all of that, too, using Dr. Camper's letter as a kind of focus. Just the same, I hoped the entire affair was over.

But it wasn't, of course.

Chapter 13

Seth: On the Big Flats Affair, Science, and Frameworks 1 and 2

Our regular Seth sessions usually take place on Monday and Wednesday nights. We met the woman from Big Flats on a Thursday. Dr. Camper's letter had come the following day. We hoped that Seth would discuss at least one of those events in his next regular session that Monday. Rob was still working on his letter to Dr. Camper. I knew I'd be mentioning both episodes in this book, so I was putting my own notes in order.

By now it was really summertime, just turning dark around 9 P.M. when sessions usually start. The front and back doors were open to let in the soft night air. I was really curious to know what Seth would have to say, particularly about the Big Flats affair; granted that he said anything at all. I knew only too well how science would interpret the incident, I thought, particularly with Dr. Camper's letter arriving around the same time.

As Rob said earlier, science would see the meeting with

the Big Flats woman as a chance encounter, pure and simple. I just happened to be at the same place as she was at the same time. She just happened to drive to that particular Elmira bookstore to buy our latest book, and I just happened to think that a fan would come over to the car, minutes before she actually approached me. For that matter I'd originally imagined that the fan would be a male passer-by so science would most certainly say that this was a classic case of someone assigning a psychic label to a perfectly normal event, and that the woman's strong intent to meet me had nothing to do with it.

I went over that explanation in my mind as I waited for the session to start. God knows it sounded reasonable enough, I thought, and I said as much to Rob.

"If it sounds so reasonable, then why don't you accept it?" he asked.

"Because I know that I didn't just *happen* to be outside of that supermarket. I *know* how I hemmed and hawed about going out that day—" I broke off. In my own intentness I hadn't noticed that Rob was grinning.

"It isn't funny," I said, but in a way it was, of course. And suddenly I sensed a vast but sympathetic amusement that wasn't mine, but Seth's. Just for a moment, I glimpsed that expansive creative psychic framework in which we all exist—a framework big enough to include the poet and the scientist, the priest, the heretic, the witches and witch hunters, and all of the living characters of historic time, living their lives rambunctiously, according to their prized beliefs about reality.

Once again I felt my consciousness begin to shift, move, take on another coloration; become somehow fuller, more assured. I sat there waiting to click into the psychological Seth slot, a state large enough to contain my own consciousness with room left over. And as I waited, I thought that the Seth trance was certainly a fact of my existence, no matter what anyone thought. Somehow in that trance my own consciousness was intact and whole, held safely within Seth's more expansive, seemingly more powerful psychological framework.

And if a scientist asked me what I felt like, right then, what would I say? I wondered. Sometimes I feel as if I'm inside a transparent psychological bubble, floating in some buoyant psychic air, peering outward *into* a vast mental universe. Sometimes my consciousness in trance feels like a small boat riding great thrusts of thoughts instead of waves. Was that my own translation of my individuality, and the power of the psyche upon which it must rest?

136   The Nitty Gritty, and Resolution

I went on thinking. Do Seth's highly individualistic characteristics sort of swim into their specific nature at some psychological point where I move out of the consciousness that I recognize as mine? Do new psychological coordinates take over? Or was Seth, after all, a kind of mental entity in a universe or field where all encounters were psychological?

And all the while I was thinking, the shifts of consciousness that I was thinking about were happening. It was trancetime. I was Seth, or vice versa. The following are excerpts from that session. As always, Rob took his verbatim notes, and Seth referred to Rob and me by our "entity names," Joseph and Ruburt. Actually the session was a simple private one, with Seth addressing himself to Rob. And as always, my eyes were open.

FROM SETH SESSION 864
JULY 2, 1979   9:06 P.M. MONDAY

"Now: Good evening.

"This is not book dictation but a discussion of intent, Framework 2, and official reality.

"I want to discuss your meeting with the woman from Big Flats, and Ruburt's immediately prior knowledge of the event; the nature of time in connection with Frameworks 1 and 2, and mostly to emphasize the importance of beliefs.

"We will call the woman from Big Flats Mrs. X for convenience's sake. She has wanted to meet Ruburt for some time. This intent was very strong and relatively steady. Mrs. X, however, is not a pushy person. She would not intrude by trying to discover your address or phone number. Her desire, however, was vivid: It was clear, simple, direct. It was implanted, of course, in Framework 2, and it waited for its time of physical fulfillment. However, there were obstacles. . . ."

Here Seth went into my own attitudes and usual disinclination to take time from my writing during the day for an outing—when Mrs. X might otherwise have had the opportunity, at least, of meeting me in a public place. Then he continued:

"The woman's desire had to wait for Ruburt's change of mind, then. Ruburt began precisely a month ago dealing with impulses once again. This indeed created a new creative impetus, and certain acts were set into motion. Whenever Mrs. X knows that a new book of ours is out, her impulse is rekindled and intensified in Framework 2; as if a bell were set ringing. This time, Ruburt had the impulse to go out in the middle of the working day, and the woman's desire helped kindle Ruburt's own impulse; so that even when he was tempted to stay home, he kept returning to that impulse once again."

Referring to the friend who visited us just before we went to the supermarket, Seth said: "Your friend always has your best interests at heart. He came in response to Framework 2 impulses, precisely so that the timing in Framework 1 could be synchronized. Otherwise, of course, you would have been at the proper location, but ahead of time.

"Ruburt was free enough of official dogma to become consciously aware of the event as he sat in the car, before he actually met Mrs. X. You (to Rob) were speaking to Mrs. X at the time, in the store. Ruburt was almost consciously aware of the fact that there was another reason for the trip downtown. He recognized the fact that the impulse to go with you was unusually strong.

"Had he not believed in, say, telepathy, he never would have been aware of his impression that someone was going to come over to the car and recognize him—a stranger. The woman [Mrs. X] also believed that in one way or another it was at least possible that her intent could somehow find fulfillment despite the obstacles.

"Now your unfortunate scientist of the letter can have no evidence of anything but official behavior, because he cannot allow his consciousness that much freedom. It is not merely that he has too much invested, but that the investment is in a closed system of reality.

"Mrs. X's clear intent in Framework 2 was to everyone's benefit. However, for some time it was blocked because the other person involved made certain decisions that made the meeting unlikely. The moment Ruburt changed, the way was clear and the action took place almost immediately. The scientist, however, has placed so many impediments for himself in Framework 1 that he cannot open the door for the impulses that would lead him toward the kind of evidence he thinks he wants.

"The fact is that science itself must change, as it discovers that its net of evidence is equipped only to catch certain kinds of fish, and that it is constructed of webs of assumptions that can only hold certain varieties of reality, while others escape its net entirely.

"The two of you started off with flying leaps when we began the Frameworks 1 and 2 material. But its implications became dulled as you began, again, to study the tangled web of official reality that so obviously clings about your social and political world, in the civilization of your times. That is natural enough—or I should say, that is <u>understandable</u> enough. Any concentration upon that tangled web, however, can help block your impulses, give you a sense of powerlessness, and prevent you from building up a sense of confidence as you learn to interact with Framework 2. . . .

"Do not look backward, comparing your ideas to those of the official world, any more than you can help. Framework 2 is a multidimensional medium of creativity and value fulfillment, in which desires from the most simple to the most complex become actualized events—if those desires are for your own good and for the good of others; not, for example, to be actualized at someone else's expense, and if you, yourselves, do not place impediments in Framework 1. . . .

"You have every right to write your letters, but do not concentrate upon the stupidity of official beliefs. That can increase their impact. Instead, remember the clarity of your own intents. Keep Framework 2 more alive in your thoughts and be more alert for its evidence."

According to Rob's notes, it was 9:42 at this point, and Seth launched into an interpretation of two of Rob's recent dreams. One, involving a white rabbit, led Seth to make the following remark:

"An aside: Scientists are enamored of magic, in terms of the magician's art, for it titillates their deep hope that a true magic of the mind exists, while at the same time reinforcing their official beliefs that all such ideas are the result of the magician's tricks."

(Then the session continued.) "Framework 2 is not distant, aloof, 'out there,' or apart from your own desires. It is as close to you as your impulses are; for your identity (now, from your viewpoint) resides in Framework 2, from which all the events of Framework 1 emerge. Going along with your nature automatically brings value fulfillment and fortunate events, for your intents, abilities, and needs work naturally together.

"When you believe in impediments, you create them, because they are <u>also</u> the result of your creativity. They take more effort, however, because they do not flow naturally from your being but are the results, say, of muddy coloration or distortions of thought.

"Your own intents, concerning your lives' work, are good. They are natural. They are held at no one's expense. Therefore they possess great power in Framework 2. They act as beneficial impetuses, causing others to have creative impulses that are also for the benefit of all. Those impulses may meet impediments in Framework 1, but they will also bide their time, as the woman's did. Their fulfillment, however, will take place. Do you have questions?"

In Seth's dream material for Rob earlier in the session, Seth had mentioned a Framework 3, so Rob took the opportunity to ask Seth to say more on the subject. Seth replied:

"You picked that up, I see. I told you that there was a Framework 3 and mentioned a Framework 4 some time ago. You must understand that I am making distinctions for your benefit.

"Framework 2 is connected with the creativity and vitality of your world. In your terms, the dead waken in Framework 2 and move through it to Framework 3, where they can be aware of their reincarnational identities and connections with time, while being apart from a concentration upon earth realities. In those terms, the so-called dead dip in and out of earth probabilities by traveling through Framework 2, and into those probabilities connected with earth realities.

"Some others may wind up in Framework 4, which is somewhat like Framework 2, except that it is a creative source for other kinds of realities not physically oriented at all and outside of, say, time concepts as you are used to thinking of them. In a way impossible to describe verbally, some portion of each identity also resides in Framework 4, and in all other frameworks.

"Some invisible particles can be in more places than one, at once. Some portions of each identity can also be in more than one place at once. It is a matter of focus and organization.

"That is all for now. I bid you a fond good evening, and I am glad that you picked up on my hint [the mention of Framework 3]. For when you do that, you are ready to ask the questions that you really want answered. The impulse is there to ask. . . . My fondest wishes. Good evening."

I was surprised that the session was so brief. It ended at 10:10 P.M. But it was certainly definitive enough: Seth was decribing not only a meaningful universe, but one that allowed for creative spontaneity and the interplay of impulses. It certainly wasn't deterministic. After I read the session, I thought of it often during the week—and about Dr. Camper. Rob completed his letter to the scientist and mailed it along with my shorter one. Seth devoted his next session to book dictation, but the following Monday, July 9, he ended Session 865 with the following comments about our correspondence with Dr. Camper:

"<u>Considering your joint feelings</u> (underline twice) you
were both wise in sending your letter or letters to the scientist. You
acted. You used your power to state your case. Had you not acted,
the affair could fester and add to a sense of powerlessness. Having
acted, however, do not concentrate on the affair, either of you. . . .

"The man wrote as he did, for one thing, because he has
come across our work secondhandedly—many times, as it was
spoken about by others. He feels such work a threat because he is
attracted to it. It stands for the hopes that he has, and also for the fear
of ridicule that he feels, caught between those who are even more
close-minded than he and those who would travel further than *he*
dares. He is afraid of the power of the scientific establishment, but
he is equally afraid of the powers of the self, so that he has no course
left but to dismiss them. End of session. [Then, jokingly:] A powerful
good evening to you both."

We hadn't really been concentrating on Dr. Camper, but
we did wonder now and then if he'd respond to our letters. Because
of the affair though, during the next several days I looked over a few
recent copies of a fairly new scientific journal devoted to studies of
"the paranormal." The magazines had been sitting around the
house for a while, but I just hadn't taken time to do more than glance
through them before.

Now I was appalled. I felt as if the magazine articles
brought me into contact with "strange encounters of the human
kind," introducing representatives of a different breed of human
beings. This was a breed whose members ignored their own psychological encounters with reality, overspecialized in exterior and
secondary intersections with life, and were comfortable with experience itself only if it were interpreted through the intermediaries of instruments, gadgets, or objective measuring devices. As if
life were too hot to handle directly, they tried to manipulate it
almost exclusively with tools, not daring to hold it in their own
psychological hands. At least that's how it seemed to me as I read
those magazines.

These were people, I thought, who couldn't trust direct
personal experience, and denied the validity of man's psychological contact with existence. They put great stress on objectivity, while
ignoring psychological reality as it naturally presents itself; a psychological reality that alone was responsible for our very perception
of a physical world.

I was also catching up on my correspondence; and the

basket of mail and the scientific journals sat side by side on the same tabletop, evidence to me of the two vastly different ways of dealing with the nature of reality. Half of the letters in that basket, I thought, dealt with experiences that simply did not exist, as far as the journals' learned scientists were concerned.

One letter in particular caught my attention. It was written by a woman who said that she was labeled emotionally ill only because she'd had an out-of-body experience. Since the psychologist who treated her thought all such events were hallucinatory, he considered the episode to be an alarming symptom of instability. He'll probably turn up next as a future contributor to this journal, I thought dourly.

What really made me angry though was finding myself agreeing with any of the journal's articles, and I *did* agree with several. The writers had a keen, if cold intelligence. They did a great job of seeing through some of the nonsense connected with the psychic field in general. Of course, they were almost vengefully gleeful whenever they could legitimately knock down some psychic performance, or show a psychic's predictions to be wrong. Only why couldn't they see their own scientific nonsense? And why couldn't their trained intellects perceive their own emotional vehemence? Because, I thought unhappily, they were definitely scientific witch hunters.

I wondered what would happen if by some fluke I got their mail and they got mine. I bet that I'd give more careful objective attention to the points made by their correspondents than they would to mine. But the tone of the journal taught me something important, too. I determined to keep the entire matter of science's limitations in perspective, to remind myself of science's accomplishments, and not to be as close-minded in my views as the writers of that journal were in theirs.

Just the same, for a few days I was discouraged. I might read the journals of established science, I grumbled, but those scientists weren't about to study Seth's material or be swayed one iota by any material that threatened their dominant stance. And the people who wrote me about their psychic experiences might just as well live on another planet as far as those scientists were involved. And *that* made me angry.

Actually, the anger cascaded into my consciousness and turned into a long poem, in which the anger itself was redeemed and turned into something else. And while I was still working on that poem, Seth gave us an excellent private session that also helped me put my recent experiences into proper perspective.

I'll start off the next chapter with excerpts from that session, which was held the night before we received Dr. Camper's reply to our letters.

Chapter 14

Seth: On Schools and Science. A Scientist's Apology and Offer of Assistance

That spring and summer Seth had taken to dictating *The Individual and the Nature of Mass Events* on Wednesday nights, leaving Mondays open for other material. Actually, Rob included some excerpts from the latter in his notes for *Mass Events,* because often the Monday sessions were related in one way or another to subjects already under discussion in Seth's book.

As you can see, though, the following session was held on a Thursday and the subject matter—science—was related to *Mass Events* and to our private lives as well. I was still brooding about scientific attitudes at the time, and Seth was nearly finished with his latest chapter, entitled, "The Ideal, the Individual, Religion, Science, and the Law." I'm presenting the session excerpts intact, with Rob's notes for a change, rather than making my own commentaries, to remind the reader that Rob is always the observer. His notes provide the exterior framework for the Seth material, just as his very presence provides an objective point of reference, subjectively speaking, for Seth and me.

That is, whether the session material is personal or book dictation or devoted to other matters, Seth speaks *to* Rob, not *at* him. Seth gestures, smiles, speaks loudly or softly as he relates his material to Rob—and Rob, I'm sure, is a surrogate reader besides the other functions he serves so well. Rob is the first person to hear the material, of course, and his attention is unwavering. I've often thought that it was as if Rob's mind was a target—*the* target, Seth's target; with me something like a booming metaphysical cannon of energy. Even when Seth speaks softly, for example, there is an extraordinary amount of power involved, with a definite focused intent.

Rob can always ask questions, as he does in the following session. I've included the personal material because it applies not only to me, but to each of us when we become discouraged about our ability to "change the world," and become overly serious and therefore, overly anxious. Rob's notes are in italics.

DELETED SETH SESSION
JULY 12, 1979   9:19 P.M. MONDAY

(No session was held last night, as was scheduled. It had been very warm and Jane had been bothered by the heat and humidity. She'd also been quite relaxed at times through the day, so I didn't ask her for a session. It seems that we also got our signals crossed, for I learned today that she'd been ready for a session; but because I didn't come out of the writing room and ask her if she wanted one, she thought I didn't want one. . . .

(But at about 9 P.M. this evening Jane surprised me by suggesting a brief session. It was just as warm tonight. All our doors and windows were open because of the heat, yet when Jane went into trance her delivery was quite energetic, almost fast, and at times very emphatic. Without greetings, then:)

"Now: Particularly to Ruburt, the following sentence:

"You do not have the responsibility to change the world for the better. That is, changing the world for the better is not your personal responsibility.

"You have a natural need to impress your world—to act through it, with it, and upon it; to illuminate it with your own vision, in which you automatically change it for the better. The original prerogative is the creative one, from which all benefits automatically flow.

"If you think that it is your personal responsibility alone to change the world, then you are always bound to feel a burdening sense of failure. The world *is* being changed through our work—but because that work is primarily a creative endeavor in the fullest, deepest meaning of that word. When you begin to hold the attitude I have just mentioned, however, you begin to insist upon immediate creative results. . . .

"The scientist's *(Camper's)* letter had good effects in crystallizing your attitudes, in Ruburt's poetry, and in the passages for his book. It also made Ruburt think, however, that he was not changing the world in any way that mattered in any important degree; that those in authority did not even read our books, and that even my latest work *(Mass Events)* would make no inroads. So he did not want book dictation, on the one hand, for that reason. On the other hand, he did, of course. And again, of course, we will finish our book in our usual style.

"I do want to emphasize, however, the existence of people like the young man who came today. You are speaking to the younger generation strongly, and they are the people who will make up the fabric of so-called official establishments in the future; and they will come to those establishments with far different values than those people now ruling. Period."

(Seth referred to Greg, a young man who arrived here yesterday afternoon in a taxi, and carried a box of a dozen long-stemmed carnations of four colors. The taxi waited, since Greg could stay but a few minutes before taking a bus out of town; he simply wanted to say thanks for the work Jane is doing, with my help.)

"Remember to keep open-minded about individual scientists also. It is against the official views of science as a field that you hold great variance."

(I didn't catch Seth's last word. "Hold great—?")

(With emphatic humor:) "Variance, disagreement—you pick the word.

"It is fairly easy to recognize the ways in which organized religion discourages vigorous intellectual speculation. It is more difficult, perhaps, to see that science fears the unofficially directed intellect quite as much as it does the unofficially directed intuitions.

"In schools, for example, there are courses in the criticism of literature, art criticism, and so forth. The arts are supposed to be 'not real.' It is quite safe, therefore, to criticize them in that regard—to see how a story or a painting is constructed, or more importantly, to critically analyze the structure of ideas, themes, or beliefs that appear, say, in the poem or work of fiction.

"When children are taught science, there is no criticism allowed. They are told, 'This is how things are.' Science's reasons are given as the only true statements of reality, with which no student is expected to quarrel. Any strong intellectual explorations of counter versions of reality have appeared in science fiction, for example. Here scientists, many being science-fiction buffs, can channel their own intellectual questioning into a safe form. They can say, 'This is, after all, merely imaginative and not to be taken seriously.'

(9:36.) "This is the reason why some scientists who either read or write science fiction are the most incensed over any suggestion that some such ideas represent a quite valid alternate conception of reality. In a fashion, at least in your time, science has as much to fear from the free intellect as religion does. And *(with irony)* any strong combination of intellectual and intuitional abilities is not tailor-made to bring you great friends from either category.

"Science has, unfortunately, bound up the minds of its own most original thinkers, for they dare not stray from certain scientific principles. All energy contains consciousness. That one sentence is basically scientific heresy, and in many circles, it is religious heresy as well. A recognition of that simple sentence would indeed change your world. . . .

". . . I bid you a fond good evening."

("Thank you. Good night."

(9:55 P.M. "I'm glad I did have the session, then," Jane said. "At least I got that straightened out, about the book sessions." When I asked her what she meant, Jane said that she'd been blue lately, wondering what good the work on Seth's books could do in the world.)

Actually I do a pretty good job of forgetting the world and its problems when I have the sessions because I do realize that if carried to extremes worry of that kind could end up blocking the sessions entirely: It would generate a frame of mind directly contrary to the one that makes the sessions possible. Reminders from Seth, such as he gave in this session, help, of course. I've deleted some other personal comments that he made, along with his interpretation of a dream I'd had the night before.

The gift of the carnations from the young man helped rouse my spirits too. So did a letter that came the following day from Dr. Camper. The letter itself helped speed up the inner processes of thought and feeling I'd been involved with since our correspondence with him began. There was no doubt that Dr. Camper was a man of honor, handling a sticky situation as fairly as he could, according to his beliefs and situation.

As we read his letter though, it was also obvious that Dr. Camper was operating in a very limited context—one that we just couldn't accept for ourselves. He started out by thanking Rob and me for our letters; then said, "I stand corrected . . . and can only say that apparently I was wrong." His statements had been qualified in his letter to the architect, he reminded us. He also said that when the novel he'd mentioned was first published, many people thought that the medium featured in it had lived in Elmira. Then, he wrote, when the Seth books came out, "It seemed reasonable to conclude that Ms. Roberts may have been the stimulus if not the model for the character." Even after seeing a copy of the author's denial of any such connection, Dr. Camper wrote that "I was still inclined to think that this was the case . . . and that [the author] might deny it for legal reasons. I see from the dates you give, however, that I was probably wrong."

"You weren't *probably* wrong," I muttered, reading. "You were wrong-wrong. No probably about it."

On the subject of "scientific validation," he wrote: "Having read little of the Seth material (which I shall now proceed to obtain), I had not realized that early attempts were made to validate the claims being made." And later on: "In science, the burden of proof for any extraordinary claim must fall on the claimant. If you wish to get the scientific community to accept the Seth phenomena, the burden of proof must be yours. If you wish to have the phenomena studied and validated, I will certainly be glad to try to help you."

The letter was several pages long. Dr. Camper agreed with most of the points that Rob mentioned in his own letter, and again it was pretty clear that Dr. Camper meant well enough and thought that he was being very open-minded.

There's no need going into several other important matters with which Rob and I took issue, but the letter did contain a suggestion that really scandalized us—and it surely wasn't scientific, either. In order to make sure that I'm not putting any words of my own into the scientist's mouth, I'm going to quote the lengthy paragraph in which the suggestion appears:

"It seems to me that we are dealing with two very different issues: (1) the source of the Seth materials, and (2) the validity of the ideas expressed in the Seth materials. These are quite independent. My major concern has been with the first issue.

Whatever the source of the materials, and I am still inclined to take the parsimonious view that while the source is internal to and not external to Ms. Roberts, the ideas can be valid. However, the paranormal aspect of these conjectures is strictly surrounding the question of source. If the ideas put forth by 'Seth' prove correct, then the genius present may simply be that of Ms. Roberts. In fact, to the degree that the Seth ideas have merit, they may in fact be largely shut off from serious consideration by specialists because they are allegedly from a paranormal source. In fact, a *prima facie* reason to be suspicious of the higher intelligence of Seth is the very fact that he would seek to put forward his messages in this fashion instead of developing a cover story which would make it easier to take the messages seriously by skeptical scientists. After all, there is no obvious reason why Seth could not dictate articles to be published in the science journals which review manuscripts blind (that is, without author designation).

"...And I do hope that you will continue to seek scientific study of the Seth phenomenon. If you do seek help in that regard, I would certainly be glad to do whatever I can. Whatever its causes, it is indeed something deserving of scientific attention."

What really shocked Rob and me was the suggestion that we should have concealed the source of the Seth material in what to us seemed to be an underhanded fashion. As Rob wrote in his reply, ten days later, "When Seth first came through (late in 1963) we joked briefly about disguising the origin of the material, but quickly realized that such a course would lead into a morass of deception that would end up destroying everything we wanted to show. To paraphrase (the Canadian writer and educator Marshall) McLuhan, 'The medium *is* the message,' and everything to do with the Seth material has to be out in the open, regardless of the consequences...."

Rob's letter went on: "Our same reasoning applies to your suggestion that Seth could write articles for publication in the science journals, were his identity hidden. Are you referring to blind peer review? We've heard of the procedure. What matter if Seth did succeed in having his work accepted blind? Sooner or later the source—the author, his credentials, etc.—would have to come out, and then where would Jane and Seth be? She'd end up labeled a deceiver by the scientific community...."

Rob also quoted passages from another letter, written to us by a professor of physics, which said in part: "At the present time there is no conceivable way that a paper which acknowledged Seth or yourself as its source of inspiration could get published in accepted physics journals. As you may be aware, it is even difficult to get very conventional work in parapsychology accepted by scientists outside of the parapsychology community, even though the work may be so hedged about as to be completely innocuous (as a threat to the prevailing scientific world view), in comparison with something as 'patently absurd' as mediumistic communications from a discarnate entity. Still, the winds of change are blowing, and it may not be too many years before the number of scientists willing to consider consciousness as an essential part of even physical phenomena will be sufficiently great that these things can actually appear properly acknowledged in the open literature."

Rob's letter made several points answering specific subjects mentioned by Dr. Camper, but two in particular caught *my* attention when I read Rob's reply. Rob wrote: "As Jane and I both indicated last time though, we can't really see that anything she can do would constitute the kind of rock-hard proof science says it wants. We think that the doubters would surely find ways to deny whatever was accomplished."

And, "We agree when you write that you take the 'parsimonious view' that the source is internal to Jane, and not external—but our definition of what's internal is evidently quite different from yours. We think that everything is basically internal, that our physical reality is really a psychological construct of unsurpassed creativity, legitimate to its smallest portion. . . ."

We received Dr. Camper's letter on July 13, and it was actually July 23 before Rob mailed our reply. In between the time that we received Dr. Camper's letter and the time of Rob's reply, though, I found myself thinking about the entire affair more than I thought I wanted to. Even as I did my household chores, I felt an inner whirl of psychological activity as if I were juggling ideas and issues back and forth in some still-troubled mental air, seeking a new kind of balance or mental resolution. As far as I could tell, Seth's material was directed to people as individuals, whether they were store clerks, truck drivers, teachers, scientists, or whatever. His ideas fell into all areas—religious, artistic, political (particularly in *Mass Events*), and scientific. I didn't think he gave a hoot whether or not science *per se* paid any attention at all. But, I thought, individuals who happened to be scientists were something else again. Science was squashing the spirit of inquiry on the part of its own membership.

But I wasn't a part of that fraternity! I got that far in my thinking one afternoon when I glanced through Dr. Camper's letter again. I read the passage: "In science, the burden of proof for any extraordinary event must fall on the claimant." And in that moment, everything began to fall into place. I was certainly familiar with the statement. I'd come across it countless times in the past, always accepting it, unthinkingly. Rob had even mentioned it in his letter to Dr. Camper, when he thanked the scientist for offering to help us "get scientific validation" for our work. This time though, I stared at the statement as if *before* it had been written in a foreign language that I was now suddenly, truly translating—discovering that it meant something far different than I'd earlier supposed. In any case, I knew that I no longer agreed with it as far as it concerned my own experience.

I was warm to begin with, that July afternoon, though it was cooler in the house than out; and I felt myself flush even more with a new keen indignation. I *wasn't* making any extraordinary claims! My experiences were psychological facts, regardless of the interpretations that might be made about them. So-called para-normal events had been reported for centuries by quite normal persons. People throughout history had recorded instances of pre-cognition, telepathy, out-of-body experiences and all such related phenomena. That data represented its own kind of evidence—an evidence that science had no right ignoring. Our own letters from people of all ages and circumstances made it clear that "para-normal" events were nearly frequent enough to be commonplace. They just couldn't all be explained away as the results of sub-conscious fabrication, neurotic behavior, or sheer fraud. They were at the very least indications that man *might* possess a highly sophis-ticated network of inner communication. Yet science hadn't even arrived at the point where it accepted the existence of conscious-ness in its equations. It refused to even consider such a hypothesis seriously, much less honestly try to gather any evidence that might support such an idea.

So, I thought, the burden of proof must fall on science as far as I was concerned: Let it prove that my experiences and the experiences of countless numbers of the world's population from past to present were, in fact, not valid, but were all the results of delusions or hallucinatory behavior. I caught myself saying that last sentence out loud, and laughed a bit sheepishly at my own ve-hement intentness. But it didn't matter, I thought. I *was* making a claim for human rights; for the inclusion of the full spectrum of psychological events into our sciences. I no longer gave science the

right to "validate" my own psychic experiences, because its thematic framework was too small to contain my reality.

Science had every right to set its rules, but not to set itself
up as the arbiter of reality. And certainly not of mine. And, I
thought, how dare science scale down the full dimensions of human
existence by denying the validity of experiences that had been a part
of man's existence for as long as history has been recorded!

I remembered my similar strong emotional reaction
after reading Dr. Camper's original letter, of course, and I knew that
I'd eventually end up with a more balanced view; but I also felt that
it was important to recognize and express my own feelings. I was, in
fact, writing them down as quickly as I could type. The ice cubes
had melted in my iced coffee. I was staring at the now lukewarm
liquid when the term "psychic manifesto" came to me. And instantly I knew that it would be the subtitle for this book, and the title
of the poetry I'd been working on all week as well. I also realized
that I'd been heading toward such a manifesto ever since I began
my latest attempt to free myself from old beliefs and started this
book.

And I thought, grinning finally, "Thanks, Dr. Camper.
If it weren't for you, I might not know yet where I stand." Actually,
again, I wasn't just reacting to this latest episode, but I'd obviously
used it as a focus point. It stood for many years' dissatisfaction with
the policies of established sciences, and was also a kind of delayed
reaction to science's past errors in the realm of technological mis-
adventures.

"A Psychic Manifesto"—I scrawled the phrase down on
the first page of my poetry and with a kind of pat passionate finesse,
I added verse after verse to the lines I already had. I'm putting that
group of poems in its own small chapter because in a way the poetry
marked a new beginning for me. It made a statement that I hadn't
been able or willing to make before. As I wrote, I was thinking not
only of myself, but again of "all the people out there" whose
personal experiences just couldn't fit into science's mold; people
whose dreams and intuitions couldn't be stilled by ridicule or
learned pronouncements.

Chapter 15
"A Psychic Manifesto"

1

My life is its own definition.
So is yours.
Let us leave the priests
to their hells and heavens,
and confine
the scientists
to their dying universe
and accidentally created stars.
Let us each dare
to open our dream's door,
and explore
the unofficial thresholds,
where we begin.

Let us refuse to be defined
as sinful selves

or creatures of a blighted species,
and instead
dare to recognize
within our dreaming hides
the grace of mental animals,
in which soul and flesh
are intermixed
with a natural alchemy;
so that awake, we dream,
and dreaming, wake,
straddling
life and death alike,
with an inner knowledge
that confounds
the dreary ministers
and scientists.

2

The flesh needs no absolution.
Its cells are innocent
as gods,
whose hidden
divine multiplications
compute our smallest acts.

How many eons did it take
for our cells to learn
arithmetic,
since they are microscopic structures,
minus brains,
and science would say,
lacking wit
or consciousness?

How did they learn
to construct
images of bone and blood,
choosing just the proper
combinations
that add up
to you and me?

3

I've yet to decipher
a fraction
of my body's knowledge,
though its molecular
mathematics
allows me to write
this line.
These thoughts journey
through my brain
by ancient pathways
that I cannot claim,
as if my body's memories
predate its own time,
rising from miniature civilizations,
whose coded arts
set my life in motion
and are expressed
through who I am.

4

The facts of life
are the heart's events,
that persist
beyond measurements.
The heart deals
with dream equations
that would dazzle a computer;
for the dreamer's
laboratory has no walls,
and his experiments
combine time and space
with a spontaneous knack
that defies
all formulas.

If hearts had to hold back
their beating,
until science proved
that life had meaning,
then we'd have

no life at all.
But the heart beats
predictably,
giving its own evidence
of a life experiment
no technology
can duplicate;
and each beat comes
like the first—
singular, mysterious,
from sources
outside the grasp
of objective
processes.

5

Each birth is unofficial,
maverick,
rising alike
from strands of love
to ancient vanished relatives,
and tied to a future, unknown self
who beckons
the dream-eyed fetus on
into life's bright scheme,
bravely daring unknown passageways
that lead
to life's threshold,
carrying
conscious cargo
from one
universe to another.
You made that journey.
So did I.

6

All that we are was once
wrapped in a tissue
parchment,
and coiled like onion skin,
imprinted

with life's hieroglyphics.
Fingers and toes were
smaller
than decimals, yet alive.
And brains-to-be,
measuring less
than an inch,
each contained
all the ingredients we'd need,
to think these thoughts.
What perfect transistors,
growing their own
future parts!
How were they wired
when, as science says,
we're only a combination
of dumb elements,
come alive in a universe
formed by chance?

Some chance, that my hands
didn't keep growing more and more
fingers, but stopped at ten,
learning to count
before I did;
and that my neck knew
where my head should be
before my eyes
could even read
a book of
anatomy.

7

So let us dismiss
all modern or ancient myths
that tell us that our genes
are flawed by primal lust,
or worse,
cursed by a revengeful god;
so that the flesh is filled
with sin's contents,
overflowing with iniquity;

or that we are natural killers—
animals run amok,
caught between
our own jealous genes
and the uncaring stars,
a schizophrenic species,
whose most magnificent acts
are stamped with the mark of Cain

Let us look instead
to our direct experience,
and listen to the messages
that arise
in unofficial ways,
bypassing dictums
and theologies.
Let us begin
by trusting once again
the personal contact of self
with self,
and self with world.
Let us observe
the facts of heart
and mind alike,
and refuse to accept
any theories that deny
our own experience.

8

My life is its own definition.
So is yours.
Our consciousness is
self-evident.
Are dreams not facts,
when each and every nighttime skull
is filled to its
nocturnal brim
with a commotion of images
to be found there,
and nowhere else
isolated from the world
like a master experiment?

But no one watches
or makes notes.
Then let us collect
our own dream species,
wander among vast
unexplored dream elements,
and discover for ourselves
those inner worlds
where mind and will are born
and merge,
and descend from dreams'
wild hilltops.

I have opened time's window
not just once,
but often,
catching just a glance
of tomorrow's evidence
before it was due;
and so have many others,
surprising some hour
before its time.
And just one such clue
is enough
to shatter all philosophies
that say we're stuck
like flies
in a jar of time.

So let us forsake
our ancient documents
and communes.
Leave the statues of the gods
to their plaster-of-paris parks,
and let the scientists
count invisible particles,
hypnotizing
themselves away.
Let us run
from doom's prophets,
whatever names they bear,
and let them sputter
of catastrophes alone—

waiting the world's end
(huddled, the survivors-to-be
wait in the worried air).

But hold the world
to your mind's ear,
and hear
the victorious roar
of life's waves
splashing against the shores
of mind and sense;
bursting tumultuously
from sources
echoed in our dreams,
as the images
of our desires
leap
into the swell
of space and time.

Chapter 16

Seth: On Creativity and Frameworks 1 and 2. Also an Out-of-Body at Noon

Again I knew, of course, that I'd moderate my attitude toward established science. In fact, I counted on it. But if my attitude has moderated, it hasn't changed. Too many events happen constantly to remind me of the capabilities of consciousness, and science's refusal to confront such issues.

In fact, two small but evocative such experiences occurred just now, nearly a year later, as I finished typing the previous chapter of this book for the final time. My habit lately is to write from 8:30 to 11:30 mornings, then do twenty minutes of physical exercise and lie down on the bed for five minutes before making lunch and returning to my desk. Two days ago I followed that procedure and lay down as usual, glancing at the clock first to check the time. It was 11:55; a sunny April day, without any leaves yet to cut down the noontime glare, so the room was very bright. I closed my eyes.

I don't remember what my thoughts were, but in the next moment I found myself in my breezeway studio, seated in a chair that I realized was actually in another room. The sunny daylight was gone. Instead, everything was gray and foggy—the small room itself and the view out the large floor-to-ceiling window. I was seated at my table, straining my neck, looking upward at Rob, who floated in the air above me like some large gray figure-shaped balloon. Why wasn't anything truly clear? As I wondered, I noticed that the furniture was all in the proper place, except for the chair I was sitting in, which by rights should be in the bedroom. And I felt odd, as if my consciousness was between gears, or as if I were somehow between realities.

While I was trying to figure this all out, Rob was talking to me. I could see his lips move in the air above me, but his words were muffled and unclear. I kept saying, "What? What?" Finally I realized that he was talking about being dissatisfied with a table in his workroom: Did I want to put it in the breezeway in place of something else? "No," I said, trying to figure out if I were actually speaking or just listening to myself speak. Rob kept bobbing in the air, floating toward the ceiling, with his earnest face looking down. "I can't figure out what's going on," I said, "but if you want to change tables, it's O.K. with me. . . . I'm not hearing you right, though."

And with no transition at all, I was back on the bed. My eyes flew open. I stared at the clock in the bright room. It was exactly twelve o'clock. I called Rob at once. He was in the bathroom, washing his paint brushes in the sink. Had anything strange happened to him? I asked.

"No," he replied, coming into the bedroom inquisitively, knowing from my tone that something had happened to me. I told him the entire incident, and even as I did, my consciousness still felt between gears, as if it hadn't entirely slipped back into its proper position yet. The feeling lasted perhaps fifteen minutes before vanishing. After lunch I wrote down everything that I could remember. Rob didn't even recall *thinking* about a table or replacing one in the breezeway with another. On the other hand, he didn't remember *what* he was thinking as he washed his paint brushes.

That night was a regular session night though; and when Seth was finished dictation, Rob asked him if he'd comment on my experience. This was Seth's brief reply, from Session 909 for Monday, April 21, 1980:

"Now, people may wiggle their feet, or doodle, or tap a desk while they are concentrating on other things. They also exercise their consciousnesses in the same fashion—doodle with their minds, relaxing in that way, wandering off to refresh themselves—and you were both doing that. But Ruburt caught himself in the act, so to speak.

"You were mentally wandering about the house, both of you, and Ruburt caught himself where his mind was, only his physical body was not in the same place. Because this was like a mental doodle, the colors were not complete. The picture was not filled in.

"The entire conversation [with Rob in the breezeway] was an attempt to make the affair reasonable, *to color in* the picture."

Anyone is free to accept or reject Seth's explanation—or just to be uncertain—but the point is that the experience was just one of the latest of a long string of unofficial events. I've had far more outstanding out-of-body episodes, but each variation of our usual consciousness is important. Each shows us a different facet of the entire spectrum of perception. I wasn't hallucinating. My consciousness *was* in another room, in a body that isn't my physical one. That is a fact of my experience. So that event and others like it constantly make me ask questions that I might not ask otherwise. What kinds of hypotheses might reasonably help us understand our own psychological mobility? What other aspects of consciousness are we overlooking? Those are questions that any science worthy of the name should be asking.

The second event happened the following day. Often such incidents do seem to bunch up. In fact, the same circumstances were involved. I was taking my five-minute rest in the bedroom, again at noontime. A few minutes earlier while I was exercising the phone rang and Rob answered it. He came into the bedroom just as I was lying down to tell me that a friend had called, saying that her twelve-year-old son was in the hospital. He'd been hit in the eye with a pole, accidentally, while playing with another boy. His eye had hemorrhaged, but he was expected to recover with no problems.

I remember thinking "I hope he's all right," just as Rob left the room. Then I closed my eyes. Instantly I saw a sparkling clear mental image, though at first I didn't know what it was. The visual data itself simply showed many dark red-brown clumps, rather large, interspersed with strings of the same color, surrounded on the left by a curved white area. In the beginning I thought I might be looking at red clumps of foliage that formed islands; but viewing them from above. Then I realized that the clumps were blood clots, seen as if through a microscope.

The feeling came to me then that "something" had to happen if the eye of my friend's son was to clear up. At once the white curved area somehow advanced on the red clumps and strings, and they began to disperse. They looked as if they were being eaten away at the edges. As I saw this happen, I "knew" that the necessary healing process had begun. Then the mental image itself disappeared all at once.

The visual data itself had intriguing connotations. We're not used to seeing things microscopically; and if I'd just had the experience itself, without prior knowledge of the boy's eye condition, I wouldn't have known how to interpret the image. I've had similar experiences of a more checkable nature, where conditions I saw mentally in a sick person's body were later found to exist there in X-ray examination. So I *was* able to bring prior experience to this event. And the more practice we have with various kinds of perception, the better able we are to distinguish between them. So of course, I am bound to ask, "Can we use a mental sight to see data not present to the eye?"

Again, I'm inclined to answer that question in the affirmative, but since official science hasn't accepted consciousness itself into its equations, the question isn't considered a legitimate one in scientific circles. So in the meantime, I'll trust the evidence of my own experience and continue to examine my own subjective states with an objective eye. And that objective eye shows me first of all that subjective states have an objective validity.

Anyhow, now in late April of 1980 I still stand behind the "Psychic Manifesto" that I wrote in July of 1979. In fact, curiously enough, no sooner had I taken my stand in relationship to science, than we began to receive a whole new flurry of letters from scientists who were interested in our work. Somewhat earlier that year, Seth had dictated some material in response to a physicist's letter, and he "came through," speaking at least briefly to a psychoanalyst, two psychologists, and a psychotherapist—each of whom visited us at various times throughout that summer. So we were hardly turning anti-scientific. Nor did my new mental independence mean that I was ignoring science's many accomplishments. It simply meant that I was returning to the evidence of my own experience, and that I refused to accept any scientific theories that contradicted it.

Within a month we heard from two other psychologists who had written papers about our work that they were trying,

unsuccessfully, to publish in scientific journals. We also heard from
several others who were using our material in their private practices. Now *that* was my idea of scientific validation, I thought; and in
a way, we *were* taking our message to the people. Besides, Seth's
material was loaded with ideas that science could check experi-
mentally if and when it ever chose to.

　　　　During this time also, Seth gave us some additional
information dealing with the "evidence of the world" in connection
with creativity, explaining how the imagination often works by
momentarily denying the given data in order to create new "evidence" that wasn't present in the world before. I'm including excerpts from that private session here, because they have many
general applications. Actually the session was held before I finished
my "Psychic Manifesto," and before Rob mailed his reply to Dr.
Camper. That is, at the time Rob and I were both thinking about
"hard" evidence and the subjective evidence of experience. Our
concerns were probably responsible for Seth's discussion.

FROM DELETED SETH SESSION
JULY 16, 1979　　9:20 P.M. MONDAY

　　　　"Now, I will be simplifying somewhat to make several
points.

　　　　"To some extent, creativity involves you in a contradiction with the evidence of reality within your world. It puts you in
a peculiar state of being—or in a peculiar relationship with the
accepted world of physical evidence.

　　　　"The state of creativity <u>can</u> be discussed <u>as if it were</u> a
separate state, like waking or sleeping. It can, in fact, involve waking
dreams. In the usual waking state, in the terms now of this discussion, you deal with the available physical evidence of the world
as it appears to your present perception, or with what you can see or
feel or touch, either immediately or with physical instruments.

　　　　"In the dream state you deal with objects that may or
may not have a physical reality. You mix times and places, and the
dream itself is a kind of completed act. Creativity allows you, while
awake, to ignore or even to contradict what seems to be the hard
evidence of known reality, either in large or small terms. The
creative act involves you in a process whereby you bring from a
mental dimension new events into the world that were not there
before.

　　　　"Some of this is so obvious that it escapes you, but since

I want to connect this with other matters, I will discuss it rather thoroughly.

"Ruburt may suddenly have an idea for a book. He wants to write it. In physical terms, that book is not before his eyes. It has not been written; it has not been published. The evidence says physically that there is no such book. It is not a part of the world's evidence. The idea for the book may come from a dream, or in that state of creativity where dreams reach toward physical actualization.

"Now Ruburt could say, 'I cannot write that book,' or wonder how many pages it might have, or think of the endless impediments that might prevent such a book from being written. Instead he ignores the physical evidence of the book's absence, and creatively begins to write.

"To some degree, creativity always involves a <u>denial</u> of life's daily official evidence, for creativity deals with that which you are about to bring into being. You are quite aware of the absence which you intend to fill. This applies obviously in the case of inventions. Creativity involves productive change.

(To Rob:) "In your painting, you are constantly involved with bringing some event into the world that was not there before. You fill the gap. You recognize the absence in the present of the physical painting you want to produce, and your creativity brings that painting into reality. With ideas, with our books, the both of you deal with such issues all the time.

"There is so much physical evidence in the world. It has been put together through the centuries, in your terms, in countless ways, bringing pictures of reality, each vivid, each contradicting the other to some extent. When man <u>believed</u> the world was flat, he used his thought processes in such a way that he had great difficulty in imagining any other kind of world, and read the evidence so that it fit the flat-world picture.

"The world's evidence, the objects, sensations, and so forth should be respected and enjoyed. It should not be forgotten, however, that such evidence gives a composite picture—not only of patterns of perception, but of <u>habits</u> of perception. . . ."

That session made a deep impression on me, and thinking of it the following day, I wrote these notes:

"Seth's material on creativity brought several issues to

mind, or made me look at them in a new way. Of course we must pay attention to the evidence of our senses, but when we begin to use our imaginations we bring a different knack into play—that of creating a divergent picture of the world, adding new data that wasn't there before, as Seth mentioned. *Then,* reason and imagination agree, because the evidence that was originally only mental becomes physical as well.

"What Seth is actually saying, then, is that as we change our assumptions and imaginatively see the world differently in our minds, we *are* actually changing the world, and in the only truly practical way. And perhaps doing that involves us in the highest creative processes that we're capable of, as a species. The world *is* our mental invention. Maybe that's been the real 'secret' all along and the one main issue that we've never understood. The natural world isn't our invention alone, of course. We share that creative venture with all of the other species. But the social, economic, artistic, political world—that *is* our exclusive invention.

"After reading Seth's last session, another thought occurred to me, one I've had before but had forgotten. Maybe it's the mental processes themselves that are important—the inner manipulations and computations that happen subjectively as we question beliefs, and creatively try to scrutinize our own subjectivity. Maybe, when we do *that,* we are almost unknowingly using different mental and psychic processes than we're used to, or putting old ones together in a completely new way.

"What I'm getting at is that our beliefs form their own level of consciousness. That is, we interpret reality so that it accords with our beliefs about it. We train ourselves to react to stimuli that can be expected according to our beliefs, and to ignore equally valid stimuli that disagree with our version of what is possible. So we end up with a coherent, even workable but limited view of life.

"But dispense with those beliefs, and new evidence that had been sifted out before suddenly becomes noticeable. It comes to our conscious attention to be dealt with, so that we have more data to take into consideration, and we actually begin to change the focus of our consciousness. Then we—and the world—*are* different than we were before.

"My new assumptions are that the universe is meaningful (no matter what science thinks), that man's impulses are basically good (no matter what religion and science think), that all species communicate through inner networks yet to be discovered, and that personal existence continues after death.

"In the past, no matter what I told myself I believed, I

was still held back by an old allegiance to official beliefs; I still measured my own development by standards I'd largely outgrown; I still looked longingly over my shoulder to make sure I hadn't strayed too far from the realm of the safe and the sane. In other words, I still reacted emotionally *as if* the limiting beliefs, particularly of science and psychology, were true.

"So I'm finally taking my stand. I'm accepting these new hypotheses down the line and I'm now free to examine the 'world's evidence' as *I* see it, with these assumptions in mind. Then why has it been so difficult to switch over from one set of beliefs to the other *all the way?* Because the more apparent my psychic abilities became, the more my daily experience varied from official norms, the more I came up against the fears that these beliefs promote: We're taught to trust subjective experience least of all. Certainly my correspondence showed me that such abilities are universal. I can understand science being skeptical of me, say, since my experiences are relatively unusual. But for science to ignore such abilities on the part of many, many people in the face of reports in all periods of history is almost incomprehensible to me.

"I suppose that makes me feel sad because sometimes I can sense a truly remarkable, sophisticated kind of psychic science devoted to an unbiased study of objective and subjective realities. I'm convinced that in time such a study would uncover mental worlds of unsuspected subtlety and abilities unsurpassed by any technology. As of now, those subjective worlds remain awaiting recognition by the conscious mind. . . ."

Shortly after I wrote those notes, on July 23, 1979, Seth began dictating Chapter 10 of *Mass Events,* entitled "The Good, the Better, the Best: Value Fulfillment Versus Competition," and I started to get the feeling that he was nearing the end of the book. I was also beginning to suspect that my own book, this one, might just involve me in my greatest creative challenge thus far—the attempt to provide a practical framework that reconciled psychic experience with the ordinary facts of life. For one thing, no sooner did I write my "Psychic Manifesto" than I began to wonder: Now, exactly how was such a manifesto to be translated in usual terms? If we were setting established science aside as the arbiter of experience, what was going to take its place?

We were going to have to be our own scientific-psychics or psychic-scientists, I thought. Yet at the same time I worried about people's ability to translate and interpret psychic events, without training or experience in doing so, and without science in the background somewhere, urging objectivity. And what about religion? I wondered uneasily. Surely there we can see what happens when we have faith without reason and belief without doubt.

But I wasn't advocating faith without reason, I thought. I was advocating the extension of reason into subjective realms. I wanted to merge reason and intuition. And as all those ideas came one after the other, I was also beginning to suspect that my "Psychic Manifesto" was only step one in what could properly be called the further education of Jane Roberts—and friends—because, again, I knew that if those concerns were accentuated in my case, they were shared by many others whose experience contradicted official precepts.

Chapter 17

The Lonesome Ex-Moonie, "Psychic Conception," and "The Armored Creature and the Butterfly"

Once summer comes I always get the feeling that it's eternal; as if somehow between June and August an inner time, that doesn't change, exists simultaneously with the usual days that go rushing toward autumn. I've felt that way as long as I can remember, and none of the other seasons give me quite the same feeling. For all of that, though, the summer of 1979 seemed to have its own impetus, and as late July arrived, the pace quickened.

For one thing, I sensed that Seth was getting ready to end *Mass Events*, yet instead of a sense of completion, I experienced an odd new anticipation. Besides that, right after I finished my "Psychic Manifesto," both our correspondents and visitors seemed to change character. People began to write more and more about specific psychic communications. There were more letters about automatic writing and Ouija messages, and all of them seemed to point up people's difficulties in interpreting such experiences. The letters almost seemed to say, "Psychic manifestos are great. But how do we interpret this stuff?"

The strangers who'd found their ways to our house since spring had, so far, been people with no particular problems. They'd been pleasant, curious, full of energy, like the boy who came in the taxi and dropped off the flowers. Then after the middle of July, the people who came here had worried, anxious faces. They seemed driven by impatience, and some by despair. Some hitchhiked across country in the mild summer weather, stopping here after having already stopped at numerous psychic centers; searching; nervously pawing through the volumes of books in psychic libraries; camping out along the way, talking about the healing powers of nature but kept from enjoying it by an edge of desperation that told them that soon it would all be over: The West Coast would fall into the sea, or a fierce depression would completely disrupt all government and law, or an unusual lineup of the planets would bring about catastrophe. It didn't matter what the reason was: disaster was approaching. And in one way or another, religion seemed to be involved, though I wasn't quick enough to catch that connection at first.

Some of these people I've forgotten, but all were healthy strong, good-looking, regardless of their states in life; and most were young. I remember several in particular, though, because of the strong impressions they made at the time. One night, for example, I sat looking through the wide-open living room windows at the mountains when a young man came up the road. He carried a knapsack over his shoulders and he looked tall and strong in the illumination of the corner street light. Then he moved toward the house, his figure blending in with the heavy tree foliage and shadows.

The doorbell rang. Rob let the young man in. I'll call him Lester. His face was an odd mixture of worry and reverence. He was willowy, with very short light-brown hair. He ducked his head as he came through the door, as if the ceiling were lower than it is or he was taller. Then he just stood there silently for a minute, glancing all around the room.

"I just had to come here," he said finally.

I nodded, waiting for him to continue, wondering how anyone with such excellent physical features could seem so lackluster. Now that he was inside, he almost looked too tall to hold himself up. Actually he wasn't much over six feet; he just gave the impression of being spindly.

"Sit down. Do you want a cup of coffee? A glass of wine?"

He turned toward me, looking alarmed. "Coffee? Wine? No. Thank you," he answered as if in some inexplicable way I'd offered him poison without realizing what I was doing, so that he had to refuse and be polite about it at the same time. My idea of hospitality really wasn't his. I might just as well have been a chief of some savage tribe in the past offering him, the missionary, a nice tidbit of cannibalized flesh. I was tempted to offer him a cigarette too, but I didn't. Actually I didn't have to. He noticed my cigarette in the ashtray in the very next moment, and he blanched.

"O.K." I said. "How about a glass of milk or fruit juice? Or water?"

He shook his head no, then sighed deeply and threw out his arms. "I give up," he said. "Where's the library and the reference rooms?"

The *what*? "The what?" I asked.

Then I realized that what I'd taken for his lack of energy was, instead, a deep disappointment that he could no longer conceal.

He said, a bit louder, "I mean, I came here to learn, and to help. I want to read all of the material you have, and join your volunteers." He stopped suddenly, his eyes going blink, blink, blink as he looked almost in despair around the living room. And I really felt sorry for him.

"No volunteers," I said, as gently as I could. "No reference libraries. Where did you come from? What are you up to? Please, *sit down*."

Finally he told me that he'd been a Moonie for several years, leaving the organization only a few months ago. "It got too restrictive," he said. "But we did a lot of good. We tried to save people from evil. But I had to get out. I had to be on my own."

"Sounds to me as if you made an excellent decision," I said.

He nodded, dubiously. We talked. I told him what Seth was discussing in his latest sessions. Rob came in and stood in the doorway, joining the conversation for a few minutes. But it didn't matter: Lester was dismayed after his pilgrimage to find just a woman and a man—surrounded by books and paintings, maybe—but alone in the private twilight, without even a few volunteers or followers in evidence.

As we talked, he took secret, quick, disappointed glances at me that I wasn't supposed to notice; or maybe I was. But here he saw no compelling presence, heard no commanding voice. My eyes didn't burn into his own, drawing out all of his secrets. (I knew I looked slightly ironical; purposefully commonplace.) For a moment I thought, almost angrily, should I really "turn on" for him? Show that I do, indeed, "have power"? Give him a demonstration that he won't quickly forget? Or more—have a Seth session; let that "worthy personage" replace me? Should I gather up all of the night's wild power that pulsed outside in the full leaves and electric air; gather it up until it filled my slim frame and seemed to pour out into the room?

Oh God, I thought, catching myself, *that's* what that boy, that young man wants. Some sly bargain between himself and me, where I pretend that such energy is mine—as opposed to *his,* or anybody's—and then he pretends to devote his life to a cause or power, or *whatever,* that he never has to contend with directly. And he was confused because I wouldn't do it! While I was thinking all of this, he told me that he'd come for a Seth session. He'd hoped for a session; dreamed of a session. He was pleading and stubborn and angry all at once.

But in that peculiar (calm and also somehow neutral) psychological area where my thoughts and Seth's somehow meet and sometimes but less often blend, I felt Seth's assessment of the situation agree with my own. The young man was still looking for the trappings of power, the exterior signs that to him gave evidence of a belief's merit—the volunteers, followers, organizations, buildings. He wanted to be dazzled: Why didn't I understand? I could almost hear his thoughts. He waited; I was supposed to overawe him. What was I waiting for?

I smiled, and drank my coffee and had a cigarette and tried to tell him to trust his *own* impulses, to make his own decisions, to have faith in the power that grew him from a fetus to a grown adult. I really tried to reach him. I felt my own belief in what I was saying. My own rather impassioned voice filled the room. But it was no good. Lester coughed and looked embarrassed and said again that he'd hoped that Seth would tell him what to do with his life. I tried to tell him that there was a God of Lester, and asked him to sense that point of direct contact with the universe. He nodded politely.

There were still a few birds singing in the evening air. I listened to them, and to the young man's voice; and I thought that in his consciousness there was a psychological area that opened up into vaster kinds of perception. Perhaps at those levels, he realized that even in our most private acts we *are* in direct contact with the universe. Only why did he seem so closed consciously to that kind of understanding? The God of Lester? No, thank you. He wanted an absolute God who told him what to do.

So, we talked as the street darkened outside the windows. I don't think I got through to him at all, and when he left I felt sad. I wrote down my impressions of the visit. I knew that Lester's conversation suggested some questions that I wasn't quite aware of yet. I could almost feel them forming in my mind. I said to hell with it for the night. The summer air blew through the house. I thought about this book again and my plans for it. The breeze nudged the edges of the manuscript (stirring the invisible molecules of the paper, I wrote; rousing the atoms).

My atoms, or *something,* were aroused enough the next day when the mail arrived, too. One letter was from a woman who had been put on a heavy tranquilizer by a medical doctor, simply because she "confessed" to having one out-of-body experience. She'd had no "other" symptoms of emotional disorder. She didn't like the effects of the drug and luckily, she discontinued its use. I was outraged.

Another long letter really put me in a quandary, though. As I read it, I didn't know whether to laugh or cry. The correspondent, a woman I'll call Sally, wrote me the following tale. She was married to her second husband and had a thirteen-year-old son living with her also from her previous marriage. This son hadn't seen his natural father, the woman's first husband, in many years. In fact, Sally didn't even know his whereabouts. Her present husband had undergone a vasectomy.

With that background, Sally began using the Ouija board. Messages came through so quickly that her fingers could hardly follow the little pointer. She was astonished. First there were brief innocuous sentences, supposedly from people she'd known who were dead. But then came a message that claimed to be from her first husband: He was dead! Sally stared at the Ouija board, in tears, filled with remorse. Why had she kept her son and his father apart?

"Oh, lady," I moaned, reading the letter, "didn't you at least question something else was involved? Didn't you wonder? Didn't you . . ."

But what she'd done was go to the telephone and call her first husband's mother, cry out her regrets, and completely confuse the woman—whose son was alive and well as far as she knew. And who, she asked, would spread such an ugly rumor? Sally, not wanting to divulge her Ouija board activities, said that a friend had given her the faulty information. She wrote that she'd nearly collapsed with embarrassment at her ex-mother-in-law's reply. She wanted to be told why the Ouija board "lied."

But this was only the beginning of Sally's Ouija board activities. She started working with the board again, after deciding to "forgive its lie." This time she contacted "spirits" who told her that she would become pregnant again—psychically. On a certain day they told her that conception had taken place. Her present husband helped her work the Ouija board. At first, she wrote, he was doubtful about having another child in the family. Then he agreed that it would be nice "if such things were possible." When she wrote me, Sally was convinced that she was three months pregnant, though she'd had no physical signs of pregnancy and she hadn't seen a doctor. Doubts were beginning to creep through, though, and she wanted me to confirm that the "spirits" were right.

Ending her letter, almost in a postscript, Sally told me that she did get the address of her first husband from his mother, made contact with him, and set up regular visiting periods for him with his son. But those events now seemed unimportant in the face of this new drama of psychic conception. Dear shades of the Virgin Mary, I thought, where do I even begin to explain?

My eyes fell on a line that read, "You always say that we should trust ourselves and our psychic information. . . ."

"And your *common sense,*" I muttered. I still can't really see how intelligent people can take such material literally, though. And Sally held down a responsible job; she wasn't dumb. But as briefly as I could, I tried to explain what had happened. First of all, I told her, the Ouija board hadn't lied. She just hadn't known how to interpret the information.

The whole affair was meant to be therapeutic; and it was. Sally's psyche actually took on the role of a shaman, taking advantage of the dissociated conditions set up when Sally decided to use the Ouija board. Then it set up two vivid psychodramas—one in which Sally believed her child's father was dead; and the other in which she played out the role of being pregnant. She was involved in a rambunctious, creative, therapeutic psychological romp that brought several vital issues into consciousness and let her express feelings she'd repressed, such as the remorse stemming from the breakup of her first marriage, and her desire to have another child.

The first issue was resolved as a direct result of the Ouija board's "lie," which was actually a psychological morality play of a kind, allowing her to act out her own feelings under a concentrated, directed (but still imagined) psychological stress. As a result, she *did* take suitable action in the physical world by contacting her former husband and resolving a conflict that had been bothering her for several years.

The "psychic conception" drama allowed her not only to express her desire for another child, but to acquaint her present husband with her feelings in a way that wouldn't threaten his own masculinity. Just the recognition of her emotions in that area may have resolved the issue. Once it was out in the open, for example, the couple might end up considering adoption.

The turmoil involved in the entire affair was most probably a vital part of the psychological therapy; at least that's how it seemed to me, I thought. And that made me wonder: How far had Sally gone in her belief that she was pregnant? Had she gone out and purchased nursery furniture? And was she going to think that the board just "lied" *again,* when she found that she wasn't pregnant after all?

I found myself muttering, "How on earth *could* she possibly have taken the board messages literally?" And then it hit me: She *had* to, or the entire process of therapy wouldn't have worked because the particular charged interplay between imaginary and physical events wouldn't have happened. It was precisely because of the "lies" that she'd taken the necessary steps in daily life to resolve the problems. Even without my letter, she'd have soon realized that she wasn't pregnant, of course; but hopefully my explanation would show her that the entire process had been beneficial.

And actually, I thought, it wasn't so strange after all that so many people took such information literally, often ignoring its very real therapeutic value. We're taught that anything that isn't literally true is false. From my correspondence it was obvious that many people felt that they must defend the *literal* content of "psychic" messages, fearing that the information must be literally true, or valueless.

And, God knows, I thought, plenty of people believed in the literal interpretation of the Bible. What was the difference, really, in believing in the second literal coming of Christ out of the heavens, and in anticipating instead the coming of glorified aliens in a spaceship to save humanity (or at least "the good people"), as many psychic messages now predicted? Or what was the difference between belief in the virgin birth of Mary and Sally's acceptance of her own possible psychic conception? No difference; except that one belief was a matter of religious dogma and the other wasn't— and both were, after all, literal interpretations of psychic messages.

The question that was beginning to bother me more and

more was this: Why did so many people hold such beliefs? And like the lonesome ex-Moonie, why did so many people need to seek the support of large groups in which they could momentarily submerge their identities? Or groups that would at least take spiritual responsibility for them? Those questions made me uneasy. I wasn't thinking of organizations in which individuals are given equal voice, but of authoritative ones. In the following days, events brought those questions even more to mind.

I also knew, of course, that psychic information could also be quite factual and literally correct, with sense data that was dependable. More and more though, I saw that we simply don't know how to interpret and process such information properly. We've concentrated all of our studies of perception on the reception and processing of *external* data. Yet even data categorized as objective is sifted through the physical senses, and colored by them to a significant degree. I was convinced that psychic data were also "objective," but in a different way—sifted and colored through the psychic perceptions.

I'd had numerous instances of receiving psychic information or having psychic experiences that were either almost completely factual or almost completely symbolic. Until the woman wrote about her "psychic conception" though, I hadn't really thought of trying to categorize and correlate all of those instances, hoping to discover what clues led me to interpret those events as either literal or symbolic ones.

Sally's experience gave me another important insight about misinterpretations of automatic writing or Ouija board messages and other such communications. It occurred to me that often we might be confusing the "psychological packaging" for the message, sometimes never opening the psychic cover to read the real contents at all. For example, we don't confuse the shape, size, or characteristics of a book with the inside message. Even though our physical senses perceive the book's color, design, and dimensions, we know that we have to open it and read the printed pages. We even ignore the image quality of the letters themselves; and when we read we automatically translate the letters' symbols into their proper sequence and meaning.

As far as psychic information or inner data is concerned, it's as if we haven't learned to read yet. We often confuse the packaging for the message, or the shapes of the psychic letters for their meanings. Besides this, just as there are many physical sources of information, there are many sources of psychic material as well.

Surely, I thought, we pick up such information constantly at unconscious levels and process it there; but whenever it approaches usual consciousness, we don't know how to handle it.

Sally's Ouija board material blended literal and nonliteral elements in a way that led her to make changes in her life. That particular blend of inner and outer events reminded me of an experience of my own that I'd had in the winter of 1979, a few months before starting this book. That experience was also therapeutic, but the events were entirely inner ones. Still, both instances involved the same kind of psychodrama.

In Sally's case, her intent in using the Ouija board, her anticipation, and the suggestive aspects connected with such performances helped set the stage for a state of consciousness amiable to the psychodrama that occurred. For her, the drama splashed over into daily events; she didn't believe that she was pregnant *only* when she was actually using the board, for example. So imaginative events merged in a directed fashion with actual ones.

My experience was confined as far as the action was concerned to the stage of inner reality, though the therapeutic results were apparent in daily life; and I described the affair in a poem, so there was a creative spillover. The event happened one afternoon as I sat staring out at the snowy yard. My body felt particularly stiff and uncomfortable, so I told myself that I could have some further insights into the reasons for my physical symptoms. Then I closed my eyes, and the experience began at once. Immediately after it happened, I found myself recording the episode in a poem, instead of writing notes about it as I usually do in such cases. The poem presents a factual narrative of what actually happened, plus my feelings about the entire affair, so I'm including it here. In fact, in a way, the poem itself was a part of the drama.

THE ARMORED CREATURE AND THE BUTTERFLY

I closed my eyes this winter afternoon
in the living room,
and saw the back yard in summertime.
It was evening *there,*
and I sat upon the porch
when a rustle from the nearby woods
made me turn my mental eyes that way.
A shadowy, murmuring mass of shrubs

was all I saw at first,
then some moving definition slowly emerged,
an animal shape approaching almost secretly.
I caught my breath. What a creature—
long, close to the ground, armored
with a tough heavy hide of dark scales
that made it move slowly
with inaudible but sensed grunts and groans.
It looked at me.
Was it prehistoric?
And what on earth had driven it
to my dream door?
Why had it left the rich deep woods?

I knew that I wasn't really outside on the porch
in a time that was at least
some two seasons off,
but the creature certainly acted as if
I was as physically visible to it
as it was to me.
Yet how could that be, when my image,
the summer night and porch and foliage
were all parts of this odd vision,
with no reality
of their own?

I shivered. Melancholy, weary—
the animal was all of that;
and I knew, without knowing
how I knew, that its mood
and mine were one.
And as I stared, much more was clear.
This mental creature was no stranger
and, in fact, was more than friend.
It was a thought creature,
slipping in from psychic worlds
so we could meet.
It needed help,
and it was coming home.

We stared at each other, two ghosts
in some undetermined mental world
while my body sat

two seasons away, eyes closed.
I said softly, "You don't need all that armor,"
for I recognized it was my own.
"It weighs you down. Take it off,"
and, as if waiting my directions,
the heavy scales flew off one by one
from the creature's hide,
disappearing
in the summer evening air.

Until now I'd been a bit aloof,
remembering
my body safe in the living room,
but suddenly the creature and I were one.
Panic roused—that the skin
beneath my scales would be so sore,
exposed,
that I would die without a covering,
or worse,
that my hide would crumble into dust
when it felt the direct contact of the air.
Then I snapped back, and as I watched—
myself again,
the creature wobbled, shook,
and its guts seemed to turn into sand,
pouring out upon the ground.

I almost called out,
but then, just as I caught my breath again,
I saw a birdlike butterfly
rise gently from the larger, crumbling bulk.
It was neither bird nor butterfly, but both,
hidden in the other beast,
and it had come to me
to be released.
Before I could move or speak,
it flew out of my vision.
And as it did
my body's eyes opened in the living room.

I looked out the window.
The snow-covered ground was there again,
and the summer foliage was gone.

What did it mean? What had I seen?
Had my own fears formed an image
to show me I was over-armored, heavy-spirited,
hiding in mental woods
that rise up at the heart's back door?
Did my fears turn
into that poor thought creature—
unable to do more than creep,
giving up freedom for protection—
so that in compassion
I would be led to set it free,
and in so doing save myself?
I freed the bird-butterfly.
Did this release
a corresponding part of me,
or must I meet more
of these mental creatures?

Perhaps I should invite them
into my company;
purposefully call them,
whistling soft mental sounds.
And I wonder: Do our feelings form
some exotic trans-species
that populate another world,
yet seek our recognition?
Thought creatures that need
to be tended and fed?
Do we set loose animals of desire,
fear and love,
all unknowing,
in an arena apart from ours—
a mental park,
where they wander and stroll,
and come to our porchstep
in times of drought
to be watered and fed,
so that in nurturing them,
we nurture ourselves?

As I read the poem, the experience itself came vividly
back into my mind. Looking at it in the light of Sally's adventures, it
was obvious that in my case too the psyche had taken on the role of

shaman, constructing its own mental landscape and charged drama. And what a landscape! I thought, because the details had been brilliant—far clearer than those in my more recent out-of-body visit to the breezeway, when everything had been cloudy and indistinct.

And that was it: Regardless of the poor perception, my consciousness *had* been in the breezeway, not in the bedroom where my body lay with its eyes closed. But in the armored creature episode, my consciousness had been split between my body and the psychic body that sat on the porch. As I realized the difference, I remembered something else about that experience; an odd, almost familiar feeling of tension, of projecting my consciousness "out" into that image. Had I entered it all the way, I could have walked (in the middle of winter) down the summer road, picked flowers, and seen the city lights through fresh green foliage. I'd been in a self-contained mental landscape, like a picture-book illustration come alive, so that you could walk into it as if having found an odd entryway *into* a flat surface. Thinking about it, I got the spookiest sense of déjà vu, as if I'd done the same thing before birth when I'd projected my consciousness into *this* body to begin with; that we all had done this, and the answers were *here*, all along, in our psychological processes.

At other, more practical levels, the experience gave definite benefits. I reminded myself that I didn't need the protection of any bodily armor; and that I was already in the process of dispensing with the beliefs that made protection seem necessary. As far as I'm concerned, those beliefs are my personal versions of the very ones we've been discussing in this book: the religious and scientific dictums that proclaim the evil or duplicity or vulnerability of our species, while denying us the very psychological properties that actually place us so securely within life's framework.

I'd begun my physical exercises shortly after that experience too, and felt considerable bodily ease. Comparing the episode with Sally's though, I was struck more by the elements of psychodrama than anything else. Were they always present in psychic information of any kind? If not, when were they vital, inconsequential, or entirely absent? What part did they play in religiously oriented experiences? How did their peculiar blend of psychic and physical events merge?

Those were *good* questions, but I had no idea of the form that some of the answers would take.

Chapter 18

The Boy Who Was a Girl.
Seth: On Psychic Development
and Impulses

I often feel as if we each have access to some immensely complicated psychological computer, and that we ask questions of a certain kind, in keeping with our current development. The questions trigger this hypothetical computer to answer at that particular level, using the types of symbolisms and beliefs we're used to, while still advancing our "education." We would each be "hooked into" this computer at our own individual place, with our own program of probable actions. At times our own program might lead to a higher organization of meaning, or bring us to a more advanced hypothesis upon which to base our lives; so that from then on we would ask questions from this more efficient level also, and trigger responses from the corresponding, more complex computer level.

This imaginary computer contains all possible information, and all probable versions of any given private or mass reality. But the material is organized by association, emotional content, and desire, and it sends us the most suitable impulses toward action—but always in line with our desires and beliefs.

This would be a universal psychological computer, of course, to which we each have access. But *sometimes* I feel that I operate like a terminal or some such, at this end, where I ask questions not only for myself but for many others as well; so that when someone writes me or visits, then click, click, click, the computer keys open. The person's question or need or situation or whatever goes into the computer. ("How do you do? How are you? Please state your name and business.") The information gets where it's supposed to go; and in one way or another an answer comes back.

And, *when* I feel that way it seems to me that each correspondent and each visitor stands for himself or herself, but also serves as a surrogate for many others, bringing questions that need answering, not to *my* attention so much as through me to the attention of the universe, or that part of its psychological computer to which I have access. It's as if I'm an input station, where someone comes and says, "Hey, universe, you there! We need a little help in this direction." And somehow the call gets through.

Anyway, I felt that way a good deal of the time during the summer of 1979. During August in particular, the people who came biking or hiking or driving up the hill to our house all seemed to have problems. Like the lonesome ex-Moonie, they weren't happy. I felt as if the key to my hypothetical computer had been left open and people were taking the universe to task for this or that oversight on its part, this or that specific need or lack.

Then I thought of Seth as some higher-up psychological computer expert, receiving the input I send, rummaging through realms of magically stored knowledge, searching through millions of mental "library cards," gathering information from the computer's most secret systems, processing it, and delivering the material, later, in a session. Then we publish the material and it goes out into the world, mixing with other information. Only sometimes I think that Seth gets all the fun while I do the fieldwork, write the letters, meet the people, live in the world; a native of the world like everyone else.

Then I realize that I really enjoy being a native of the world. I'm in no rush at all to trip off to other realms of whatever natures. I know the world has problems, and I have my own. But for me, even the quietest moment is somehow potent with excitement. But for our visitors that month, troubles seemed to have overwhelmed any exuberance. The odd thing to me was that few of these people had any serious health problems or even real financial difficulties. They were fairly young, intelligent, gifted; but they felt as if life's meaning always escaped them.

One boy did have a problem, though. It was a bright sunny morning, and he'd just arrived in town after hitchhiking from another state. He greeted me by saying that he wanted to meet me just once—before he committed suicide.

I do remember wanting to squawk mentally at the universe or Seth or my higher consciousness or somebody, "Now, what?" Was there a sign that read "Bring your unhappiness to my front door this month"? I'd had several recent calls from either prospective suicides or their families; and how could I try to get some comprehensive answers to such distressing problems, if I had to stop to deal with specific ones all the time? That attitude struck me as so unreasonable that it ended up restoring my sense of equanimity. And while all of those thoughts were going through my head, the big, dark-haired young man sat down. I'll call him David.

"Did you hear what I said?" he asked.

"Uh huh. Want a cup of coffee?"

He shook his head; his fingers and ears and facial muscles were shaking too. "Coffee isn't good for your health," he said.

"Neither is suicide," I replied. "But, to each his own." I was saying what I felt like saying, trusting my impulses completely. Yet that didn't stop me from wondering whether David might not storm out of the house and kill himself on the front lawn after my last remark.

His mouth, which was wide and generous, did lots of incongruous things: puckered, pouted, trembled and quivered sideways all at once.

"Yeah, well, I just want to get rid of my body," he said finally. He had veiled, almost feminine eyes; they looked about thirteen years old, while the rest of him looked a rambunctious twenty-one. His face was wide and open (except for the secretive eyes) and he had freckles. I like people with freckles.

"Your body looks great to me," I said. "Why do you want to get rid of it?" The morning sun glinted on his arms; touched his ear lobes. "Your body's drinking up the sun right now," I said.

Suddenly his head was almost in his arms, like some nearly decapitated flower. "If you knew . . . if you knew . . ." he said, "you'd probably throw me out of the house."

"It can't be *that* bad," I said. "Since you're here, you

might as well tell me. Anyhow if you're going to commit suicide, why worry about my reaction or anybody else's?"

"It *is* that bad," he replied with a soberness that drained all color from his face. His secret feminine eyes looked desperate.

"Bad, huh? Let's see. You want to 'do it' with animals?" I said, as if that was the conclusion I'd come to. ("Good God, Jane," I thought, but I could already tell the shock treatment was working.)

He looked suddenly more scandalized than desperate. "That's terrible!" he stammered, blushing. "Boy, you don't fool around, do you? That's awful. No, it isn't *that*."

"Well, I wouldn't throw you out of the house if it *was*," I said, grinning. "And after that, anyhow, what do you think could shock me that much? So, come on. Out with it."

First he looked stubborn. Then he glanced away from me toward the window, and his voice, coming sideways at me, said, "A friend who took some psychology courses told me I was sick. And a woman I know who's familiar with the Bible said that I was unnatural."

"You want to 'do it' with little boys?" I offered; and this time I got a stronger response than before. He really looked horrified. What kind of a cad did I think he was?

"That's terrible. Homosexuality is wrong," he declared, his eyes flashing for a moment. Then he hung his head and muttered, "It's not like that with me. I just . . . feel that I'm a female trapped in a male's body. And worse, I just fell in love. With a man."

"Oh. Is *that* all?" I said.

He stared at me with those feminine eyes, too confused to commit suicide for the moment anyhow. "*All?*" he said, angrily now. "My parents think of me as their son. *I* think of me as their daughter. My sisters think I'm their brother—"

"What makes you think homosexuality is morally wrong, by the way?" I sneaked the question in, interrupting him.

"Well, it's not natural," he replied, this time with a slight male rumble in his voice.

Just about then, Rob came into the room from his studio. The two of us talked to David for more than an hour, and we gave him a copy of Seth's *The Nature of the Psyche* to take with him. By the time the two of us were finished counting his blessings for him—excellent health; a quick, inquisitive mind; youth; a good, sturdy-looking body—he was grudgingly beginning to admit that his situation might at least be bearable; or that he'd be giving up an awful lot to get rid of it. He promised to read *Psyche,* in which Seth discusses sexuality. We tried to explain that, in a way, he'd chosen a unique and valuable focus in life that could give him insights that were available only to few people.

And, in a way, it was almost humorous as Rob and I tried to share what knowledge we have about the great variances sexual expression and affiliation can take. David came from a "hill-billy, factory town," filled with fundamentalist preachers. I think his curiosity about sex finally got the best of him, and that his hopes of learning more made him decide to put off his suicide for a while. We *did* hear from him over a year later. He wrote that he'd decided to go along with himself and see what happened. And, no sex-change operation for *him*. He declared that he had more freedom in a man's body than he would in a woman's. Interesting?

Actually, what we tried to do was to reestablish David's trust in his own nature, and inspire him to take a chance on his own integrity as a person. In fact, several days after David's visit, Seth dictated some material for Chapter 10 of *Mass Events* that em-phasizes the importance of self-approval in connection with ordi-nary living, and with the development of creative or psychic abilities.

This material seemed particularly pertinent in the light of the kind of visitors we were having at the time. David's problem was fairly unusual, of course; but quite a few of our visitors seemed to feel the same sense of alienation from themselves and the same disenchantment with life, but lacked any severe problem to account for their feelings. I'd also received several phone calls and letters involving people who were would-be suicides. The correspondence usually contained a small percentage of people who wrote about taking their own lives; but, again, such letters bunched up in this period.

It seems to me that in most such instances the clear lines of effective action become blocked. And as I read the following ma-terial from *Mass Events,* I saw how important impulses were in keeping alive our zest for life, and in pointing us in those directions that would promote our sense of power and action. The first excerpt is from Session 870 for August 1, 1979, and can be found along with the next excerpt in Chapter 10 of Seth's *Mass Events*:

"Examine the literature that you read, the television pro-grams that you watch, and tell yourself to ignore those indications given of the body's weakness. Tell yourself to ignore programs or literature that speak authoritatively about the species' 'killer in-stincts.' Make an effort to free your intellect of such hampering beliefs. Take a chance on your own abilities. If you learn to trust your basic integrity as person, then you will be able to assess your abilities clearly, neither exaggerating them or underassessing them.

"You will not feel the need, say, to 'justify your existence' by exaggerating a particular gift, setting up the performance of one particular feat or art as a rigid ideal when, in fact, you may be pleasantly gifted, but not endowed with that ability enough to give you the outstanding praise you might think you desire.

"On the other hand, there are many highly gifted people who continually put their abilities down and are afraid to take one small step toward their expression. If you accept the rightness of your life in the universe, then your ideals will be those in keeping with your nature. They will be fairly easily given expression, so that they add to your own fulfillment and to the development of society as well.

"Your impulses are your closest communication with your inner self, because in the waking state they are the spontaneous urgings toward action, rising from that deep inner knowledge of yourself that you have in dreams. You were born because you had the impulse to be. There was no exterior cosmic Pied Piper, singing magical notes . . . urging the universe into being.

"The urge to be came from within, and that urge is repeated to some extent in each impulse, each urge toward action on the part of man or molecule. If you do not trust the nature of your impulses, then you do not trust the nature of your life, the nature of the universe, or the nature of your own being.

"Any animal knows better than to distrust the nature of its own life. And so does any infant. Nature exists by virtue of faith. The squirrel gathers nuts in the faith that it will have the needed provisions, and that spring will follow winter. Your impulses are immersed in the quality called faith, for they urge you into action in the faith that the moment for action exists. Your beliefs must interact with your impulses, however, and often they can erode that natural beneficial spontaneity that impulses can provide.

"When I speak of impulses, many of you will automatically think of impulses that appear contradictory or dangerous or 'evil,' and that is because you are so convinced of the basic unworthiness of your being. You have every right to question your impulses, to choose between them, to assess them; but you must be aware of them, acknowledge their existence, for they will lead you to your own true nature.

"With your belief systems, this may involve a lengthy journey for some of you. For many of your impulses now are the result of the pressure caused by perfectly normal unacknowledged ones in the past. But your impulses reflect the basic impulse of your life. Even if they appear contradictory at any given time, overall they will be seen to form constructive patterns toward actions that point more clearly toward your own path for fulfillment and development.

"Natural attributes show themselves quite clearly, for example, in early childhood, when you are allowed greater freedom to do what you want to do. Some people as children love to work with words, some with images, some with objects. Some show great ability in dealing with their contemporaries, while others naturally lean toward solitude and private meditations. Look back toward the impulsive behavior of your childhood, toward those activities that mostly pleased you.

"If you painted pictures, this does not mean that you necessarily should be an artist. Only you know the strength of those impulses—but if they are intense and consistent, then pursue them. If you end up simply painting as a hobby, that will still enrich your life and understanding. If your impulses lead you toward relationships with others, then do not let fears of unworthiness stand in your way. It is very important that you express your idealism actively, to whatever extent you can, for this increases your sense of worth and power. . . ."

And from Seth session 872 for Wednesday, August 8, 1979:

"Many of you, for example, keep searching for some seemingly remote spiritual inner self that you can trust and look to for help and support, but all the while you distrust the familiar self with which you have such intimate contact. You set up divisions between portions of the self that are unnecessary.

"Some correspondents write, saying, 'I realize that I am too egotistical.' There are many schools for spiritual advancement that teach you to 'get rid of the clutter of your impulses and desires,' to shove aside the self that you are in search of a greater idealized version. First of all, the self that you are is ever-changing and never static. There is an inner self in the terms of those definitions, but that inner self, which is the source of your present being, speaks through your impulses. They provide inbuilt spiritual and biological impetuses toward your most ideal development. You must trust the self that you are. Now.

"If you would know yourself in deepest terms, you must

start with your own feelings, emotions, desires, intents and impulses. Spiritual knowledge and psychic wisdom are the natural results of a sense of self-unity.

"Again, impulses are inherently good, both spiritually and biologically. They emerge from Framework 2, from the inner self, and they are based on the great inner webwork of communication that exists between all the species on your planet. Impulses also provide the natural impetus toward those patterns of behavior that serve you best; so that while certain impulses may bunch up, say, toward physical activity, others, seemingly contradictory, will lead you toward quiet contemplation; so that overall, certain balances are maintained.

"Some people are only aware of, or largely aware of, impulses toward anger, because they have inhibited those natural impulses toward love that would otherwise temper what seemed to be aggressive impulses. When you begin trusting yourselves, you begin by taking it for granted that to some extent at least, you have not trusted yourself or your impulses in the past. You have thought that impulses were dangerous, disruptive, or even evil. So as you begin to learn self-trust, you acknowledge your impulses. You try them on for size. You see where they lead you by allowing them some freedom. You do not follow impulses through physically that would hurt others, or that seem in direct contradiction to your present beliefs. But you *do* acknowledge those impulses. You <u>do</u> try to discover their source. Behind them you will almost always find an inhibited impulse, or many of them, that motivated you to move in some ideal direction—to seek love or understanding so idealized in your mind that it seemed impossible to achieve. You are left with the impulse to strike out.

"If you examine such troublesome impulses, you will always find that they originally arose only after a long process, a process in which you were afraid to take small positive steps toward some ideal. Your own impulses naturally lead you to seek creative fulfillment, the expansion of your consciousness, psychic excursions, and the conscious knowledge and manipulation of your dreams.

"No methods will work if you are afraid of your own impulses, or of the nature of your own being. Most of you understand that All That Is is within you; that 'God' is within creation, within physical matter, and that 'He' does not simply operate as some cosmic director on the outside of reality. You must understand that the spiritual self <u>also</u> exists within the physical self in the same fashion. The inner self is not remote either, not divorced from your most intimate desires and affairs, but instead communicates through your own smallest gesture. . . .

"This sense of division within the self forces you to think that there is a remote, spiritual, wise, intuitive inner self, and a bewildered, put-upon, spiritually ignorant, inferior physical self, which happens to be the one you identify with. Many of you believe, furthermore, that the physical self's very nature is evil, that its impulses left alone will run in direct opposition to the good of the physical world and society, and fly in the face of the deeper spiritual truths of inner reality.

"The inner self then becomes so idealized . . . that the physical self by contrast seems only the more ignorant and flawed. In the face of such beliefs, the ideal of psychic development or astral travel or spiritual knowledge, or even of sane living, seems so remote as to be impossible. . . ."

I thought that those passages contained some of the most helpful information that Seth had ever given. I certainly applied it to myself, and during this time I was still making a concerted attempt to acknowledge and follow my own impulses. I still am, for that matter. This meant that several times a day, while writing at my desk, I'd feel an impulse to do something else—catch up on the housecleaning, paint an acrylic of some object that caught my attention, phone someone, or whatever—all impulses that I would have ignored not too long ago.

Now I acknowledged them and let my feelings about them roll or tumble or thunder out. They still followed the old patterns and beliefs: I needed discipline to sit at my desk and write because I couldn't trust myself to do it otherwise, because my inner self, being a reservoir of chaotic impulses, needed to be held down and directed. And each time, I'd go through the entire round of counter-arguments: The scientific and religious beliefs that gave me such ideas were themselves flawed; spontaneity knew its own order; and so forth. After the 872nd Seth session though, I often read excerpts from that material instead, discovering that it covered all bases.

What I was trying to do was to substitute conscious acknowledgement of impulses to move, and conscious decisions about them, for the almost automatic rejection of such urges that I'd allowed my physical symptoms to handle for me. I'm mentioning this here because it's clear to me that in many instances of health problems, we allow symptoms to handle our reactions for us, and so cleverly that we forget starting the mechanism to begin with.

In any case, following my impulses led me to do a good deal of painting that summer—ink sketches and acrylics; to write lots of poetry; and to consent to more appointments than I would have otherwise. Besides this, I decided to take over the entire living room as a work room. A friend helped Rob move the couch and TV out to the new back room that I had used sometimes as a study. I felt as if in rearranging the exterior objects in the house, I'd really rearranged the furniture of my mind or psyche. (Uh, that belief is *heavy*. Let's move it to the corner of the room—or better, *out!*)

And in the meantime, Rob's brothers and their families visited us several times. I went over all the notes I had for this book to date. And we decided to have the outside of the house painted. There was no doubt of it: the acceleration that I'd felt earlier began to quicken. I felt that the notes I had for this book, including the God of Jane idea and my emotional "Psychic Manifesto," were leading me in a direction that I could finally sense, even if I wasn't consciously aware of it. And, also in the meantime, our visitors changed character again. They were energetic. They had a sense of purpose. They had a million vigorous questions, or so it seemed, and they wanted answers.

Chapter 19

Trial by Glass and Session 871: Seth on Weather, an Earthquake, and People Who Love Danger

There I was, all alone in my own kitchen, safe in my own house one August afternoon, minding my own business when *suddenly* . . . but rather than tell the story myself, I'll let Rob's notes in Session 871 tell you what happened. Not that I'm likely to forget! The last Seth sessions I quoted were 870 and 872, devoted to book dictation. Session 871, however, was given over to Seth's explanation of the rather frightening event of Thursday, August 2, 1979; and Rob and I both found Seth's explanation nearly as fascinating as the episode he was discussing. In any case, I'm presenting the session in its original format. Rob's italicized opening notes set the scene.

SESSION 871   AUGUST 6, 1979   9:40 P.M. MONDAY

(At about 3:30 P.M. last Thursday, Jane participated in a startling experience—one that we hoped Seth would at least mention this evening. At that time Jane was sitting at the kitchen table, perhaps six-and-a-half feet from the open porch door. The day had been hot and humid. A thunderstorm had been threatening to develop for some time; finally it began to rain and blow as I helped Jane prepare a dish she was fixing for our evening meal.

(The wind increased in intensity, blowing across the valley from the south and racing up the road just east of the house. Sheets of rain rolled before the wind. I went into the bedroom to close the windows. As I did so a terrific blast of wind struck the house. Dimly in the racket, I heard Jane cry out. I thought she may have yelled at the cats. On returning to the kitchen, though, I saw her sitting at the table with great shards of glass littering the rug at her feet. For some reason that day I'd forgotten to put a stopper at the kitchen's storm door, and the sudden blast of wind had slammed it shut with enough force to shatter the bottom of its two large glass panels.

(At first I couldn't believe my eyes. The broken glass had cata-pulted toward Jane, yet she sat unharmed by the razorlike edges. Underneath the table I found a large jagged piece of glass, close to a foot across, propped up against an inner table leg on the side where I usually sit. In some strange quirk of speed and physics, this knife-edged piece had not only been blown into the kitchen, but had managed to turn nearly a right angle, missing Jane, in order to come to rest opposite her legs against the table's leg. It could have cut her severely.

(Almost at once the strong wind began to subside, although the rain continued. Just as quickly—as we realized that she was unhurt—we also realized that something unusual had indeed taken place. We felt that she had been spared injury, for whatever reasons. As I cleaned up the dozens of pieces of glass and put them in a heavy carton, we talked about why she might have been protected, and decided to ask Seth to comment.

(Jane became so relaxed as session time approached that she told me several times that she'd have to put off her trance until tomorrow night. At the same time, she had a lot of material in her mind from Seth—on the glass experience, a dream I'd had on August 1, in which I'd found her lying on the floor in the bathroom doorway, and some material about a fairly strong earthquake that had struck south of San Francisco this afternoon. Seth, she said somewhat wonderingly, planned to tie all of these episodes together. They seemed to make a most unlikely combination, though....

("I guess I'm confused," Jane said as we sat there. "I'm so

relaxed, yet I feel all that material there. I want it, but I don't feel like doing it. . . . Oh, all right," she laughed as I worked on these notes. "I'll have the session. At least I'll try."

(The first portion of this session is deleted.

(9:53.) "Because of the changes in routine, you 'forgot' to put the stopper in the door. You must remember that you have an inner knowledge of all weather conditions, so you were both at certain levels aware of the approaching storm.

"Ruburt had a good point (today): The behavior of weather is like poltergeist activity. To that extent, so was the slamming of the door and the shattering of glass. You both knew that Ruburt would remain unharmed and that there was no danger, regardless of the 'frightening' aspects of the physical situation.

"Even if he had seen the glass begin to break, Ruburt could not have run out of danger in time. So you each saw him in a position in which the physical evidence certainly was against a favorable prognosis—yet the glass stopped before it came close to Ruburt's bare legs or arms.

"This was meant to reassure you both, and it happened as a result of your dream *(of August 1, in which I saw Jane fallen in the bathroom doorway)*. It reassured Ruburt of the good intent of his own inner self. It assured him that he did indeed have an important place in the universe; that he was meant to live and thrive.

"Now, many people visit California for the same reason. They live in the midst of danger, and are unharmed. Some people, of course, need constant reassurances of that nature. Others may visit California during the time of an earthquake, as in today's episode, and then return home, to feel that they were somehow spared—and spared for a reason.

"Perhaps the best way you can understand your relationship with the weather is to think of it in terms of regional and national poltergeist activity. We are speaking of interactions of energy, however, and not, say, the power of men's minds working upon 'inanimate' matter. We are actually talking about the interactions of consciousness at certain states of activity.

"If you can hold that idea in your minds, and think simultaneously of the behavior of viruses with body organs, then you may perhaps gain an intuitive feeling for the relationship of the body and diseases. For here you are dealing with what you might call a kind of inner poltergeist activity, where, say, viruses instead of clouds are swept through an inner environment.

"The weather, storms or not, represents an overall stabilizing framework that makes personal reality possible; and the storms resulting represent an immense distribution of natural resources and necessary elements. In the same fashion, disease represents an overall larger organization quite as necessary for physical survival as the storms that affect the weather.

"This is difficult to express, but as there are always some storms upon the earth, of varying degrees and intensities, so there are also always some diseases within the body, and these play an important part in maintaining the stability that you call health.

"I do not like the terminology, but with your beliefs and language I will have to stick with the word 'disease' for now, using that term with misgivings, for the purposes of this discussion. I must say that in those terms, all life is composed of diseases.

"Thunderstorms are caused by characteristics that are always present in nature. They cause difficulties only under certain conditions of what I will call here 'exaggerated status.' The same applies, say, to viruses that you think of as deadly. Your thoughts affect the viruses in your body. Your thoughts affect the air outside your window. These are all questions involving the behavior of consciousness at different levels of activity.

"You note a certain activity and name it as a disease when it makes itself known in the interior landscape of the body. Then it becomes identified by certain symptoms. That same 'disease,' whatever its label, existed in the body beforehand, 'dispersed,' before its parts came together to form the thundercloud of disease. It was then a part of the body's natural inner landscape; brought to a head, so to speak, by the behavior of consciousness at that level of activity.

"Thunderheads come and go. They distribute rain where it is needed. Ideally, diseases would do the same thing; redistributing, say, the body's resources, and establishing an overall state of health. I am speaking ideally here. The treatment of specific symptoms can be unfortunate, since it undermines whatever intent the body had. Your medicine, however, is such an important part of your world's belief system that it must, of course, be taken into consideration.

"The kind of natural treatment that is ideal can only exist in a society that understands its place within nature, and understands the survival of the personality beyond death. Overall, you will use medicine and its technologies to live or die, as each individual decides. You lose, however, your feeling of oneness with the body and nature as a result [of your beliefs]. People who decide to die young, for example, may now have automobile accidents rather than dying from childhood diseases.

"Ideally there should be no 'battle' against disease, but a vast project in which man tries to study the interactions of all kinds of consciousnesses with his own, and a study that teaches him how to understand his own motives and desires.

"There are biological, spiritual and social aspects to the entire matter, as there are in the questions of natural disasters in terms of extravagant weather. . . .

"For now I bid you a fond and somewhat jaunty good evening."

("Thank you, Seth.")

"My fondest regards to you both."

("Good night."

(10:31 P.M. "All I know is that it was a great session," Jane said. "I'm glad I had it. I was pretty far out, but I remember thinking that it was a great stroke when Seth pulled together the weather, the behavior of diseases in the body, and poltergeist activity. I thought that was brilliant," she laughed. And so it is, I agreed.

(Thus, it developed once again that when she didn't feel like having a session, Jane came through with an excellent one. I've seen this happen often. Her delivery had been good, her—Seth's—manner, active and animated. . .)

When I typed the excerpt from this session, I was interested in *what* Seth said, rather than *how* he said it, I suppose. So almost without thinking I cut out all Rob's indications of time, and references to any pauses Seth took, or gestures he made. On rereading the session I realized that it read as if it were originally written rather than verbal material. Again, I was impressed by the rightness of Rob's notes and their way of preserving the immediacy of the sessions.

So remember that all that material was spoken spontaneously on the spot, as it were, accompanied by Seth's characteristic manner, smiles, and gestures. And Seth never uses "uh"s, "ah"s, or other connective devices or hesitations that I use in normal speech. He does pause now and then, and sometimes he says, "Give us a moment, please," We do not change his material without so indicating. When a word is underlined or in quotes it's because Seth requested it.

The change of routine Seth mentioned referred to the fact that we'd started getting up around 4 A.M. to work, so we could enjoy the dawn and also work when it was quiet and cool. A few of our chores fell by the wayside, though; hence Rob forgot to put the stopper at the door. According to Seth, Rob's fears caused his dream of me falling in the bathroom, and the incident of the shattered glass reassured both of us.

I certainly remember thinking "Thank you, God of Jane," when I realized that I was surrounded on all four sides by fragments of glass, and not one had touched me. I'd worn shorts and a sleeveless blouse at the time, so I certainly hadn't been protected by any clothing.

One other incident happened that day, though, that Seth didn't mention. After Rob cleaned up the glass, I put the casserole I'd fixed in the oven and we took brief naps while it cooked. I had a dream that I couldn't remember, then I started to wake up. As I lay there half asleep and half awake I realized that I was looking at a small, card-sized document with a drawing of a person at the bottom left edge. There was also writing on the document, and though I forgot the wording later I knew that the script signified that the attention of the universe had been "lavished" on the person in question since birth. I squinted mentally, and finally made out the year of birth which was printed on the lower right. It read 1929. And I realized that the person referred to was me.

That small incident happening right after my "escape" that afternoon really had a big effect on me. I knew that the same kind of attention was "lavished" on each person, but this was like a private message, applying specifically to me, of course. I thought about it often that evening. Later, when we ate the dinner I'd prepared (summer squash, onions, peppers, ground chuck and rice), I thought about how privileged we are to eat each meal—how great it was to enjoy that domestic supper. And I felt that despite all the cosmic comings and goings and incomprehensible programs of the universe, we were charmed. We live a charmed existence, each of us, I thought; but only if we realize it. Because if we don't, then our own negative beliefs make us blind to our true state. And I kept thinking: That portion of the universe in which I'm centered, that portion that turns itself into me, looks out for my safety and well-being. And the same applied to everyone.

We ate supper on the coffee table in front of the couch, and watched television while I was thinking all of this. A newscast told of the death earlier in the day of a famous sports hero in a private plane crash. He was still in his thirties. And I thought: What happened to *his* charmed life? Then the anchor man said that there had been rumors that the sports idol had been having health difficulties that might have forced him out of the sports field. I wondered: Did he want to die, then, young, in a blaze of glory? Did he choose to become a legend: How conscious or unconscious was his decision? What prior decisions did he make? And what ones did he change or not change at the last moment? How strange and intimately mysterious it all was! And in what recesses of our minds do we form the shape, the beginning and the ending, of our own lives?

As I thought about the sportsman's death, my own scary episode earlier in the day, and the strange document I'd seen in my mind, I began to get so relaxed that I could hardly keep my eyes open. Tension was leaving my body at a quick rate, but so was all ambition. It was then that I told Rob I didn't think I could have a session later unless I pepped up. I felt so lax that it just didn't seem possible that I could end up speaking for an energetic Seth, no matter how good the session might be. It was also in here that somehow I "knew" if we *did* have a session, Seth was going to connect the glass door episode with poltergeist activity and the earthquake that had also been mentioned on the T.V. news.

Obviously, I did have the session later that night though. Afterward, Rob read me the parts of it concerned with the broken glass affair, and in bed I kept going over *that* in my mind. I remembered the tumultuous energy of that wild wind and driving rain; the gusts that blew in from the screened porch through the open doorway. I'd been excited by the storm. The last bout of wind had finally risen to a crescendo just after Rob left the kitchen; so that when the door blew shut and the glass shattered, I didn't even know where the extra clashes of sound came from. It was then I must have yelled. In the next second, the glass was falling all around me.

So, according to Seth, Rob and I had both been involved in a different kind of psychodrama, but how did it work? Rob's dream showed him he was worried about me. He told me the dream, too. So somehow the two of us together set up the situation. He "forgot" to put the stopper at the door. When the storm came, in some unconscious but wholly natural way our emotional energy mixed with the storm's power (collected and directed it), and whoom! The glass explodes into the kitchen—but avoiding me completely. Dear God of Jane!

Anyhow, my thoughts kept me awake. I got up about 3 A.M. And I wrote:

"The night seems very spacious, as if it has more psychic room in it than daytime; and with so much of man's consciousness turned toward dreams, the earth itself seems more dreamlike, while at the same time endowed with a peculiar kind of wakefulness. My people-portraits stacked around the studio seem more alive, for example, as if they possessed a rudimentary consciousness or a kind of trans-life that shows itself to my own night-eyes.

"Outside my open windows, the night earth seems like an abstract of itself, with fluid, flexible forms that aren't static but ever-changing. The house across the way loses several feet to the night spaces, first on one side and then on the other; and the windows look as if they move to the right or left just a fraction of an inch. It all makes me feel as if the world doesn't keep its precise shapes at night; or knowing so few are watching, it lets up its discipline—letting rocks, leaves, grass and flowers all interweave; turning a bug on a grass tip into grass and back again. Anyhow that's how it looks. All shifting.

"And my consciousness seems more brilliant at night too; more alert. It gets a primitive feel around the edges as if the night rearouses perceptions native to parts of me that I've forgotten."

I read over what I'd written, wondering. At what level, then, did our energies merge with the contents of the natural world, mixing with the wind, slamming porch doors, forming the events of our lives from our births to our deaths? I wondered if we'd ever know. But I did know that we weren't at the "mercy" of nature. Instead, we were a part of nature's events.

Chapter 20

Seth Comments on Christianity's Early Days, the Crucifixion, and Other Allied Subjects that I Sometimes Wish He'd Forget

On August 15, 1979, Seth finished *The Individual and the Nature of Mass Events* in Session 873. Rob and I weren't surprised. We'd both felt for some time that the book was coming to a close. Besides that, I began to understand my sense of anticipation as I started to "pick up" hints about Seth's *next* project. He had been throwing out hints about it in our recent private sessions. In late July, the phrase "Dreams, 'Evolution,' and Value Fulfillment" came into my mind, and I was pretty sure, though not certain, that it would be the title of Seth's next book.

Just the same, when Seth finished *Mass Events* I was shocked in a way difficult to describe; and I always feel that way when Seth ends a book. *Mass Events* had dominated our sessions, of course, which automatically organized themselves around the book. The events of our lives seemed to mirror the book's thesis and to fall into place, as if to serve as living examples of whatever aspect of reality Seth was discussing at any given time. So if we weren't surprised, we were still taken back in a fashion.

We had no idea when Seth would begin his next book. We didn't even ask, preferring to let the sessions' own rhythm have their way. We did have some ideas about the subject matter because at the end of *Mass Events* Seth began speaking about the importance of dreams in the process we usually call evolution.

My part in producing *Mass Events* was over. I felt a strong sense of accomplishment, of course, but one that, as always with Seth's books, arouses questions that sometimes seem unanswerable. These questions involve the nature of creativity itself, and psychic creativity in particular. How was that book organized and dictated, beyond the normal domain of my own consciousness? Of course Seth was *real*, but how did we define or explain or understand that reality?

Those inquiries are often in the background of my mind, but when I'm finally presented with a new completed Seth book they rise again, more vigorously than before. As you'll see, some comments Seth made toward the end of August headed my thoughts about all of this in a slightly different direction; one that intrigued and also distressed me to some degree.

If my part in *Mass Events* was over, though, Rob's certainly wasn't. Now it was up to him to finish all the notes and references, "frame" the sessions by showing the daily context in which they happened, type the entire manuscript, and prepare it for publication. So while he was enthused at the idea of Seth starting a new book, Rob certainly hoped for a chance to catch his breath in the meantime.

And in that meantime, several developments were taking place. I began preparing my presentation for *this* book to Prentice-Hall. As I did so—trying to keep the book's many subjects in mind—I was struck again by the amount of conscious work this book required, in contrast to Seth's. Also, a new minor theme seemed to enter our lives right after Seth's discussion of people who loved danger. Though I didn't notice this at first, our letters began to stress questions about accidents, sports, and daring exploits. Several of the people who visited us during this time went in for sports that involved danger. That minor theme turned into a major one, with a strong religious cast.

This odd merging of themes happened, as clearly as I can tell, during a Seth session on the night of August 26. We were visited by a physics professor who often participated in several exciting and dangerous sports. I'll call her Greta. She had just recovered from a life-threatening illness. After we'd talked for a while, Seth came through. He began speaking with a quiet humor:

"I have been listening, and I simply have a few comments. I will tell a story. If this were class, I would say: 'I will close my eyes, so no one knows who I am talking about.' Now, there are certain kinds of people who thrive on excitement. They thrive on contrasts. There are certain kinds of people who thrive on excitement and thrive on contrasts who also have a certain distrust of energy and power. Power overawes them. They admire it. They fear it. They seek it and they hide from it at the same time. So when they manage to satisfy their appetites for contrasts and excitement and energy, they get it in one great dose, which then convinces them that energy is exciting *and* dangerous. It is to be run from and sought at the same time.

"Now, some people want to live a quiet life, safely tucked in between the night and the dawn. And they are satisfied with that. But we are not dealing with that kind of story this evening. . . . There are people who run race cars down tracks at fantastic speeds. They love the excitement although at any moment they might be killed. And so it seems to them that the edge of living is sharper. It seems to them that their senses are keener. . . .

"There are others who become very ill . . who find themselves in a situation that they have themselves formed. It seems to them that they must fight for their very existences, and therefore, from that vantage point they look at life and its experiences, and stop and say, 'Shall I go on, or shall I not?' And to such people, it is as if they are standing at the top of a vast mountain, with all of the energy of the universe flowing through them, and they think: 'This is life. How dangerous and fascinating. How filled with contrasts. But how frightening!' And they stop and make a choice."

Seth spoke the above passages kindly but energetically, with an elaborate pretense of not including Greta in his list of kinds of people who behaved in the ways he mentioned; while, of course, accurately pinpointing her own characteristics—a device Greta saw through and enjoyed. As Seth continued, though, he spoke to her more seriously and directly:

"There is nothing to be feared in energy. You can take tiny sips of energy from a spoon. You can take a shower of energy if you want. But there is nothing dangerous in energy. It will not overwhelm you. . . .

"You do not need to drive yourself to the heights. . . . The heights are yours, even when you breathe quietly; even when you are tucked safely between the night and the dawn. The excitement is not dangerous, unless you want it to be. . . .

"Use the abilities that you have, and in that way you will reach your own heights. By using the abilities that you have, you become more the person that you already are. And you can be that person, easily. You are that person, easily. You do not need methods. . . . All that you have to do is to realize that this energy is your own. I merely show it to you. It is the biological energy within each of your cells. You do not have to seek it, to punish yourself for it, or drive yourself to attain it. It is yours, and it has always been yours. Simply ride the natural energy of your own being."

Seth ended the last passages with rolling rhythm. His voice seemed to exemplify energy transformed into his rousing vowels and syllables. I deleted a good deal of material here that dealt with Greta's private life, so I've had to disrupt much of Seth's delivery, and the build-up of rhythm isn't nearly as obvious as it was at the time.

I came out of trance feeling more energetic myself than I had earlier. Greta, Rob, and I sat around the table having a general discussion that I've quite forgotten. Then Greta brought up the subject of Christ's Crucifixion and the central part that the Crucifixion drama played in Christianity. Seth came through almost at once:

"You do not need to die to achieve spiritual rebirth. Again, I am looking nowhere in particular. You need not suffer to attain knowledge. . . . The Crucifixion story represented, in your terms, now, the self-destructive aspect of the species at the time. And it represents the self-destructive elements of the species in this time for those who still accept it.

"Many religions set up their methods and their dogmas, offering the hope of great knowledge, great understanding, and wisdom. There is only one catch: You have to die first! . . . Some of the basic tenets of Christianity were very good, but for all of that, you still have the story that when you suffer and die you will go to heaven, gain knowledge and beauty and truth, and escape this 'vale of tears.' "

Again, with a kind of broad, kindly humor: "Think what might have happened, and think of how your religious books might read, if the myth read differently. Supposing the story read thusly: Christ was not crucified at all. He was not persecuted. He was not chased. He was not scourged, and no one gave him vinegar to drink. Instead, they handed him purple robes, set him up in state at Rome, called him Christ, the Son of God, but said that the kingdom of God is upon the earth, and salvation is now. What would the priests do? For, indeed, knowledge and joy and salvation would be within your grasp. Many religions believe that you must go through trials or walk through fire first. But Christianity believes that you must die first. Now, in your terms, that is certainly the most severe trial of all. And a poor way to prove faith. For if you believe in life, you prove your faith by living it. You dare love it. You do not need suffering or trials. . . ."

Seth went on to explain that Greta often used her participation in dangerous sports in an effort to set up trials for herself, and answered several questions she asked about other issues. Then he ended the session by saying to Rob: "I thought I would give you a note on Christianity for your evening's mental snack."

Mental snack! Not for me, I thought. I always get at least slightly uncomfortable when Seth mentions Christ. Whatever its merits, Christianity has caused as much war and dissension as any other field of activity, it seems to me. Any material on Christ is bound to be controversial if it doesn't fit Christianity's framework; but more, I usually feel that any such information, however accurate, would just add more fuel to the fire.

In fact, when I came upon Seth's passages just yesterday, I said to Rob, "Are we really ready to *publish* Seth saying that the Crucifixion story reflects the species' self-destructive tendencies?"

"Sure. Why not?" Rob asked. He glanced up at me briefly then looked back to his own work, obviously oblivious to my misgivings.

"Well, uh, Christianity is *based* on the Crucifixion and Resurrection," I said nervously.

"So?"

He still didn't get it, but his innocence in that area always gets *me*! I had to break out laughing. "God, I don't know what I'd do without you," I said. And I meant it.

In any case, Seth's comments were just the beginning. He was to give two other sessions in a short period of time on Christianity and related matters; and one in particular was to lead me into areas I'd pretty well avoided in the past. That session was held the night after Greta's visit, and in it Seth also referred to two specific letters I'd received that previous Saturday—letters that weighed on my mind.

The first—what a coincidence!—was from a man "in contact with Seth" who wanted to inform me that I'd distorted Seth's material on Christ, and that Seth had told him so! My correspondent had the proper material which reinstated Christ's life and affairs as given in the Bible. "Good Christ!" I muttered irritably to Rob when I read the letter. "What about the other two people who wrote last year, each with their *own* versions of Christ's life, each contradicting the other, and each supposedly containing corrections from Seth?"

Rob just shook his head.

"Will the real Christ please stand up?" I said. I'd written the man a brief note explaining that he was free to believe what he wanted about Christ's life—that he wasn't in contact with Seth, but with his own symbolized version of who or what he thought Seth was.

The man had mentioned that at first he was bothered by his own material, but felt much better now since he realized that *he* wasn't responsible for it. And *that* brought my own attitude to mind, one that I'd so taken for granted that the correspondent's words really shocked me. I take the responsibility for the Seth material and I always have, in that I would never make it public if it didn't meet my own standards of integrity and excellence. I think that we must all be responsible for our own "subconscious acts" or trance revelations, or whatever.

The second letter had exciting implications, yet also gave me some moments of disquietude. It was from a woman I'll call Linda who told the following story: She was the driver of a car that slammed into another. As a result of the accident Linda suffered a broken leg, and a young girl in the other car was the victim of unknown injuries that sent her into a coma. She and the young girl (aged 7) were sent to the same hospital, and Linda suffered anguished guilt feelings when the young patient remained in a coma day after day.

According to her letter, the doctors didn't know exactly why the child was in a coma to begin with; but Linda got it in her head that the little girl didn't want to live, or at least that she didn't fight for life. Over a week passed. Finally one night Linda had a dream in which Seth appeared to her, went with her into the child's hospital room, touched the little girl and healed her. Linda knew that the coma would break in the morning. And that's exactly what happened. As mysteriously as it had come, the coma vanished. The little girl was perfectly all right. "Of course," Linda wrote, "she might have recovered anyhow." But Linda didn't think so. She was convinced that Seth had healed the child.

I thought that the entire affair was fascinating. Since nothing could be proven one way or the other, I went along with the evidence of Linda's experience. But I didn't think Seth healed the child. I thought that the dream-Seth was the woman's own creative accomplishment, the dream-manufacture of a personality who could use the healing abilities she possessed, but didn't realize were hers. I told her so in a brief note. But again, I found her interpretation disquieting.

In any case, both of those letters plus Greta's visit were on my mind when Seth gave the following session. This time I'll include the entire session, with all of Rob's notes and other designations in italics.

SESSION 876   AUGUST 27, 1979   9:12 P.M. MONDAY

(This afternoon I took our female cat, Mitzie, to the vet to be spayed. We may have her back by Wednesday. Now, Billy, her litter-mate, squirmed in my lap as I tried to write these notes. This is the first time that the two cats have been separated. I couldn't tell whether Billy missed his sister or not, although Jane said this was the time of evening when the two often played together. We speculated about what kind of communication might go on between them while they're separated.

(Last night we were visited by [Greta Darrow]. Seth came through several times. Greta taped the session on her own recorder; she's to send us a transcript. We'll call that Session 875.

(Jane was very relaxed as we waited for the session. Perhaps she was a little tired too, since we'd been up with Greta until after 2 A.M. "Don't be surprised if it's a brief session," Jane said. She laughed. "I'm really relaxed. Tonight it's more like Seth is saying, 'Come on, Jane,' instead of me being after him for a change. . . . I'd just like a freebie tonight. I don't want to worry about questions, or what Seth will talk about. . . . "

(Then, with many pauses:)

"Now. A few notes on Christianity in fact and fiction."
(This was one of the subjects we'd discussed with Greta last night.
So had Seth.)

"It seems to you, in your time, that the Christianity you know is the inevitable form taken by Christianity. It seems that Christianity as you know it was the result of a more or less single line of development, beginning, say, with Christ's birth."
(Pause.) "This is far from the case. During those times, and prior to Christ's birth as you think of it, there were many attempts to initiate the kind of religion that was later called Christianity."
(Pause.) "There were many, many individuals in various parts of the then-known world who had similar concepts, visions, and psychic experiences. Any one of these could have served as the focus of the religion that finally emerged as Christianity.

"There were many differences between your world and that one. The import of dreams, visions, and psychic events was considerable. You must remember that science had not yet defined the limitations or boundaries of reality in those days. A man was not considered insane if he received a mystical vision; and the literature of the Jews is, of course, filled with such instances. Mystical experience provided an inner, rich pageantry against which the most miserable of daily physical existences could somehow seem redeemed and meaningful.

"In your day, ordinary people may pray to God to punish a despot, but their practical actions will more likely involve them in actions of revolution. They do not expect God to come out of His heaven, for example, and overturn the government for them. Not in your time.

"In the days of which I am speaking, however, the lives of many people were involved with psychic content. People looked for a new God, a new Messiah who would, by His might, put them in their rightful place of power. Most people did not read or write. The world myth took the place of television."
(Long pause at 9:29.) " 'Supernatural events' had a place in that world, and the heritages of many peoples were carried down orally, in dramatic form. The use of exaggeration and hyperbole was expected. 'Supernatural events' were psychic facts to those people. There was not the same kind of distinction made between the material world and the spiritual one that you make. The most skeptical worldly rabbi in those times still looked over his psychic shoulder now and then, lest Jehovah be watching.

"The world believed in the intervention of gods into human events in a way that seems quite unacceptable in your times. The same kind of following—the same kind of followers—that Christ had also found many other men, and all of the followers hoped that their messiah would be the Messiah. The outcome was not inevitable, but the expression of psychic need and desire was.

"Now, look to the present. A woman wrote that she was involved with . . . correspondences in which I was communicating with her; and she was certain that this would prove beyond a doubt my own independent nature, since I [would have given] messages to another medium besides Ruburt. The woman was quite convinced of that.

"Other people have written that I have given them such messages. Another woman dreamed of me, and had an experience in which a child was definitely healed. Now, I did not communicate with those women—but their belief in me helped each of them use certain abilities. One woman has done some writing—not very good—but still, those abilities came to the fore. The other woman was able to use her own healing abilities.

"Now: Back in those times of which I was speaking, generally events more or less of the same nature occurred frequently, and some were far more outstanding. But the results were attributed to the various individuals who aroused their followers' hopes and abilities."

(Pause.) "You must remember that without books, magazines and newspapers, television and radio, information and social discourse all had to come from personal contact—and rumors ran wild."

(Long pause.) "The man who was crucified agreed to the execution because he did believe he was a messiah who had to be crucified. He sought the experience on the one hand, while dreading it on the other. Some of those early Christian ideas were a conglomeration of other beliefs, even while they served to build upon Jewish lore most deeply.

"There were, indeed, several 'Christs,' several people whose preaching and exploits merged to form the composite figure historically known as Christ. There are all kinds of contradictions in the Bible, and in Christ's own attitudes as depicted, because there were more Christs than one.

"Some of the [Christian] heritage was of Indian origin. Reincarnation was definitely a part of those early beliefs. The Sermon on the Mount is probably the closest interpretation of the best Christianity had to offer—but the tenets of that (underlined)

Christ, who gave the Sermon on the Mount, did not suit some of the people involved who looked for an earthly king. 'Blessed are the meek' did not fit them or their idea of political power. The Christ who gave the Sermon on the Mount also said that the kingdom of heaven was within—and that dictum did not fit in either with those who wanted a politically effective Sire."

(9:54.) "Another Christ was the one who cursed the fig tree.

"Give us a moment. . . . You must remember, also, that in those days one person was often talked about as being a new incarnation of a past prophet in Jewish tradition. People were being converted to one faith or another all the time. A man would have a vision, attain a new spiritual identity, and change his name accordingly.

"The spirit of the prophets was said to touch the souls of other men. So a person 'inspired by Christ' could speak as Him; and his words, in that tradition, would be considered Christ's words.

"The individuals whose existences added up to the composite picture of the historic Christ overlapped in time, both preceding the time given for Christ's birth and following the time given for His death. Those who felt themselves inspired could alter the records with immunity."

(Long pause.) "The Roman Empire had served its purposes for itself, and for the species. A new kind of organization was needed politically—one that would be strong enough to enlarge even Rome's sway, and move into new areas more competently. In those times, religion was the basis for politics, and Rome's religious base was weakened. Few believed in its gods any longer. Rome was tolerant then. But people were not ready for tolerance."

(Long pause at 10:04.) "Christianity was, then, a rather rich blend of beliefs that were gradually weeded out. You had many probable roads that Christianity could have followed. Each of them represented various probable developments in culture and philosophy; and each of those developments, of course, would have given you a different present. Each of those alternatives has happened also.

"Behind the power of Christianity lies the unending reality of man's inner source, which he continually tries to explore, express, and define. And from that attempt emerges all religions, civilizations, sciences, and philosophies."

(A one-minute pause at 10:08.) "The New Testament marked the beginning of Christianity, but in a form that brought an end to the continuing saga of the Jewish traditions—for there were no new prophets after that. <u>To that extent,</u> (underline twice!) the Bible ceased to be a living document of a people's spiritual search, a gathering together of psychic events, myths, historical wars, people's fears and yearnings. With the coming of the Christ, no more was added to that book. There were many records that could have been added, but they did not correlate with the version of Christ that was settled upon.

"The composite [historical] picture of Christ is based upon the settled-upon events taken from the lives of three people in particular, though there are a few events that simply do not apply. Any events that happened to those people that did not fit the picture were hidden or [evidence of them] destroyed. You must understand that an 'event of the psyche' was considered a fact. Saul heard God's voice—or rather, Paul heard God's voice. To him, that was a fact.

"There was a God who spoke, who could send flashes of light to blind men—people tried to take psychic events and turn them into literal facts. *(Long pause.)* But the very term 'literal fact' adds a different meaning. Exaggerations were expected in those times. They were not thought of as lies.

"That is enough. I sneak this [kind of material] in now and then. Do you have any questions?"

("Was part of this based on your own observations when you lived in the first century A.D.?")

"It was based on my own knowledge—most of it gained <u>after</u> that life, as far as the overall conception of Christianity are concerned. The mores I knew—for example, that exaggerations were expected in all walks of life. No one spoke in terms of what you think of as bare fact. It would not have been polite.

"I bid you, then, a fond good evening."

("Thank you very much, Seth. Good night."

(10:21 P.M. "I still have to watch it," Jane said. "Even in trance, I could feel part of me uneasy because Seth was discussing Christ." She grinned. "Maybe we got the material tonight because I was so floppy," she said. "I do take responsibility for what Seth says, though."

(I thought Seth's remark, that he'd gained most of his knowledge about Christianity after that life in the first century, was quite revealing. It was another of those insights into his own reality that he extends to us every so often. Unless we're very careful, such comments can get lost in the sessions; I try to keep track of them in a separate notebook. Obviously, they'd add up to a book in themselves. . . .)

That Seth session intrigued me. I kept thinking of the similarities between the Christ era as Seth described it and our own times. Even if the mores *were* different, people were far more interested in "psychic content" than they were, say, even when our sessions began in late 1963. Now there were new religious sects everywhere. I decided that Linda's belief that Seth had healed a child bothered me because of the religious connotations. I wasn't out to start a new religion! Neither was Seth.

But I could feel myself trying to make some new connections that certainly had a *kind* of religious implication. And even that made me uneasy. There was some extension of the God of Jane idea that kept trying to surface. When it did, it seemed perfectly obvious, of course.

In the meantime, I wondered uneasily why Seth had really gone back to the Christ material. I certainly didn't feel like taking on Christianity and science to boot! At the same time, I reminded myself that my reaction was exaggerated. Still, Rob and I both suddenly became aware of all the letters to the editor written by religious fundamentalists and published in the local paper.

I read over Seth's last "Christ session" to be sure of what he said, and thought vaguely about checking through all of our records for past references made by Seth on Christ and allied topics—a chore we *will* get to one day, by the way.

I said to Rob, "As far as I can recall, Seth stated some time ago that the Christ spirit, as it's thought of, touched Paul, John the Baptist, and Christ—who were all parts of the Christ entity. The exploits of the *historically known* Christ, though, involved three people, only one being a man called Christ. Once Seth said that the man who was actually crucified was drugged. So I suppose he's the same person referred to in the last session—the one who believed he *was* the messiah, but was frightened too."

"You've got it," Rob said. "But one of these days I'm going to check all of our records and make up a series of questions for Seth on Christ, based on what we have so far."

"Just what I was thinking earlier," I replied; but I didn't mind if he took his time, I thought.

Chapter 21

God-Making and God-Makers. Also More on Christianity from Seth

The feelings I'd had about summer's eternal quality were suddenly just memories. As September came, everything inside the house and outside seemed poised only between small but innumerable changes. There were already a few less leaves in the treetops, and through the spaces where they had been more light splashed down into the living room that was my studio. The leaves winked. The new autumn light winked, and sometimes the world seemed to change from one moment to the next, becoming with each change more intense, more charged. Autumn's acceleration had begun and though the leaves weren't falling, swirling through the air yet, the wild rhythm that would drive them was already stirring everywhere. At least that's how I felt.

I kept thinking of Seth's session on Christianity, and in the meantime people kept sending more letters about Ouija board communications and "automatic" messages. And what messages they were! There was a personality from another star system, ready to land with his starship any day now to whisk away his followers from Earth's "corrupt and dying environment." There were personalities who gave economic advice, in the face of certain nationwide depression and anarchy. There were warnings of planetary disasters and world's end. But the communications also contained advice as to how these various events could be avoided by those who believed in the messages; and finally, all of the catastrophes were to result in a new consciousness, either on a purged but pure Earth, or "beyond."

The people who wrote took these messages literally. But what did they really mean? I wondered. They were the rumblings of the mass psyche, I thought, expressed by the various individuals in their own ways. The messages reflected the fears of our times, exaggerated and magnified through the psyche's natural sense of drama and personification. The religious aspects bothered me, though. I remembered what Seth had said about all the sects flourishing during the birth of Christianity.

"And speak for yourself, Jane," I thought. The Seth material had never been inflammatory, though. Seth never gave dire predictions. He didn't promote himself as a leader of a chosen group of spiritually elite. And when I told people to trust their own psychic information, I didn't mean that it should necessarily be taken literally. Still, why should people get psychic horror tales? And of a religious nature? Because, I thought uneasily, such messages contained the seeds at least of variant religions, based on the old ones but updated—starmen coming from the heavens instead of God and His angels; and the chosen few selected from the rest of the masses for salvation.

At the same time I kept thinking of Seth's latest book, produced in those now-forgotten trance hours—organized, dictated and delivered with a psychological ease that I still found astonishing. Then there was his projected new book, *Dreams, "Evolution," and Value Fulfillment.* What would *it* contain? And someplace in these musings the word "evolution" in Seth's title attained a special significance that I felt strongly but couldn't quite identify. At the same time, all the questions I'd had in my mind about religion intensified. I had to go back to my own experience for answers, I thought, and forget other people's "messages." Again, who or what did I really think Seth was?

I started writing down my thoughts, calmly enough at first, but I could feel undercurrents of understanding rushing beneath my sentences. Finally I wrote faster and faster, teetering on the edges of new perspectives, or at least seeing my work—and life itself—from a different viewpoint. I wrote all morning and afternoon. It was Friday, September 7. This is what I wrote; and *as* I wrote, I realized that this material was the next natural development following the God of Jane ideas and my statements of psychic independence.

"The Seth experience offers as many questions as it ever did, even though each day seems to bring new clues and insights. I do think that Seth represents a kind of psychological extension from my normal state—the self 'ascending' through itself, using itself as a psychological steppingstone to vaster realities. As long as we believe that information comes to us only through the physical senses, we'll need such psychic extensions to gather the knowledge that we believe to be beyond our own capacities.

"Seth may be myself at another level of activity, so transformed that even to me the psychological distances between us seem insurmountable. *There, nowhere,* I'm Seth. Here, anywhere, I'm me, embarked on my own journey in space and time, living a life that may be perceived in its entirety by Seth in the proverbial twinkling of an eye.

"But more is involved too; and as I write these lines I see in the Seth experience dim glimmerings of the psychological activities we may have used to create our gods—Zeus with his exuberant divine crew, Christ, Jehovah, Buddha, Allah, Zoroaster, and all the rest. But what purposes would we have for such activity?

"It suddenly occurs to me that such activity may *represent* our highest creative abilities to date as a species—the creation of a series of personified psychological aspects, representing our own inner knowledge as it exists outside of space and time; giving directives that appear as commandments or new guides to action, and thereby communicating the knowledge of the species to its individual members. The catch is that these directives, assuming the guise of visions or revelations, would still have to push through the conscious mind's beliefs and the culture of the time. The knowledge is there, but usually we didn't know how to interpret it.

"Within that kind of framework, perhaps I've been practicing the mental art of god-making all along; and understood within that context, then I couldn't be in better service. Maybe the Seth experience brings those ancient psychological abilities into the light of day, where if we will we can study them devoid of religious superstition and perceive them as evidence of our own highest genius; a genius that is behind all of our creativity and that propels our civilizations.

"All of this (almost magically, mysteriously, yet clearly) leads back to the validity of private impulses. And visions. For it seems clear to me (at least right now) that man's private visions, alone or grouped together, formed the basis of all our civilizations. Those visions and intuitive concepts about the nature of 'God' and the universe directed the form those civilizations took, and provided a psychological mobility that gave us the ancient civilizations—Egypt, Babylonia, the Roman Empire, Islam, and our modern culture as well. What distinguishes each of those civilizations is the characteristic concept of God and nature around which it evolved.

"The *processes* by which we originated civilization seems lost in antiquity's rich psychological bed of myths and facts, hidden in the heady mixture of subjective and objective events. But perhaps in times of upheaval when old values are crumbling, those processes actually become visible in the world again, if we know where to look.

"In the past, as a species we were blinded by our own psychic contents when they emerged through the visions of a prophet, shaman, or prospective 'God.' The religions, formed around such events, didn't understand that they were dealing with dramatic symbols that *represented* aspects of an ultimate Divinity, and *stood for* a reality that was not expressible in usual terms. Instead, the religions insisted upon a literal interpretation of psychic events; just as today, many people involved in automatic writing insist that the spaceman or saint or other such communicator is 'real' in usual matter-of-fact terms.

"So we ended up with nationalistic gods, parochial supermen, each supposed to be absolute, or with a series of divine rivalries in which various gods jealously guarded their own earthly devotees. The trouble was that we invested these gods with the cloak of absolutism. If the god of our civilization said, 'Go slay your neighbors; they are evil and your enemies,' then off we went, engaged in another holy war, our own motives neatly hidden beneath a sacred banner.

"Actually, the visions that gave birth to our religions provided powerful symbols around which we did, indeed, group all of our other activities. They served as intense focuses for the organization of everything from agriculture to science or its equivalent. That's no small accomplishment, but it's sometimes easy to forget when we consider the problems brought about by the rigid dogmas that finally clogged those visions. Ultimately, the dogmas smother the very intuitive insights they were meant to protect: The gods die, and with them the civilizations that grew up about them.

"Yet we are natural god-makers, a fact that certainly should be taken into consideration by our psychologies. In fact, our god-making tendencies characterize us. Throughout history we've consistently formed these mental models of godly beings who then, through visions and revelations, make their messages clear to the conscious mind, laying down the rules for our civilizations, structuring our institutions and directing our military establishments also, whatever their sophistication or lack of it. Again, our gods must represent our unconscious knowledge that some source exists from which our own world springs.

"The birth of a world religion takes place very seldom, but in between times there are innumerable trial runs as each individual continually receives his or her own intuitive knowledge (through dreams, inspiration, and altered states), and checks this against the official religion or religions. As long as this private knowledge fits into religion's framework, there is no slack to take up. Individuals project their private psychic experience into that charged, prepared, religious mold. Unless world religions accept new psychic content, however, they grow more and more out of phase with private experience. A slack appears.

"When this happens, as in our time, private psychic events become more intrusive and noticeable, because they are no longer smoothly projected into the drama of official religious form. Psychic material that was hidden before then begins to emerge, as once again the individual is forced to seek the meaning of his or her life in the larger context of existence itself, unbuffered by dogma.

"Religions often predict their own eventual downfall and the resulting end of the era of civilization that they supported (as in Nostradamus). In our own times we can see the psychological climate in which old gods die, and new ones begin to take their place. In our case, the old god is not quite dead and may, in fact, blaze with an intensified glow for a final time; while the new god or gods are still shimmering in probabilities, as yet unborn, but definitely seeking expression and form.

"To some extent, the Ouija board personalities, the cults, and the new age religions, are each attempts to free psychic content from its ancient rigidity and to seek a new, larger context in which the full dimensions of human existence can be creatively expressed. Most of these cults or sects will be too bizarre or extreme to suit the overall psychic purposes of large masses of the people, and will simply fall by the wayside or continue with only a few faithful followers.

"In this time of transition, some groups, such as the fundamentalists, will try to infuse new life into old Christian doctrine. Others, and their numbers seem to be growing, turn to Eastern religion, with its equally rigid dogmas. *Those* dogmas at least appear novel, and many Americans tired of competition may find a momentary sense of peace by letting go a compulsive desire for advancement, success, or achievement. Some Western scientists are intrigued by certain Buddhistic concepts which are akin to some of the ideas in modern physics.

"In any case, I don't agree with the *content* of any of our organized religions. I'm convinced that the religious *process* itself involves the translation of inner intuitive knowledge into conscious form, but the content of that form is also dependent upon our own understanding at any given historical point. And, unfortunately, we still haven't learned to distinguish between psychic morality plays (psychodramas) and psychic facts applicable to literal interpretation. This is true because we haven't realized that there *is* an entire spectrum of inner perception, as varied as the exterior one.

"Yet in a greater sense, we are all god-makers—forming our own models in response to our unconscious recognition that we and our world *do* spring from another source.

"These ideas would have really startled me not too many years ago. If there was one thing I wanted no part of, it was religion. But I see that all of our philosophical questions of whatever nature lead back to the basic question of man's source; and our beliefs in that regard color our sciences, arts, and psychologies.

"Seth makes no claims of omnipotence, of course, and he claims no miracles at midday, beyond those that are within our own reach, at least theoretically. He has no intention of starting a new religion. Neither have I. We do both hope to help spark a new, wider view of reality; a new cultural climate; and to provide some kind of philosophical structure vital enough to be used as a springboard into areas of knowledge and performance that have been closed thus far to all of us."

As I wrote that material, I felt excited and sensed new connections between myself as an adult and that child who used to sit writing poetry on the porch steps, wondering about her relationship with the universe. I was still doing the same thing, in a different, concentrated way—but I hadn't quite realized it.

As I thought about it, I saw other connections between the processes of writing poetry and god-making. Rob had asked me to write the Introduction to Seth's *Mass Events*, and as I made notes for that the following Monday, I found my god-making ideas appearing in the Introduction; I began to see my relationship with Seth in a clearer way. Because portions of that material are important here, I'm including the following excerpts:

From My Introduction to Seth's
THE INDIVIDUAL AND THE NATURE OF MASS EVENTS

". . . And what is my part in all of this? I see it as harking back to the poet's original role: to explore the reaches of his or her private psyche, pushing against usual psychological barriers until they give, opening up a new mystical territory—the psyche of the people, of the species itself—perceiving a spectacular vision of inner reality that the poet then communicates to the people, translating that vision through words, rhythm, or songs.

"The earliest poets were probably half shaman, half prophet, speaking for the forces of nature, for the 'spirits' of the living and the dead, voicing their visions of man's unity with the universe. They spoke their messages, sang their songs, chanted their sagas aloud. And maybe that's why Seth *speaks*—communicating first through spoken words rather than, say, through automatic writing. Seth's books are first of all spoken productions. Perhaps the Seth sessions themselves harken back to some ancient time when we received much of our pertinent information about ourselves in just such a fashion—one of us journeying for the others into the 'mass unconsciousness,' a journey that somehow altered and expanded the personality; and then communicating our findings as best we could.

"If so, though, such altered 'between world' personalities can be remarkably stable; and if they form according to our ideas of individuality then they certainly outdo us in their unique complexity. For if Seth is only a psychological model filled out by *my* unconscious trance material, then he puts our usual concepts of personality to shame, and by implication shows that we ourselves have a long way to go if we are to use our full potential.

"So I do think that more is involved. I think that Seth *is* a model of ourselves as we know we can be; that he speaks for the part of ourselves that never for a minute believed all that nonsense about flawed selves. . . .

"But however we attempt to define Seth's reality, I'm convinced of one thing by now: He is delivering to our conscious minds our deepest unconscious knowledge about ourselves, the world, the universe, and the source of Being itself. Not that Seth claims any kind of omnipotence, because he doesn't. His material, however, is clearly providing such translations of unconscious knowledge, and intuitive disclosures; disclosures, according to Seth, no more remarkable than those available in nature itself, but we have forgotten how to read nature's messages; disclosures no more mysterious than those available in our own states of inspiration, but we've forgotten how to decipher those communications too. Instead, many people are even frightened of inspiration itself.

"I think that such phenomena were important in evolutionary terms, helping to shape man's consciousness. Not that such material wasn't often distorted, or just as often discounted. In any case it would have to be interpreted again and again so that it applied to the species' experience in time's framework.

"Talk about psychological complexities. I was just presented with an excellent example of the ideas I've been discussing. As I wrote the previous few paragraphs of this Introduction, the words themselves seemed to carry me on with a certain rhythm. I felt as if I were drawing on energy and knowledge beyond my usual capacities. Then, since it was late afternoon, I took a break for a brief nap. More ideas came to me that I scribbled down in the bedroom. The subjective pace quickened and kept accelerating—then I hit a psychological brick wall and I could carry the concepts no further. At that point I suddenly recognized Seth 'around the edges' of my mind. The next moment, I fell asleep. When I awakened a half hour later, I prepared dinner. Rob and I ate and watched the television news. Then I went back to my study.

"No sooner did I sit down again than such a rich vein of material opened that I could hardly write fast enough to get it down; and it began where my earlier ideas ended off. I was being given many of the subject headings for . . . Seth's *next* book, even as I was writing the Introduction for this one! Behind each heading or subject I sensed realms of information available to Seth, but not (in usual terms) to me. . . ."

The experience I just described was fascinating and frustrating at the same time. I sensed the full emotional scope of Seth's next book and I *did* pick up a good amount of specific material; but most of it vanished from my mind before I could writ it down. I did retain notes about the subject matter, but they are so fragmentary in comparison to the fullness of that momentary inner vision of the book that I'm not including them here. But I knew the book would be terrific, and I wondered when Seth would begin its dictation. In our next session he *did* confirm that the title, *Dreams, "Evolution," and Value Fulfillment*, was correct, but he didn't say when he would start the book.

In the meantime, while I was thinking about the implications of god-making, events involving religion began to intrude into our lives, as ones concerning science had earlier. This time, for example, a fan sent us a book about the history of the popes; and in his next session, Seth commented on that subject and went on to discuss the conditions in Rome just after the time of Christ. The first part of the session was devoted to other topics. However, at 9:57 P.M., according to Rob's notes, Seth paused and then launched into this material. (We hadn't read the book about the popes yet.)

FROM SETH SESSION 879   FOR SEPTEMBER 17, 1979

"A very brief note. A few of the early popes were not martyred by the Romans, but killed by their own people for various reasons—to avoid schisms, to make the Romans look worse than they were, and sometimes simply because the popes were greedy.

"At that time Church <u>doctrine</u> was being formed. Some of the popes wanted Rome as an adversary to further unite the new [Christian] sect against the common enemy. Many documents were destroyed on several occasions by popes who feared that their contents were inflammatory. Sources were given for other papers that were imaginary. What Christianity had, however, was largely the common man's stamp of approval, for ideally it said that the slave was the equal of the emperor.

"The wealthy Romans had indeed been undermined even before the time of Christ—undermined for many reasons. For one thing, there was an unwieldy group of what you might call small businessmen, freemen, and Roman citizens. Their numbers were swelled by the ranks of foreign businessmen as well who came to that capital of prosperity, and also by former slaves who had, one way or another, gained their freedom.

"This was as lusty and exuberant an era, in that regard, as the time that you think of as giving birth to the rise of small businesses, say, in the Middle Ages. Some businessmen barely made a living, but they guarded their freedom jealously, and would think nothing of lying or cheating in order to keep their established ways of livelihood. Many such people were ripe for the ideas of Christianity. They needed a cause to unite them, and one that would give them a sense of dignity: A sense of dignity that Roman citizenship had once provided for all of its citizens—at least ideally. By the time of Christ, that pretense scarcely existed.

"Rome was overextended. Its tax structure was beginning to collapse. The small businessman was taxed most severely, and in retaliation he usually cheated. Merchants made a habit of keeping one set of papers for legal purposes, and a set that had very little to do with the actual business. Those small businessmen, the slaves and the foreigners, mixed and merged in the marketplace, and they were rambunctious. They did not dare defy Rome openly, and so they managed to bore from within.

"The Jewish rabbis were as bad as the rest, and the Jews were twice bled [since] in one way or another they paid tribute to the temple, its priests, and Rome as well. That identity as Roman citizens began to erode. It was each man for himself, and that kind of feeling needed a philosophy that would go one better than Rome's ancient dictum: the equality of each Roman citizen. It would be the equality of each man, Roman or not, under a God who would be greater than the state.

"You would have a spiritual, more expansive version of Rome's equal citizens, with nationalized boundaries dropped. People needed a new framework.

"Give us a moment. . . . The Jews were excellent in business matters. They mingled with the Romans. They were underneath Rome's regal paw. They also had a tradition of a religious nature right there. They had numbers and enthusiasm. They were the only people, as a people, closely allied and under Rome's domination who had an available, intense, magnetic tradition of the kind needed at that time.

"The Greeks, for example, were in a fashion too cultivated, too philosophical and lenient, in those terms, to form together any cohesive approach. Even as slaves, and angry, they still looked down slightly at the Romans as, for example, engineers rather than original thinkers.

". . . There was a great deal of vitality waiting to be tapped. The prophecies of the Jews, according to their ancient books, referred to a Jewish messiah who would deliver the Jews— but in that time of great creative turmoil a remarkable, intuitive leap of world-shaking proportions was made. For Christ when He came (in the terms usually understood) refused to ally himself with the

Jews alone, but said he was to be the Messiah for all people, regardless of nationality."

(With amusement:) "If one government or empire couldn't unite all those diverse peoples, by God, one God could—a Messiah that could rouse alike the energies of the Jews, the Greeks, the slaves, the businessmen, the wanderers. Now, that would be some Messiah indeed!

"An immediate triumph of the old Jewish traditions of prophecy would have culminated with the coming of the Messiah and by the foundation of a Jewish state in political terms. Such a threat would instantly be countered by Rome; so in another fascinating interpretation, you have Christ really saying that the kingdom of heaven is within you—that He will not, for example, lead a physical army to conquer Rome. Such an attempt would have been ludicrous.

"Rewards were offered, then, but put off for a while. The inadequacies and injustices of the times were grossly apparent to everyone. Man had to find a framework to hold him over so that the idea of justice was at least preserved. In spite of the competition between slave and slave, and slave and businessman, there was still a camaraderie that began to stir the people, and that materialized more fully in the idea of Christian fellowship."

("Can I ask a question?")

"You may."

("Are you saying that a man called Christ actually lived?" I had in mind various earlier statements by Seth to the effect that the Christ we know of was a composite of several individuals.)

"This goes along with other material that I gave you. I meant that the official words of the [Biblical] Christ were finally interpreted as saying certain things. . . ."

"It's so complicated," I grumbled, when I'd read the session. "And it was so long ago. And it's all been so distorted through the years. Who cares what happened then?" Because, I thought, I bet that we were all involved in god-making right *now.* This minute. The process was happening *now.* Probable new gods were peeking around the edges of the world.

And I didn't want to think of old gods or sciences already growing senile. But I wasn't to get off quite so fancy-free.

Chapter 22

A Christ in Every Living Room, Dr. Jekyll and Mr. Hyde, and Heaven for the Good Guys

Each season seems to characterize itself for me in one way or another. Whenever I think of springtime 1979, I think about beginning this book, for example, and my meeting with the woman from Big Flats comes instantly to mind. Then I think of the morning when the dawn landscape gave me the idea for *The God of Jane.* I associate the hot July weather that year with Dr. Camper's letters and can almost see myself writing my rather impassioned poem, "A Psychic Manifesto," as I sat by the living room windows, staring at the fully foliaged hills.

That autumn reminds me of several things that all seemed to be happening at once. For one thing, Seth began to dictate his Preface for *Dreams, "Evolution," and Value Fulfillment* on September 25. The month before we'd turned the small back room into a den of sorts. The couch and coffee table and television set were now there, so that's where we held the Seth sessions for a change. (I'd taken over the living room to use as my studio.)

The den is strange: At night it seems cozy and small, but in the daytime the patio door connects it to the outside world and almost gives it a public air. Maybe it was the room's intimate nighttime quality, plus the excitement of the autumn air, but the sessions seemed newly rousing as Seth began to dictate his latest book. My trancetime had new highlights in it, difficult to describe. It seemed odd to have the sessions in a different corner of the house, almost as if I'd turned another corner of consciousness at the same time.

We'd decided to have the outside of the house painted. The man who did it for us came around 5 P.M. and worked until dark, so when sessions began at 9, the smell of paint was still around. Probably because Rob is an artist, I really like the smell of almost any kind of paint—or turpentine—and the circumstances all seemed to fit together evocatively. I'd come out of trance, feeling that I'd been light years of consciousness away, and return to the specific smell of that paint and think how intimate our house was, after all that psychological distance.

But that room also reminds me of a different kind of event entirely—one that also actually led me further along the way I wanted to go, though I didn't know it at the time. We were in that same den on a weekend afternoon. The patio door beside us was open. Rob and I were both relaxing, ready for lunch after having worked all morning. Though it was autumn, a warm wind rushed down the back hill, and the air almost felt like summer. Our two cats lay on the screened-in porch outside the patio door, basking in a patch of sunlight that splashed in under the rolled-down bamboo blind. Rob turned on the television set with a flick of the remote control button. I plunked down on the couch, smiling out at the innocent yard.

Rob was watching television. He chuckled, and I turned to see what had made him laugh. He had the sound turned off, but the picture was on. And what a picture! I frowned at once. There in brilliant supercolor was a face you knew belonged to a hell-fire preacher in the middle of a holy frenzy. "Oh, get another channel," I muttered, seeing those earnest, tear-filled eyes on the screen, the holy perspiration glittering on the fat, pained forehead. The furiously moving lips were mercifully silent with the sound turned off on the set, but the agonized magnificence of the face and glazed eyes made the message clear anyhow: An awful retribution awaited those who didn't believe in Jesus.

I picked up my peanut butter sandwich and looked out the window.

Rob *grinned,* and turned up the volume.

I'll call the preacher Reverend Grover. His voice instantly, triumphantly, revengefully (or so it seemed) filled the room. "Aha. Oha. Yes. I believe in hell-fire! God is merciful. Oh, yes, the almighty God is merciful, but hell is where the sinners go. Woe to those who do not listen to God's holy word. And who are the sinners?" Shaking his dyed, black, expensively coiffed head, he whispered, "Oh, we are all sinners." Then, in a voice loud enough to blast the neighborhood: "We are all sinners who must place their hands in the hands of the Lord. Be saved. Go to Jesus. Do it now."

Rob and I hadn't been inside any church in twenty years, except to attend one or two weddings, and we'd never paid any attention to televised religious programs either. So nothing prepared us for this sudden emotional confrontation. I stared, nearly stunned, as the preacher ran up and down the stage, jumped up and down, screamed, waved his hands, and did just about everything but stand on his head.

"Oh, yes," he shouted. "Yes. You have to believe in the Bible, friends. God's word is there. In the Bible. That's where it's at, friends." His eyes narrowed. His lips trembled, and his preacher's arm suddenly sliced the television air like a blade. "Oh, the Lord knows what goes on! He knows that the devil sends you dreams and visions that pretend to foretell the future and mislead you into a love of power and the sin of pride."

Love of power! I thought incredulously that I'd never seen anyone so orgasmically involved with power before. To me the audience looked as if their collective eyestems were stretching out of their heads in an effort to glue themselves to *his* eyes—and his eyes looked ready to roll out of their sockets. I almost felt sick.

On the other hand, I remembered Seth's latest material on early Christianity, and the many letters I'd been getting with a religious cast. Well, here was a demonstration of *modern* Christianity, or a segment of it, and I didn't like *it* much either. Still, I couldn't deny that some magnetic-like attraction had drawn all those people in the audience to that service. The huge stadium was crowded. I imagined all those people dressing in their best clothes, leaving

their houses, walking city blocks or across fields or down state
highways to board the buses that the announcer now listed during
a break in the preacher's sermon.

And how incongruous, I thought, that such religious
superstition should be made available through technology's auspices; the televised image of the preacher formed almost miracu-
lously before our eyes; the threats of hell and damnation riding the
transistorized airwaves, as the preacher's form once more filled the
screen and his voice filled our small den. Perspiration was trickling
down his broad forehead; not just from the holy effort to deliver
God's message, but also from the heat of the invisible television
lights as the cameras swooped in for another close-up.

"Oha. Aha. I bring you Jesus, sweet Jesus," the Reverend
Grover cried. "Give up the demon, tobacco. Give up the demon,
alcohol. Yell out, 'Oh, demon tobacco, leave me! Oh, demon alcohol, be thee gone! Leave my body beautiful and pure for Jesus.'"

I glanced at Rob. He was eating his sandwich, looking
relaxed, detached and somewhat curious; watching the screen as if
the entire production was an exhibition of religious practices on
another planet. I just nibbled at *my* sandwich; even the peanut
butter was beginning to look wicked. And preacher-boy went on. In
the few minutes it took me to drink my milk, he'd managed to
denounce homosexuals, "free thinkers," rock musicians, card
players, movie-goers, and anyone or anything else not "holy."

"Embrace Jesus," he shouted. "Embrace Jesus, or when
you die—and oh, yes, friends, we all die—then you'll be consigned
to the flames of hell with the rest of the sinners."

"Damn," I said. "Hon, get another channel, will you?"

"Why? It's fascinating," Rob said, grinning at me.
Then, more soberly: "Don't let my relative detachment fool you.
The entire performance is really obscene, isn't it? I just can't
imagine expending any energy on Christianity: It's too filled with
contradictions. What we're watching is a beautiful or deplorable
picture of a belief system at work—according to your point of view.
And I guess in our book, it's pretty deplorable."

I didn't answer because just then the Reverend Grover's
voice boomed out so powerfully that for a minute I thought the
volume on the T.V. set had gone out of control. The preacher was
screaming with exultation, triumph, and passion. In a quick but
commanding gesture, he held up a Bible to the screen, its title
facing a million living rooms.

"I dare you. In your homes, come forward. Put out your
hands. Touch this Bible on your television screen. Those of you

who are sick, say, 'Oh, dear Jesus, I embrace You. I'm ready to be healed.' And you will be! Does Jesus need to touch you directly? Oh, no, dear friends. Merely touch the televised image of the Bible, and be healed. Come forward. Receive your healing from the hands of Jesus."

I shoved myself further back on the couch, as if the preacher could see me if I sat too far forward. "Jesus," I muttered. I stared at the Reverend Grover's heavy jowls: They were shaking. His lips were fluttering furiously. Then, amazed, I stared at his eyes: *They* were almost childishly merry, filled with a strange unabashed tenderness and wild expectation as if he did, indeed, already see the crippled throwing away their crutches; the deaf their hearing aids; and the blind their useless glasses. Yet, at the very same time, his eyes were also somehow hard and revengeful. One minute his face looked like a rather sweet, fat boy's face, hungry all the time but for more than food; but then the sweetness was replaced by that glittering fanaticism. He was hooked on himself, I thought. He believed it all now, if he'd ever doubted. He'd left himself no way out. And for a moment I felt sorry for him. But only for a moment.

His voice grew more frenzied. I yelled to Rob above the racket: "Boy, if I had to accept all that rubbish—if I had to accept that kind of a petty tyrant of a God in order to lose my own physical symptoms, well, I'd keep them and consider each one a badge of honor!" My eyes stung. I remembered that my muscles hurt. I looked at the Bible whose image almost entirely filled the television screen and I wondered how many people, hesitantly or bravely, defiantly or desperately, reached out for that promised healing. How many pressed their hands against the Bible's televised image, waiting; ready to give up anything, if only bones or eyes or tissue or minds were suddenly renewed?

I cringed at the emotional blackmail. But was I secretly tempted? What if I did ("Aw, what the hell have I got to lose?") touch that screen? Suppose I did? And what if my body was suddenly as free as Rob's? Or the cats'? Free as air? For that release, could I bend my mind and spirit backward into dogma's creepy, closed closet? Not even if I was fleet enough to run in the Olympics, I decided fervently.

Rob must have been watching me because he said, "This whole thing really gets to you, doesn't it? Why? It's the same old stuff."

"That's it," I said. "What about the miserable beliefs those people accept in return for whatever comfort they receive? Salvation has its drawbacks, it seems to me."

"Don't forget though, some healings *could* take place under those conditions," Rob replied. "The benefits might not last long, because the beliefs in evil and sin are too strong. Still, healings could happen."

I nodded in agreement: A shared belief system on the part of the audience *could* certainly produce healings under certain conditions.

"But listen to *that!*" Rob directed, and I looked at the television screen again. The Bible was gone. Reverend Grover was rolling his eyes again. He was also shouting: "Let your sins be washed away in the blood of Jesus."

"I don't want any part of me washed in anybody's blood," I said indignantly. "The worst part is that this guy is sincere. At least I think he is. He's not just a confidence man out for a fast buck. God, I'd trust a confidence man more than a fanatic any day." Not that this holy boy wasn't doing famously in material terms, I thought. As Rob pointed out, men in the aisles were now taking up collections in the background where, now and then, the cameras focused on a group of enraptured faces. And sincere or not, there was no mistaking the fanaticism in the Reverend's now honeyed tones; no mistaking the sense of power he enjoyed as a "mouth-piece for Jesus."

And thinking of Christ, I said, "With friends like that, Jesus doesn't need any enemies."

Rob shook his head. "I just never believed any of that stuff," he said. "My parents were supposed to be Presbyterians but they didn't go to church even twice a year. They taught my brothers and me to be honest and kind and so forth, but they didn't have any real religious convictions, for which I've always been grateful." He paused for a moment, eyeing the television screen, and went on, slowly: "What I can't understand is why, as a species, we keep up with Christianity or any religion that concentrates on sin, chosen people, the vengeance of God, and the like. We've spent two thousand years messing around with those ideas, and they don't seem to have made people any better."

Rob's remark made me think of something that had never occurred to me before. "Wouldn't it be something if as a species we survived *despite* Christianity or any of our organized religions?" I said. "I mean, maybe it's a tribute to the human spirit that it *did* manage to thrive despite such limiting beliefs."

I broke off, fascinated by the screen again. The Reverend Grover was yelling about hell-fire once more, in a vehement per-formance that made the Catholic Church of my childhood seem innocent by contrast. I actually shivered as I sensed the crushing weight of the preacher's beliefs. At least the Catholics had purgatory for those not ready for God or devil; but for the Reverend Grover, you were saved or not. There was no in between. And if you weren't saved, then that was the end of it.

For the third or fourth time, he held up the Bible. "Believe in this blessed book, and be saved. Believe in this book, God's holy word, and be healed of all your difficulties. Lose your aches and pains. Only surrender to sweet Jesus." This time he somehow changed a terrible grimace into a sudden enticing smile. And once more he held the Bible up to the screen.

I fidgeted. I was hot and cold by turns. Again that sneaky question returned: If I *could* possibly accept "sweet Jesus," might I spring right up in the next moment, completely flexible? Suppose I knew ahead of time that I would definitely be healed if I accepted the preacher's premise. Under those conditions, would I accept the idea that life was created by a God who punished his creatures for the sins of ancestors who transgressed at the beginning of time?

I thought angrily that I'd rather crawl with honor if I had to, instead of accepting that kind of bargain. I knew my face was flushed, but I didn't care. I told myself dramatically that I'd nag that kind of god through the very corridors of hell and heaven, even if I was the only hold-out in the world. But (I relaxed a little) I wouldn't be the only hold-out, of course. Rob would be one. And there would be millions of other people too. I felt rather ashamed of myself: Had I, for a minute, been afraid of Jehovah's wrath? Good God, I thought: People must have felt that way in ancient times when they turned away from Zeus: still wondering if he'd destroy them with thunderbolts, even after they'd decided that he didn't exist at all.

By now I was nearly exhausted. I hardly glanced at the screen where telephone numbers now flashed, so that viewers could call for information about the chartered buses. Vaguely I imagined the preacher and his high-powered crew coming into small towns and large, taking over the local stadiums, glaring at local reporters, giving out their literature, and "collecting souls for God."

"I give up," I said. "Give me the channel selector. I've had all I can take of the Reverend Grover."

It would be in that same small den that we'd hold our next Seth session, and for a few minutes I played around with a fantasy of my own. I imagined that Reverend Grover's image still flickered on the television screen at our next session, only this time the preacher could see into the room. He could watch me neatly turning into Seth, and hear Seth's voice continuing dictation of his newest book, giving *his* version of the beginning of the world.

After all, I thought, Seth's personality is projected onto the screen of my mind as surely as any image is projected on a television screen. And Seth doesn't have any script to follow. He doesn't spout ancient nonsense. And the "channel" is original, formed by a psychological meshing of my reality and his, so that each of our existences is implied in the other's. Anyway, I imagined Seth "coming through" to confront the Reverend Grover's TV image. I don't really think that Seth would bother confronting anyone. But in my mind, the Reverend Grover's eyes *freeze.* He yells dramatically: "Get thou behind me, Satan."

Seth, in this imaginary encounter, says: "I don't see anyone behind you but an audience of emotionally battered people."

"And television lights and cameras, and men going up and down the aisles, collecting the faithful's hard-earned cash," I think, wickedly.

"I confound you, Satan," shouts Reverend Grover.

"I'm not Satan," Seth answers, reasonably enough.

"Then he sent you," the preacher yells.

"There just isn't any Satan," Seth replies.

"Now, I know you're the devil," Reverend Grover cries triumphantly. "No one except the devil himself would make such a statement. How do you account for man's evil if there's no devil? Ah, no. You'll not deceive me."

"Man's nature is basically good," Seth replies, more quietly than I would have. "Fear of a god's vengeance doesn't teach man to be good. It just teaches him to be fearful. Again, man's nature is basically good."

And in my mental theater the Reverend Grover's head snaps forward. He screams: "But no one but the devil would ever say that man is good. That's the most evil thing I've ever heard!"

"I thought you were going to change the channel," Rob said. "You've got the strangest look on your face."

And *that* broke me up! I laughed, tried to forget my gloomy mood, and found an old Dr. Jekyll and Mr. Hyde movie on the one channel not devoted to sports or religion. Purposefully, I prepared myself to enjoy the old-fashioned saga. I grinned: There were the foggy London streets seen in countless spooky melo-dramas; there was Dr. Jekyll's Victorian laboratory with its home-spun but dangerous ingredients. There, in other words, was science at its mythological center; its potential benefits and dangers barely sensed and, in any case, safely hidden back in time, back in the mystery of those probably-faked London movie streets.

I nibbled the last edges of my sandwich crusts. My pleasure in the saga was eroding. There, I thought, was the poor fool Jekyll, whose desire for knowledge was about to lead him to drink the deadly potion—the potion that would unleash those disastrous hidden elements of man's being. There was that nice, sincere Dr. Jekyll forsaking all the good people's society, opening up the Pandora's box of man's soul, releasing all of those primitive, deadly, wicked, selfish *impulses*!

"God almighty," I sputtered.

"What's wrong now?" Rob asked. "You sure are having a rough lunch hour."

"Oh, I feel cheated," I grumbled. "I used to love those old Jekyll-Hyde movies. And all of a sudden, I realized that it's the same old thing again. Poor Mr. Hyde starts out fun-loving and innocent enough when he's first released. He's a friendly, frolicking dude in the beginning. But he changes. Oh, he changes! The idea behind the whole thing is that man's true inner nature is evil and dangerous and that his hidden impulses will lead him to destruction."

"Dear Seth," I thought. "You wrote an entire book on the opposite premise: that impulses are good and that they connect us with the great impulse of life itself. Do you think anyone will listen?"

There was no answer. At least not then.

"I think I'll make some cornbread," I said.

Rob was grinning at me. "Why? What's the connection?" he asked.

"Because it's a lovely, simple task that I can do. And the results show right away," I answered. So I sat in the kitchen by the open door and made the cornbread; working, I thought, with ingredients that you could get your hands into; following certain instructions that led to a dependable product. Bread-making was much more reliable than god-making, no matter how you looked at it. And as a project in god-making, I gave Christianity and its organized offshoots a very poor rating indeed. The "product" wasn't fit for human consumption.

The day's mail didn't improve my mood. A correspondent wrote about the efforts of a fundamentalist Christian group to prevent a "psychic fair" from being held at a shopping mall in a small Ohio town. The group contacted all of the businessmen involved with the projected fair, told them that psychics "got their information from the devil," and threatened a local boycott of the mall. As a result, the fair was called off.

Also in the same day's mail was the latest copy of a scientific journal that is devoted to what I can only call scientific fundamentalism. It contained a bibliography of books debunking "the paranormal." The only difference between the two groups of fundamentalists was that religious fanatics stated that psychic activity was the work of the devil, while the scientists said that it didn't exist at all. But both groups obviously found it threatening.

And so it is, I thought, to both groups, because psychic activity represents the individual's ability to discover certain kinds of knowledge for himself or herself; because psychic activity is *personal* and direct; and regardless of the many complications arising from interpreting such knowledge, it always offers alternate versions of reality or at least suggests their possibility. People with rigid belief systems *do* find that kind of activity threatening.

And it really didn't matter, I thought. Monday, in that den where we'd watched the preacher on TV, we'd have our own psychological television channel turned on again; the unofficial, private channel tuned to trancetime instead of clock time. We'd hear Seth's version of the beginning of the world. Trancetime would spin out its alternate vision of reality. And as long as there *were* alternate visions there was hope. And room for creative excitement.

Chapter 23

Psychic Naturalists, "Spirits Who Walk in the Light," and Psychic Chauvinism

I spent the rest of that weekend writing the notes that gave me the basis for the previous chapter on Reverend Grover. To do that, I wrote a description of the television program and my reactions, jotted down my version of the running conversation that Rob and I had engaged in at the time, then checked with him to see that I'd quoted him correctly. You can be certain, then, that any such recreated episodes are pretty faithful to the actual events, since I always follow the same procedures.

I did change Reverend Grover's appearance and make other substitutions so that he couldn't be identified. To do *that,* I watched four or five other such programs hoping to capture the flavor of fundamentalism as it appears on our television screens; and that was an education in itself. Of course I realize that fundamentalism is only one segment of Christianity, but it is rapidly coming into the mainline of political and social activity.

In any case, I discovered that Reverend Grover was no more hell-oriented than any of the other fundamentalist ministers, and he was actually less harsh than most. The entire spectrum included preachers with all kinds of personal characteristics and approaches—from one who adapted a rather supercilious intellectual pretense, speaking the most utter nonsense in the quietest, most reasonable of tones to holy rabble-rousers. There was only one television preacher who seemed at all genial or sensible, and he was a free-wheeler, using Christianity as a carrier for positive thinking concepts.

During the following months I also kept track of the Reverend Grover, tuning into his program now and then just long enough to see what was going on. There was no doubt of his good intentions. He clung to his belief in sweet Jesus as if his life and everyone else's depended upon it; successfully reconciling the ideas of a loving, merciful God, faith healing, and heaven for the good guys, with the contradictory beliefs in God's vengeance, the devil, eternal damnation for the bad guys, and man's sinful nature.

Reverend Grover's production is a huge commercial venture, of course, like most of the other showcases of the TV salesmen of God. In other words, there *is* a "holy market." People *are* attracted to those beliefs. But why? The question was in my mind all that autumn. Why on earth would we, as a people, want to believe in sinful selves, in an authoritative father-God given to temper tantrums, and in all of the other frightening tales that tinged even Christianity's better edges?

And that week, while I was involved with those issues and checking my notes, we were busy in other ways too. Earlier, following my impulses, I'd agreed to do a two-hour taped radio interview, and it came due that week. Seth even came through briefly, much to the interviewer's surprise. Several nights later we were visited by a psychologist who was using Seth's ideas in his treatment of clients. In the meantime, the house painter was just finishing up his work; and Seth continued dictation of *his* latest project.

Before I realized it, the next weekend had arrived; this one far cooler and more like autumn. Our friends, Peg and Bill Gallagher, were coming for a Friday night get-together. We'd been so busy that we hadn't seen them in more than a month. As it was, Rob spent the time right after dinner typing Seth's last session, hoping to finish before the Gallaghers arrived. Then another group of events began that were to extend through the weekend in one way or another, bringing many of the philosophical challenges I'd been concerned with into new focus.

The first incident happened as I prepared for company. I'd just used a small carpet sweeper on the green rug in the den, dusted the coffee table which would later hold wine glasses and our eternal cornbread (I always make two at a time and freeze one). I was frowning at a small end table, thinking that it *really* needed waxing, when another, completely intrusive thought suddenly came into my mind.

"More guests are coming tonight than you expect. Some fans will drop by." The thought was definitely mine, despite the use of "you." It was as if one unknown but more knowledgeable part of me were passing on some useful information. If my own usual thoughts were colored green, then this odd thought would have been blue; just different enough to be noticed.

For a minute I reacted almost automatically, putting the idea down without giving it a chance. For one thing, I argued silently, in all the years of our frequent Friday night get-togethers with the Gallaghers, no fans had ever intruded. Maybe I secretly wanted more company, I thought; and the buried wish surfaced, pretending to be a precognitive impression.

Then I caught myself firmly: No hint of the mind's abilities, however small, was to be overlooked or judged beforehand or without examination! My earlier ideas about psychic naturalists came to mind. So what was I waiting for? Here, I told myself, we have a tiny wrenlike thought, similar to the others in my mental flock; only this one is "marked differently"—it seems to carry information about the near future. And if the model of reality in my hypothesis was true, then precognition itself would be predicted in the model. Right? Right. So mentally I "tagged" the intrusive thought, then scribbled it down and marked the time and date. Then I promptly forgot the whole thing as I went about my chores.

Ten minutes later a cold draught of air rushed against my legs, and Rob's laugh suddenly rang through the house to the back den where I was still working. I realized that someone must have rung the front doorbell, and Rob was answering it. In a moment I heard the door close. "Who was that?" I yelled.

"A kid selling raffle tickets. I bought one," Rob called, and went back to his typing.

Hmm. Had that kid been the "visitors" my impression had predicted? I opened the back patio door for a breath of night

air, and frowned: Nothing was ever simple! If the kid had been
selling tickets in the neighborhood, it was possible that I could have
heard him, say, knocking at a neighbor's door, and not been aware
of it; then mistakenly assigned the event to the future. No, that didn't
even make sense, I thought. The question was: Was a distorted
perception of *some* kind involved instead of a legitimate hint about
the near future?

How strange it was that we still didn't know how our own
minds worked. And the worst part of it was that our pat explanations usually hid our own ignorance from ourselves. For example, I
thought, could my perceptive mechanisms somehow have leapt just
a little bit out of their usual close fit in time, picked up the boy's
approaching visit but then interpreted "boy" as fan, because a visit
from a fan seemed to make more sense? That didn't seem likely
either, since the original impression had definitely referred to *two*
people at the very least. These questions were still going through
my head when the Gallaghers arrived about twenty minutes later.
Then I relaxed and once again forgot the entire affair. But not for
long.

We all sat chatting. It was past 10 P.M. and dark outside.
A wind had started blowing down the back hill, so when we first
heard a knocking noise nearby, we just assumed that a trick of wind
had caused the extra racket. When it continued, though, Rob went
out on the back porch to check while the rest of us continued with
our conversation. Then we heard the sounds of footsteps and voices
and of metal being dragged across the porch as people opened
folded-up chairs to sit down. Obviously, unscheduled visitors had
arrived at the back door.

Rob returned in about fifteen minutes. Two young men,
driving through town, had stopped to call. Usually he invites such
unexpected guests in, but he didn't want to disrupt our visit with
the Gallaghers. So, as he told us, he chatted with the young men on
the porch and sent them on their way.

So my earlier thought about guests had been literally
correct all along: For the first time in all of our fourteen years of get-
togethers, fans had come on a Friday night! It was a small enough
instance of precognition (or, perhaps, telepathy) I thought, but
again, if the world conformed to scientific dogma, then *any* such
event would be impossible. Each such occurrence, however trivial it
seemed, gave further evidence of the gap in official versions of
reality, and each one should be lovingly collected, classified, examined, and preserved. How many other people had similar experiences that very night? I wondered. How many instances of telep-

athy or clairvoyance did we all throw away by discounting them or their implications? Why was it so difficult for us to look at such mental events with any objectivity?

The answer was pretty obvious, I thought unhappily. A part of me was still playing around with the idea that coincidence was responsible for the entire affair, for example, even though I knew better. We were all so well trained to ignore the evidence of our own experience if it conflicted with scientific theory that we almost reacted automatically in that way. Was I still worried about accepting an unproven hypothesis? Once more I reminded myself that in incidents like that night's, science couldn't *prove* that coincidence was responsible any more than I could prove that it wasn't. It was open territory. Then I remembered the boy selling raffle tickets. Where did he fit in? And the entire texture of the event seemed richer than I'd realized.

I'd made a brief note about the initial impression but hadn't had time to tell Rob about it before the Gallaghers arrived, so in a lull in the conversation I described the incident along with my reactions. When I was finished, Peg told us about a "reading" given to one of her cousins by an old woman in the country a few weeks earlier.

"Mary, my cousin, and a friend of hers heard about this woman from an acquaintance," Peg began. "Anyway, they went to see her. The very first thing that the woman said to Mary was: 'You shouldn't wear other people's clothing. The vibrations are wrong.' Mary was really shocked. She looked great, she always does; and her clothes are always in style—but she buys them all at a thrift shop, secondhand! No one could possibly tell that just by looking at her, though; and if the clothes don't fit perfectly, then she has them tailored to fit. The woman gave some other equally good specific impressions, according to Mary, but I've forgotten what they were. And she gave some pretty general stuff that could apply to anyone."

Peg continued: "But the point I want to make is that ordinary people *do* know that there's more to life than they've been taught. In a way they look for evidence even if they get it from someone else. I think that many people take so-called scientific experts with a grain of salt—particularly nowadays."

Peg told the story so earnestly that I had to smile. "I hope you're right," I said. "But look at what Mary's kids are being taught in school—that evolution is more or less scientific fact, that the species is basically predatory, and that survival of the fittest is the rule of existence."

Rob broke in: "Then they probably go to Sunday school

where they're told to forget all *that* nonsense and believe, instead, in a mean-tempered God, heaven and hell, and all the rest." Rob grinned ironically, as if to soften his statement a bit. I thought he just felt like relaxing and really wanted to change the subject.

Before I could think of a way to bring the conversation around to a less charged topic, Peg brought up an issue that I'd momentarily forgotten. A short time before, Rob had written a letter to the editor and sent it to the local newspaper where both of the Gallaghers work. The letter was in response to the paper's report of a scientist's lecture at a nearby college.

The scientist's point, to which Rob objected, was that the premise of any divine existence had been simply an ignorant attempt to explain phenomena for which science as yet had no answers: As science continued to explain away one mystery after another, the idea of a God would no longer be necessary. Then, in a sentence that really outraged Rob and me both when we read it, the scientist was quoted as saying that in the future, children would build consciousness with electric erector sets.

Anyway, Rob's letter to the editor was too long, and the editor had written a note asking Rob to shorten it to meet the newspaper's requirements. Rob had decided not to bother. For one thing, he'd sent a copy to the scientist involved; and for another, he just didn't have the time to do the work of cutting the original version. The editor, knowing we were all friends, had asked Peg to bring up the subject, suggesting again that Rob make the changes so that the letter could be published.

I followed the rest of the conversation only dimly, lost in my thoughts: How like science to refuse to study the *insides* of consciousness—its subjective nature or contents—while imagining that the complex processes involved were so mechanistic that tomorrow's bright child could *construct* a dash of consciousness to while away a boring afternoon!

I almost got dizzy, thinking about the implications of *building* consciousness with any kind of erector set. Fantasies flashed within my inner vision. I saw *living* dolls, arms akimbo, consciousness trapped within plastic eyes. Why not? I asked, imagining a future television commercial, the announcer saying: "This baby doll not only cries, eats, and wets its diapers, but it thinks and has feelings, too." Then, in my mind, a mother asks her five-year-old: "What kind of consciousness do you want for your birthday, darling?" So my thoughts went, at least for a while.

Finally I surfaced back to the ongoing conversation. Peg,

Bill, and Rob were still discussing Rob's letter, but this time I remembered some material that had come in the mail that very day. Our correspondent had enclosed another letter to the editor (without knowing about Rob's), written by still another Rob Butts. *That* Rob Butts lived in a distant state and was himself the editor of a newspaper. The enclosed letter expressed ideas similar to many of ours and the correspondent wanted to know if we thought that the two Rob Buttses were probable selves, or what?

Or what? We didn't know, of course, I thought. There was so much that we didn't know. We *did* know that the answers didn't lie in scientific formulas, or in any formulas for that matter. The thick coat of official reality had frayed again, if only slightly; and again for a moment I really sensed that different kind of organization described by Seth as underlying all of our lives. I could feel its subjective texture: Its mental invisible threads were composed of those odd, quirky, unrecognized, unofficial events that we've been taught to ignore. Studying them might get us somewhere.

Even our present conversation contained all kinds of clues, I thought. The answers were really "all there," even for the four of us in that small den. They were "all there" for all of us, whoever we were, but for some reason we didn't hold the proper focus. We kept looking at ourselves and the world in the old fashion, putting reality together in habitual ways.

But, I reminded myself again, come Monday Seth would continue dictation on his newest project. All the edicts of official science and religion together couldn't stop that from happening, and couldn't stop any of us from trusting ourselves and our impulses if we were determined to do so. Now the den seemed like a cozy mindcave, flickering with eternity's images. I *am* safe, I thought. Seth is right: We live in a safe universe once we believe that we do, because the belief creates the reality. I'll remind myself of that in a thousand stunning ways, I promised myself. I didn't need defenses; and one of these days I'd run as swiftly in my physical body as I did in my dream body now, as the new evidence replaced the old.

The Gallaghers left around midnight. As Rob and I cleaned up, fed the cats, chatted, and locked the doors, I started getting excited again about the entire idea of psychic naturalists. Once more I imagined "the people" making their own determinations about existence—recognizing, classifying and identifying not exotic species of plants, but those subjective oddities of thought, impression, or vision with which science and religion refused to contend. I saw all of us together, collecting evidence of a different kind of reality; gently but surely enlarging the range of our experience.

Once more events seemed to shoot that fantasy down, though. Two visitors the next day made me question the entire idea. I'd spent the morning and afternoon scribbling down notes about the events of the night before, and I'd planned to answer the mail after supper. Rob and I were sitting on the couch, unfinished dessert still on the coffee table, the third game of the World Series playing on television, when a knock came at the patio door. I grimaced; a blob of mayonnaise had fallen on my blouse a few minutes earlier, leaving a round circle of grease; my hair needed combing; and I just didn't feel like seeing guests. Rob grinned fatalistically, shrugged, told me that I looked fine, and answered the door. This time he let the strangers in.

She came into the den first, resolutely. She was tall, large-boned, dressed with studied nonchalance—good sports jacket, expensive slacks, silver earrings showing at the edges of her short black hair. He came in behind her, wearing a rumpled business suit and tie. He had thick blond hair that was turning gray, a narrow face, and broody eyes.

They'd driven down from Canada just to see us. The woman said that her name was Dorothea and that she was a lecturer on psychic matters. I believed her. Her voice was jolly but with a brisk no-nonsense ring to it, and I bet that she could really bellow out if the need arose. She'd read all of our books, she told us. So had her husband, Phillip. Phillip nodded as if he wasn't used to speaking for himself very often, so I grinned at him. He blushed. The two of them were companionable enough though; comfortable together. I asked them to sit down.

"There are several people in our psychic group who 'channel,' " Dorothea began enthusiastically. "They're a pretty neat group of people. Whenever anybody has any doubts about speaking for another personality or entity in trance, then I tell them: 'Just ask the entity if he or she walks in the Light. That's all. If it's a good spirit, it will gladly say that it knows the Light of Christ. And if it refuses to answer—well, that's it. Don't give it any psychic room at all. Say you want nothing to do with it.' So we've never had any trouble," she said.

Listening, for a moment I saw my ideas of psychic naturalists go down the drain. Bitterly I thought that I'd forgotten the most important issue of all: In so-called psychic matters, people had to decide first if they were dealing with gods or demons. Any unofficial information of any kind had to pass the acid good-or-bad test. Any idea of objective examination was so far down the list of priorities that Dorothea's group probably never got that far at all.

I just stared at her.

She thought that I didn't understand. "*You* know," she explained further. "If an entity won't say it's from the Light, well, then, it's from the other camp. Maybe not the devil. I'm not necessarily saying that; but one of the demons, or maybe just a mischievous spirit. But anyhow, not uplifting."

Silence. Dorothea paused, stopped by the expression on my face most likely. I said: "Look, if people believe in evil spirits or demons, they shouldn't be fooling around trying to contact anyone, as far as I'm concerned. In a way, they set themselves up for trouble because they'll interpret their experiences so superstitiously."

"Oh, I don't believe any of it for a minute," Dorothea declared quickly. "But in case some people *do*, or for those people who do, it's a good idea to calm their fears and clear the air."

I didn't want to hurt her feelings, but I couldn't understand how she could have read our books and not know our position on such subjects. So I huffed and puffed for a few minutes, trying to be diplomatic on the one hand, and clear away the psychic debris on the other. "If you've read Seth at all, you should know that he doesn't go along with such ideas," I said. "I mean, you're free to believe anything you want; but if you're familiar with our work, then I just can't see why you thought I'd agree with what you said. Taking that line with people just reinforces religious superstition, to my way of thinking."

"Oh, yes," she said quickly, her face suddenly solemn when I mentioned Seth. "I'm sure *Seth's* above all that!"

"But so are you and Phillip and anyone else who wants to be," I exclaimed.

"Hypothetically, hypothetically," she murmured. "Oh, you're so lucky to be at the level you're at. . . ."

"Level? It's using common sense," I said, not as patiently as I thought I should have. "Why on earth would anyone want to believe in demons and evil spirits?"

"Well, no one really *wants* to, I suppose," she answered Her husband didn't say anything. One look at Rob's face told me that he'd abdicated for the time being; he just didn't think that we were going to change Dorothea's ideas in an hour's conversation. Dorothea smiled. "But beliefs *do* change for the better," she said. "It all takes time, that's all."

So I just smiled back, and after a few more minutes of

conversation I said that Rob and I had plans for the rest of the evening, and the couple left.

I felt uncomfortable about the encounter though. Surely I must have seemed ungracious at best; hammering away at Dorothea's beliefs, I thought, even if I did find them deplorable. For one thing, I really liked Dorothea, and Phillip too. For another, I could imagine her—sporty and jovial—up before an audience, her hearty voice booming out, trying to be as down-to-earth as she could be in her discussions of psychic phenomena. Only, hey, I thought, how factual can you get, dealing with gods and demons? And when that kind of nonsense was mixed in with mediumistic behavior, the implications went beyond the ridiculous. So, when Dorothea left I found myself brooding not only about her visit but also about the other appalling misconceptions connected with psychic activity in general.

Quite a few of those beliefs include the sexual stereotyping that runs through nearly all psychic literature, drama, and folklore. There's the classic picture of the languorous lady collapsing in a trance or near-faint while in the shadows of the boudoir or parlor or séance room lurks the powerful male spirit or vampire. Since the poor woman is in no condition to protect herself, another powerful but good male (spirit or human) stands guard. He banishes any malignant spirits and defends the spiritual and physical virginity of the entranced psychic princess. And in cases of mediumship, the "susceptible" woman, God bless her heart, gives up all responsibility for her trance utterances, letting "the source possess her" completely. And it's goodbye, common sense. (There are male mediums too, of course, but they don't operate under those particular gothic traditions.)

In any case, I found myself thinking of several women who had written or visited me during the years. They were intelligent women, but their psychic abilities *and* intellects were blanketed beneath religion's stereotyped counterpanes. Their creativity was smothered, the wide possible ranges of their psychic experience limited, and any originality buried beneath banal conventions.

And in the psychic field, I thought, all of the most superstitious of religious beliefs and the most rejected of scientific theories unfortunately met and merged. The religious hangover was the most destructive, as far as I could tell. It was responsible for the uneasy blend of gods and devils, good spirits and bad with telepathy, clairvoyance and telekinesis, and for the almost unthinking acceptance of the "communicators" of automatic writing and related phenomena at face value, without any exploration of the nature of the psyche itself.

Maybe people just wanted the God of Abraham instead of any individualized version of divinity, I thought, growing more discouraged. Even the Biblical apocalypse was being combined with U.F.O. tales—the prophets of doom now receiving their messages through telepathy from spacemen, as if determined to make the ancient prophecies work out one way or another. I grinned weakly, suddenly sorry for the bleary-eyed scientists; feeling almost indulgent toward science's errors for a change, as I contemplated the idiocies that often pervaded the psychic field. Now we had the superstars from other galaxies reciting the old exhortations: "Repent, repent, for the end of the world is at hand." And if there are any space people watching (a distinct possibility, I thought), then they must wince at the nonsense spouted in their names.

But then in the midst of all those rather unhappy considerations, another more optimistic idea presented itself: Nonsense or no, people *were* taking up the slack that science and religion have each left in their wakes. For the first time in several generations, people were realizing that science didn't have all the answers, and that religion never did. Peg Gallagher was right, I thought, remembering our conversation of the night before. People did "know better." They *did* strain against the limitations of official beliefs; and many, like Peg's cousin, went to psychic "readers." Those readers could be found almost anywhere—in storefront rooms, trailer parks, cottages, suburbs and city slums. Even if their readings might be cluttered with superstitions, they provided some certain instances of legitimate unofficial information.

Amateur knowledge-seekers were springing up everywhere. It's regrettable, I thought, that they dragged so much official debris with them. The resulting combinations of religious concepts and bastard science were bound to be hybrids. Still, overall, the development certainly seemed healthy to me, representing people's rebellion against established dogmas.

Even Dorothea was trying to loosen herself from old beliefs. She and Phillip must be miles away by now, I thought. They'd visited us for their own reasons, of course, but had they also come to bring some of those issues to the forefront of my mind? I wondered. I even started directing some of my thoughts to Dorothea, imagining her sitting in the car, staring through the windshield at the passing street lights.

"Listen, Dorothea," I was saying, mentally. "If science

has stressed the intellect at the expense of the intuitions, well, religion has almost divorced itself from reason. So neither science nor religion can ever even hope to do more than define a half of reality to begin with. We have to combine the intuitive and reasoning faculties." I hoped that somehow she heard me.

In any case, I thought, the events of the weekend, insignificant as they appeared topside, contained in capsule form all of the issues I'd been dealing with for so long. Once again there had been an unofficial event, one that science without proof would assign to coincidence, but one of a kind that was familiar to all of us at one time or another. Once again, there was my insistence that each of us must define reality for ourselves, thrusting away any dogmas that hampered us. And once again I was presented with a disturbing example of the ways in which some people interpret psychic experience through superstition's thick overlay.

Click, click, click—the questions were all going into my "psychological computer," I thought. And somehow everything would be resolved.

Chapter 24

A Decentralized God and an American Vision

The month of October has always been exciting and magical to me—orange leaves falling everywhere, piled in gutters, flying across lawns, flapping against windowpanes like orange birds peeking into living rooms. In the October of 1979 I heard about another psychic fair. This one was coming to town, and I hoped that it would fare better than the one I'd read about earlier. The coming event struck me as peculiarly American in character, even though gypsies have traveled through Europe for centuries, telling fortunes and reading tarot cards. The gypsies, though, were often mischievous, and the people who were to conduct the fair were more or less ordinary people, from all walks of life, whose distinguishing gift was psychic. In rather typical American fashion, I thought, they were taking their wares to the marketplace, displaying their psychic products out in the open, forsaking the old seance rooms and spooky cubbyholes for the bright malls at noon.

Yet, I thought, there were some neat spooky implications. I imagined consumers, arms filled with packages, pausing at the rows of card tables set up outside the shops. People knew what to expect when buying coats, apples, beer, or souvenirs. Those products have recognizable purposes. But, as the newspaper ads explained, the psychics hoped to show the powers of the mind at work. They hoped to display psychological products that were as real as any physical wares. The term "fortune telling" was never used in the advertisements but the word "parapsychology" was; predominantly, as if this implied relationship with science made the entire fair more respectable and worthy.

In any case, the fair was almost canceled. I could hardly believe it when a group of local religious fundamentalists began an impassioned campaign to intimidate the merchants at the mall. Nice American housewives met in spotless spic-and-span kitchens, to drink coffee and dial the telephone until all the businessmen at the shopping center were contacted. Those good upright ladies warned that the psychics' information came from the devil; that Satan was behind the psychic fair. As good proper Christians, their obligation was clear: They would boycott the entire mall if the fair were held.

Now *that* was good American ingenuity at work, I thought: Hit the pocketbook. But I was very uneasy. I hadn't expected that kind of bitterness in Elmira, or realized that fundamentalism's peculiar blend of fanaticism had reached into this comparatively small town. Was it crisscrossing the country? Was it taking advantage of October's great natural exhilaration, riding it to the hilt, using nature's excitement to emphasize the prejudice of an ancient god? You can bet your booties it was, I thought.

The fair *was* held, in a central spot rented out by the mall to any community or business or professional group who had the cash. But as people lined up at the psychics' tables, they were handed pamphlets proclaiming that the psychic readings were satanic, inspired by the devil to deceive people and steal souls away from God.

Shortly afterward, another religious group took over a local park one afternoon for a rally. It might seem like a typically American scene: a small parade in the town square; people carrying brightly colored banners; statues resplendent in the bright autumn air. Only this was a protest march against homosexuals. People waved their Bibles and shouted that homosexuals were evil and unnatural, according to God's holy words. Reading about that event made me uneasy too. It wasn't my idea of Americana.

I found myself thinking, "Thank God we have a constitution and separation of church and state." In any case, the fundamentalist activity at the fair and at the rally turned my mind toward public and even national events as they were related to religion and psychic activity. I could feel myself trying to make certain important connections that had so far escaped me.

At the same time something else made me consider the public or sociological implications of trance material—my own in particular. Sue Watkins, a close friend and former student, had been writing a book, *Conversations with Seth*, about her experiences in my classes. Actually the book was to be almost a biography of the class itself, and would feature many previously unpublished Seth sessions. I was reading Sue's manuscript for the first time the same weekend that the psychic fair was being held, so that the two events became related in my mind.

At first it was strange and even a bit unsettling to read about class, Seth, and myself, as seen from someone else's viewpoint. Perhaps that jogged me into looking at my experiences from a slightly different perspective too, and before I realized it, I was thinking about the state of the nation again when the Seth sessions started. It seemed certain that some interaction between public affairs and the events of my private life must have caused a particular kind of tension that generated my psychic initiation.

That peculiar tension must happen only when certain types of persons encounter particular kinds of historical events, I thought. Again I remembered my concerns back in late 1963. John F. Kennedy had just been assassinated. There had been talk about a big showdown with Cuba. (Rob and I had stocked survival food, a rifle, and other supplies in a closet.) Those national events made a deep impression on our private lives. And surely the Seth sessions provided a new framework or platform from which we could consider what was going on in our own lives and in the world.

Looked at from that perspective, my private trances were originally triggered, at least partially, by national need and were a response to the problems of the times as they infringed upon my private life. In a fashion then, I had been responding to the needs of others as well as myself in that strange shamanistic tradition of which I'd been unaware.

It *was* quite possible then, I thought, that when the problems of the species became too great for its framework of understanding a new psychological acceleration began in response to the tension, until one way or another we broke free to a larger context. And surely now was the time.

We'd become exteriorized to an alarming degree, I mused, acting *as if* we were, indeed, science's living machines: manufactured by some automatic, brilliant mechanics that ran itself without cause or reason—mindless survival machines. Or we acted as if we were a god's sinful creatures, tainted with evil since birth. Our thoughts became so identified with exterior organizations that we'd invested them with parts of ourselves, then lost sight of those portions. We stopped asking the important questions for *ourselves.* Instead we turned over the questions to science or religion, and largely accepted their prepackaged answers and explanations.

The orange leaves spun in dizzying patterns outside the windows day after day, and I'd stare at them, thinking: Is it possible that we really are only thinking machines; our thoughts the automatic by-products of the brain's processes? Could our thoughts, could *these* thoughts, be just psychological shapes flickering in the fire of consumed energy—as meaningless in themselves as the fantasy shapes that flames make in a fireplace? That was what science would have us believe. But that framework was too narrow to contain our experience. It was too narrow and limited to offer any real solutions to the problems of the world.

So no wonder, I thought, there were psychic fairs in village malls. No wonder historic heroes, wisemen, spacemen, and saints were all communicating through automatic writing or Ouija boards. No wonder there were new cults springing up everywhere. And no wonder that the prophets of doom were taking over the television screens and the ancient religions were trying a new revival. The psychological acceleration had begun. The mass psyche was pushing at its boundaries, reaching, searching, using all of its energy to pull free. The old dogmas might blaze with new fire for a moment, but the people were busy: In their own ways, they were again ready to approach the universe and their experience directly. What did it all mean, I wondered, and what were they—what were we—really up to?

We were rediscovering our ancient tools of god-making, I thought; polishing those psychological skills that had grown rusty from disuse throughout many centuries. We were ready to come out from behind our dogmas and ceremonies, to encounter the universe through our own eyes and to try once again to push against our recognized boundaries. We might make errors again. We might even drag along dark vestiges from the past—gods and devils, martyrs, evil spirits and divine curses—but we *were* on the move again, and maybe one day we would shake off that pesty pack of superstitions.

The phrase "god-making" still struck me as perfectly apt and strange at the same time. I felt the same way about this emphasis on religion. One day that fall I wrote the following notes, trying to organize my thoughts on the subject. As I did, the leaves outside were falling everywhere. By the time I'd finished writing, one whole portion of clear sky was exposed that, before, had been filled with still-clinging foliage. The sky seemed almost severe, glad to be rid of the clutter of leaves; exposed, and somehow closer to earth. So I imagined the mass psyche, shaking off ancient beliefs, impatient to be free of them. My notes read:

"I think that religions originate in our own creative abilities, which are more powerful than we suspect, as I wrote a short time ago; and that the birth of any great religion represents those creative energies wedded to psychic events, as man seeks to dramatize and express the vast scope of his own subjective reality and looks for the source of Being. The result is a transdimensional spectacular event, an exalted vision superimposed upon historical fact.

"We often forget that there *are* different kinds of reality, and that our experience of any of them is dependent upon our perception. The events of the psyche are quite 'real' and have their effect on usual experience, whether or not they happen historically. For example, whatever physical events actually were involved in the birth of Christianity became carriers of supercharged psychic vision, bringing about a union of psychic creativity and historical fact. Physical events become the medium with which the mass psyche works at such times. Instead of using paint or stone, the psyche sculpts the facts of history into a living psychodrama. In this process all actions become supercharged, superintense. Hallucinated events are allowed to supersede physical ones, and cast their light over time's landscape.

"The birth of a religion, then, involves a peculiar blending of psychic and historical events, and when that process is over man is left with a hybrid dramatization that he apparently takes literally, following the form rather than the spirit of the originating revelatory material. This happens, I think, whenever we try to translate psychic data into *absolute* terms, and we make that error because we've not yet learned to distinguish the gradations of reality.

"Science deals with a predictable world in which the events of the psyche have no meaning. My first startling out-of-body experience (see *The Seth Material*) would be considered as a hallucination by science. Yet it initiated my psychic adventures and is certainly responsible in part for the Seth sessions and all of the books published as a result.

"What I'm trying to say is that mind forms matter, but usually this process is psychologically invisible. When religions are born, the balance tips in favor of the mind, and the nonphysical events that are always behind physical ones begin to show. But we mistake the psychic product's source; we think that it comes outside of ourselves, and we objectify the events into the stream of historic fact. We ignore the *process,* the state of consciousness in which all this happens, and it's the process itself that is so important.

"At such times the mass psyche opens up, sensing a greater psychological reality; and in an action we never quite glimpse its energy goes splashing out, striking the world of historic events, marking this individual or that one with an imprint of magnetic significance."

And it was happening again, I thought, as I read my notes. Even science was a religion of sorts, involved in a search for man's origins. Only how odd it was that such an orderly discipline could accept random chance and natural selection as explanations for a complicated, orderly universe. And when you really thought of it, how strange that religion itself in its long history couldn't come up with any better explanations than its curious assortment of unbelievable gods, underworlds, and heavens.

I felt as if I had some excellent insights but was missing an important point that would pull all of my ideas together. To clear my mind, I began an acrylic painting of the maple tree in the front yard. I finished reading Sue's manuscript, astonished again by the various interpretations that different individuals would place on a seemingly single event. Sue's book was fascinating and very well-written. Finally I forgot god-making and its implications for a while.

When I finished my painting and Sue's manuscript though, my questions were still waiting, with a new one added. Seth had been dictating his *Dreams, "Evolution," and Value Fulfillment* in our regular sessions, delivering material that Rob and I thought offered a brilliant alternate explanation of the origin of the universe, and described a new vision of man and nature that was far superior to the dogmatic answers of science or religion. But in man's long history, why hadn't he—why hadn't we—developed such a philosophy centuries ago and built our civilizations around it?

Why had we ended up, instead, with people like the Reverend Grover, shouting about hell and damnation on modern television screens? Or with supposedly well-meaning men and women holding antihomosexual rallies in *city* parks, all in the name of God? Or with a science that had no reverence for life? And what significant ambiguity did I sense in all of this, that I couldn't quite mentally locate?

The answer came in a way that was both commonplace and surprising. Actually, it was an unexpected visit from three lively young people that finally drew my ideas together into clear focus, and set me down smack in the middle of a philosophical place where I'd never really been before.

The three strangers came on one of those exciting days in late autumn when the air is crisp and shiny, the wind high in the nearly empty treetops, and the shadows moving everywhere. I'd just reached a stopping point in my writing when I heard the sounds of laughter coming from the back porch. This time I felt like seeing company. So, apparently, did Rob. Hearing the voices, he came to answer the door, and the three young people trooped in, full of health and vitality, eyes alert, not missing anything.

I was in the small breezeway studio so everyone crowded in there. Rob felt like taking a break from his work too, so he poured us all glasses of wine and sat down himself. I'll call our visitors Charles, Anna and Sarah. They said, breathlessly, that they couldn't *believe* that I was actually seeing them! Drinking wine with them! Rob and I started laughing at their enthusiasm. Finally we all ended up laughing and joking.

Charles did most of the talking. To me he resembled pictures of "the poet as a young man" that I'd seen in old anthologies. His body seemed to fall into natural poses, and when he stopped smiling a kind of self-conscious soberness gave his features a dramatic cast. Anna and Sarah were beautiful young women, both out to show that they had brains as well as beauty. And all of them had a kind of European formality that showed now and then, usually when it seemed to temper their impulsiveness.

After their initial burst of enthusiasm and display of high spirits, for example, all three suddenly quieted, as if afraid that they'd gone too far, or thought that they might be reprimanded. You could see them compose themselves. Anna and Sarah lowered their bright eyes and smoothed out the few wrinkles in their blue jeans over their knees. Charles sipped his wine in an almost formal fashion.

In a few minutes we discovered the reasons for their reactions. Charles told us that they'd just returned to "the States" from Europe, where all three had attended a particular school specializing in the expansion of consciousness. Even though the arts were specifically featured, the entire structure of the courses had been highly authoritative.

"They offered us each a scholarship so that we'd be able to teach there ourselves when we were finished," Charles said. "But after a while the atmosphere was really smothering. So we thanked them—and we've come back home, at least for a while."

"Still, Europe has that ancient culture," Sarah said, nostalgically. "I mean, those cathedrals and castles dating back through the centuries. But it *did* get stifling. And even the teaching of art in the school followed the founder's philosophy."

And right there something happened, as if this visit from the three young people home from abroad, and the discussion of European culture, were just the precise data needed to release the insights I'd been looking for from that invisible psychological computer to which I sense we're all connected. I could actually feel certain ideas being moved around in my mind, rearranged, as if an entirely new sorting out process were occurring to make room for the newest information. And that information came with a strong emotional surge. I started talking so quickly and spontaneously that my own words startled me, so that I had to hear them like anyone else before I knew what they were saying myself.

"That's it," I said, and to me my words sounded wondrously clear. "Europe *is* a place of ancient beliefs and authoritative doctrines. Now it just occurred to me that it's no coincidence that I started my own work here, in this country. And when our country was founded, it *was* a land for the do-it-yourselfers. Modern spiritualism started here too, but it didn't go far enough. Christianity itself came here from Europe, and we should have left it behind too. But we didn't. The new country needed a religion uniquely suited to a democracy; maybe religion isn't the proper word: a *vision.* An authoritative, absolute God doesn't fit a democracy any more than an absolute king or dictator would!"

My own words startled me. The idea was completely new to me on a conscious level, but it was so obvious once it was spoken that it seemed inconceivable I hadn't thought of it before: An absolute God whose word was to be obeyed without question didn't belong in a democracy! Luckily the Constitution *did* provide for separation of church and state, but behind that was the implied belief that the Christian God stood invisibly behind our presidents: And when our presidents sent the people off to war, it was in God's name as well as in the name of the country.

I was making so many connections that I couldn't wait to

write everything down, and I was even somewhat dazed by what certainly seemed to be a uniquely American vision, since I'd never been particularly patriotic. But I suddenly sensed the national roots of my work, and felt them reach back to the country's beginnings. Even then we were determined to free our minds from the past. We just hadn't gone far enough.

I can't remember exactly how I ended the conversation with our guests, but after they left I found myself thinking of the school they'd described, and of many other such establishments devoted to "esoteric knowledge." They were all authoritative in nature, given to disciplinarian activities, stressing European rather than American traditions; while others followed Buddhistic principles, emphasizing not individuality but selflessness.

Early American spiritualism did make an attempt to break away though, I thought. It represented an attempt to tackle the questions of immortality with a unique "do-it-yourself" zest tied to the American literal-mindedness. If the dead really survived, well, let them talk for themselves; let them produce good evidence. Anything physical would do; raps, voices, ectoplasm that could be seen—or almost seen. Let's bring the entire question into the democratic light of day where even the scientists can get a good look! That had been the attitude. But unfortunately spiritualism carried along with it all of the good and evil spirits of religion and superstition. Good doses of chicanery were also involved, as the well-intended tried to manufacture the evidence for survival that seemed so elusive. Besides all this, a touch of exotica was added as spiritualists deserted native American "guides" for Tibetan masters, monks, and assorted gurus.

But now maybe television would do a real service, I thought, remembering the Reverend Grover. Seeing the various evangelists on televised spectaculars, people might finally make certain comparisons between such programs and other TV fare. They might understand at last that the Bible is a far bloodier and violent drama than they'd realized. So the more I thought about it, the more I approved of such exposure in the public forum. I also remembered several American writers from the past that I wished were represented there too, though.

I thought of Walt Whitman, Thoreau, and Emerson. They were peculiarly American as thinkers with their stress upon individuality, mysticism, strength, expression, and responsibility. Darwin and Freud were both European, their theories tinged by ancient prejudices and pessimism. But mostly I remembered my own conflicts: for years I felt caught between the philosophies of

T. S. Eliot and e e cummings, as expressed in their poetry.

Once I almost knew Eliot's poem *The Waste Land* by heart, and would read it aloud at a moment's notice. I thought that it represented a devastating but true picture of reality. In contrast, there was e e cummings, and I knew his poem "My Father Moved Through Dooms of Love" by heart also. Eliot's pessimism pervaded the arts and sciences, and it became fashionable to be bored with life. No one really paid much attention to e e cummings. His optimism went out of style. He was called simplistic, for caring.

It hadn't occurred to me before in just the same way that Eliot was so buried in European tradition—for although born and educated in America, he became a British subject. I just never thought much about it. But e e cummings had a vision of America, and no one listened. His vision was swallowed by Darwinism and Freudianism; and so was Whitman's and Thoreau's and Emerson's.

I felt a certain sorrow for those now rather unfashionable American writers, and it was during this period that I wrote the poem "e. e. cummings' ghost" that appears in the frontmatter of this book. At the same time I saw that my impulses had led me truly, from the God of Jane idea, through to my "Psychic Manifesto," to the realization that what we needed was a decentralized God; and I knew that my work for this particular book was finished.

Overall, then, I envision us as being part of an indivisible Godhead or Source to which we each give individual expression through the actions of our lives, but for which no one person or group or dogma or book can presume to speak in absolute terms. *This* Divinity or Ultimate Reality endows us with inner direction that's provided, as Seth states, though our natural impulses. Those impulses are uniquely suited to bring about our individual fulfillments and accomplishments in a way that also benefits all life. This stress on impulses in no way denies the importance of the intellect, however. As a species, we are impulsively intellectual; we have the impulse to reason.

We will, indeed, have quite different visions and versions of God, All That Is, Ultimate Reality or whatever other term we may use to describe our unknown source, as we each interpret reality through our unique experiences and abilities. Such diversity should be taken for granted. But we should allow no one such vision to be accepted as absolute, or as carrying the indelible stamp of Divine approval.

Since we are, apparently, natural god-makers, it's about time that we begin to examine the psychic and psychological processes involved. Ultimately we form our entire civilizations around such beliefs. Obviously then, the processes themselves arouse the deepest levels of the psyche. The events of any religion become supercharged. The heady mixture of psychic and historic events fuses and henceforth cannot be separated.

I think that the preliminary stages of such new explosive psychic rebirth are upon us now. People are looking for alternate explanations of reality. Growing numbers of them can see little sense either in Christianity's or science's version of the nature of man and his place in nature's framework.

Again: An authoritative absolute God doesn't fit a democracy any more than a king or dictator would. How is it that we haven't realized that before? True, our president must at least check with Congress before sending our people off to war. But the president's authority has always been backed up by the certainty that God was on our side, and based on the assumption that war's mass murders were justified if committed in the combined service of God and country.

So, no more! The next time it's shouted from national podiums that God is on our side, we have the right to ask, "Which God? Jesus? The Jesus who said 'Blessed are the meek' or the Jesus who cursed the fig tree? The God of the religious fundamentalists? Of the Jews? Which God?" The gods of Jane and Rob and the gods of my readers are apt to be a bit more loving, certainly less terrible and less sure of themselves: Their messages are for private persons. And I'm convinced that in those terms, we do have individual gods; that the portion of the universe that formed us continues to do so, and that the universe and the selves that we are meet and intersect at those psychic levels where our own creativity begins. But we've been taught the opposite. We've been taught that as a species we're cursed from antiquity, flawed by original sin or by science's "selfish genes." No wonder we couldn't trust ourselves and our lives. No wonder we've had such difficulties worldwide for as far back as history is recorded.

Maybe the time *is* ripe for a change. We need a democracy of spirit, an end to divine hierarchies—and this country may well be the most auspicious place for such a rebirth. If Christianity's authoritative God clashes with democratic ideals, the idea of a Divinity expressing itself equally through each citizen fits in quite well. In fact, that divine quality in man would provide the self-reliance and trust that would truly enable a people to govern themselves.

Such a people would never give war a divine sanction, but would consider it a deplorable example of man's own distorted beliefs about himself and the world; beliefs that do indeed pit one nation against the other. And such a people would no longer hook up the idea of individualism with Darwinian survival of the fittest doctrines that foster competition rather than cooperation.

There is no doubt that we need to believe that life has meaning. That belief may well be a biological imperative. If we were as science maintains—only creatures formed by elements combining mindlessly in a universe itself created by chance, surrounded everywhere by chaos—then how could we even conceive of the idea of meaning or order?

Science would say that the idea of meaning itself is simply a reflection of the state of the brain, as is the illusion of our consciousness. But a science that disregards consciousness must necessarily end up creating its own illusion. It ignores the reality of experience, the evidence of being, and in so doing it denies rather than reinforces life's values.

We need a division of scientific dogma from national policy-making so that those values not considered by science can be given some voice in issues involving public welfare. An authoritative God coupled with an aggressive science sanctioned by national policy could have disastrous results indeed.

This Universal Divinity or Ultimate Reality or All That Is wouldn't be confined to one people or nation or species though, but would include all species of life. Each creature, each life *whatever its degree* would have its rights as an expression of that Source and as an inhabitant of Earth and contributer to planetary existence. Divinity, then would be dispersed throughout creation.

I become more and more convinced that the mass psyche is preparing for another intuitive upthrust, and that within its vast ranges it does possess the solutions, visions, and wisdom that we need. That power is making itself felt in the private arena. It's expressed and personified in the psychic experience of large numbers of people. It speaks through the spacemen and saints and psychic heroes of automatic writings and Ouija board messages; even in the cults and the frenzied activities of the fundamentalists. The mass psyche is looking for a way out of official beliefs. It's ready to form a more comprehensive vision.

But we must stop automatically taking such information at face value, translating it automatically through ancient beliefs. We must look directly at our own experience again—and learn to trust it. We must be our own psychic naturalists, combining reason with intuition. We must refuse to let old theories define our realities for us, limiting and distorting the very scope of our lives.

Instead, we must learn to acknowledge and interpret our own psychic perceptions; to distinguish between, say, psychic newscasts, documentaries, dramas, fantasies, and educational programs. We have to learn to read the language of the psyche and to discover far more about the psychodrama's strange blend of inner and exterior events. And to do all of that, we have to trust ourselves and our impulses.

In order to be sane and healthy, in order to even begin to understand our potentials as a species, we have to cultivate ideas and philosophies that provide us with a secure psychological base as good creatures, alive in a good universe. Otherwise, by our own definitions, we condemn ourselves as meaningless subjective mechanisms, or as the sinful children of an ancient revengeful god.

And, as Seth states in his *The Individual and the Nature of Mass Events,* we must redefine our ideas of good and evil and reexamine the characteristics of idealism so that we really understand that the end cannot justify the means taken to achieve it. Our ideals must be reflected in the methods we use to fulfill them. These are all issues in which each of us can be personally involved by studying them as they appear in our personal lives.

It's vitally important that we examine and explore the reaches of our own consciousnesses, gather evidence of those unofficial psychic events held in such disgrace by science and religion, and build up our own confidence. We need to examine the very contents and processes of our minds—not with instruments but with our consciousness itself.

As I type this final chapter, Rob has just finished his work on Seth's *The Individual and the Nature of Mass Events,* and Seth is already on Chapter 9 of *Dreams, "Evolution," and Value Fulfillment.* I've clocked many more hours of trancetime, of course, and I'm still trying to map those contours of the psyche in which my subjective travels happen. There is a point, though, where the private psyche opens up to the mass psyche and where they both become aware of a still greater Source from which all reality emerges.

The completed manuscript for *Mass Events* sits on Rob's desk right now. And even if we can't *prove* Seth's model of reality any more than we can science's or religion's, certainly Seth provides a more intellectually and emotionally satisfying one as far as I'm concerned, and one that leaves us room for gallant, meaningful action

And how strange that my private impulses led me to a kind of public vision in which we all uphold a democracy of spirit, and insist upon interpreting not just the Bible but the nature of reality for ourselves!

Index